Prophecies

Daniel's Seventy Weeks:
The Keystone of Bible Prophecy

Published by

PalmoniQuest LLC

Copyright © 2015 by William Struse

All rights reserved. No part of this book may be reproduced, scanned, or distributed in any printed form without permission.

ISBN 978-0-9979609-0-7

www.the13thenumeration.com

This book is dedicated to all those who love the words of YHWH.

Acknowledgments

YHWH, thank You for another adventure in Your Word. May these words honor You.

Win, once again I thank you for helping to make this book a reality. It has been a joy to rediscover this together.

Maranatha, Hope, Hannah, Zane, and Noah, you inspire me! Never forget how much YHWH loves you.

Rachel, once again I am indebted to your editing skill and knowledge of the Scripture. You helped make this book better than it would have been. Thank you.

INDEX

Introduction

Part I – Keystone of the Covenant

1. Bridging the Covenants
2. The Forgotten Covenant
3. The Holy Mountain
4. Redemption in 70 Sevens

Part II – The Second Temple Era

Introduction
1. The Commandment to Restore and Build
2. Cyrus the Great: A Decree to Rebuild the Temple and Jerusalem
3. Darius 'the Great' Artaxerxes: A Decree to Continue Construction on the Temple
4. The Seventh Year of Artaxerxes: A Decree for Ezra to Beautify the Temple
5. Ezra, the Priest and Scribe: His History and Lineage Relative to the Second Temple Era
6. The Twentieth Year of Artaxerxes: A Decree to Rebuild the Walls and Gates of Jerusalem
7. Nehemiah the Governor
8. Queen of 127 Provinces
9. The Fifth Decree: The Word to Return and Build Jerusalem

Part III – Countdown to the Messiah

Introduction
1. Timing the 70 Weeks
2. Biblical Time and the Messiah Factors

3. The Elusive 13th Month
4. Of Circles, Cubits, and Context
5. 70 Sevens and the Messiah Factors
6. 7 Shabuwa until the Messiah
7. The Messiah Cut Off
8. The Final Shabuwa
9. Daniel 9, the Flood, and YHWH's Redemptive Purpose
10. Strengthening the Covenant
11. The Final Shabuwa of Living Witnesses
12. The 70th Shabuwa Fulfilled
13. The 70th Shabuwa and the Times of the Gentiles
14. Daniel 9 and the Messiah's Purpose
15. Daniel 9: Keystone of the Covenants

(You may view or print a high resolution PDF copy of the charts in this book at the following link: http://www.danielsseventyweeks.com/Daniels70Weeks%20ChartsPicturesTables.pdf)

Important Notice

I believe the information in this book is far too important to limit its message to those who can afford it. Various digital versions of this book and my other books in the Prophecy and Patterns are available for free to my blog subscribers. It's free to subscribe and I will never share your email address. The only thing I will share with you is my love for all things Biblical. To become a subscriber to my blog, *Where History and the Bible Meet* go here: http://www.the13thenumeration.com/Blog13/subscribe/

If you are not sure whether you are a subscriber feel free to email me at: wstruse@the13thenumeration.com

Introduction

If someone asked you to explain how the Bible is different from any other religious text in history, how would you answer? I believe there are several good ways to answer this question, but to my mind the one that stands out is that the Bible predicted future events that came to pass. It is this use of predictive prophecy that is the divine stamp, if you will, on the Bible's authenticity as a genuinely inspired record of events past, present, and yet to come.

But the Bible is more than just an organized collection of ancient prophetic texts. The Bible is ultimately a tragic yet redeeming love story. It is the story of a Creator who, in a desperate attempt to save His fallen creations, humbles Himself in order to pay the righteous penalty for their transgressions; transgressions which, according to His unbreakable word, require the death of those He loves. In order to accomplish this task, the One who made us humbled Himself and became like us. And when the sentence of death was passed and the time came to pay the penalty, He stood in our place and received the righteous judgment so that we might live.

There are many prophecies in the Bible that speak of this coming Redeemer who would suffer so that we might live. But in the entire biblical record, there is only one prophecy that tells us specifically *when* these events would take place. That prophecy is found in the book of Daniel, chapter 9. It is known to most of us as the prophecy of 70 weeks, and it is the only prophecy in the Bible that gives us a secular date by which we can accurately calculate the first coming of the Messiah.

But the prophecy of 70 weeks is so much more than a messianic prediction. This prophecy, given to a Judean captive named Daniel, is really the bridge between the Old and New Testaments: a keystone, if you will, that connects old and new. You see, it is the prophecy of 70 weeks that spans the five hundred years of silence between the Bible's two testaments.

To give you a clearer picture of why this is so important, the word we understand as "testament" (as in Old and New Testaments) also means "covenant." In other words, the Old and New Covenants are the record of mankind's reconciliation with our Creator. The Old Covenant texts follow the promised "seed" of the Messiah from Adam, Noah, Abraham, and David up to the Second Temple era and the prophecy of 70 weeks, which foretells the date of the coming of the Messiah, Yeshua. This prophecy then spans the next five hundred years and brings us to the New Covenant when the Messiah at last appeared. The documentation of this covenant, as found in the collection of books commonly called the New Testament, is made up in part of the eyewitness accounts of the Messiah Yeshua fulfilling the Old Covenant promises concerning mankind's reconciliation to YHWH. The prophecy of 70 weeks is the central biblical proof text to show that a Hebrew man named Yeshua, born during the reign of the Roman empire, was the expected Messiah, who strengthened, confirmed, yea, *fulfilled* the Old Covenant promises of a coming Redeemer.

> And he shall send Jesus Christ, which before was preached unto you: whom the heaven must receive until the times of restitution of all things, which God hath spoken by the mouth of all his holy prophets since the world began. (Acts 3:20–21)

If you've read Book I in this series, *The 13th Enumeration: Key to the Bible's Messianic Symbolism,* you saw how Yeshua fulfilled the sacrificial symbolism found in the Old Testament and how it was the apostle Matthew, in his inspired arrangement of Yeshua's lineage, who provided us with the key to understanding this symbolism. How appropriate, then, that we find this lineage of Yeshua anchoring the first chapter of the first book of the New Testament. It is here in Matthew 1 that it is recorded that Yeshua is the son of David and of Abraham. It is also in Matthew 1 that we find clues that point us back to Daniel 9 and the prophecy of 70 weeks, thus inexorably linking both covenants together.

Let's take a look once again at Matthew's amazing lineage of Yeshua:

Lineage of Yeshua (Jesus)
As <u>Summarized</u> in Matthew 1

14 Generations From Abraham to David		14 Generations From David to the captivity		14 Generations From the captivity to Yeshua/Jesus	

As <u>Given</u> in Matthew 1

Abraham	1	Solomon	1	Salathiel	1
Isaac	2	Reaboam	2	Zorobabel	2
Jacob	3	Abia	3	Abiud	3
Judas	4	Asa	4	Eliakim	4
Phares	5	Josaphat	5	Azor	5
Esrom	6	Joram	6	Sadoc	6
Aram	7	Ozias	7	Achim	7
Aminadab	8	Joatham	8	Eliud	8
Naasson	9	Achaz	9	Eleazar	9
Salmon	10	Ezekias	10	Matthan	10
Booz	11	Manasses	11	Jacob	11
Obed	12	Amon	12	Joseph	12
Jesse	13	Josias	13	Yeshua	13
David	14	Jechonias	14		14*

2nd Column with missing kings and details

	Solomon	1	
	Roboam	2	
	Abia	3	
	Asa	4	
	Josaphat	5	
	Joram	6	
3 missing names → 3	Ahaziah		(6+7 = 13)
	Joash		
	Amaziah		
	Ozias	7	
	Joatham	8	
	Achaz	9	
	Ezekias	10	} 70
	Manasses	11	
	Amon	12	
	Josias	13	
1 missing name — 1	Jehoiakim		Daniel's captivity begins between 13/14
	Jechonias	14	

* implied not stated

Look closely at the second column with its missing kings. Notice the single missing name between the 13th and 14th generations. The missing king is named Jehoiakim. As we saw in Book I of the Prophecy and Patterns series, Jehoiakim means "YHWH raises up." Indeed, it was Yeshua, the 13th generation of Matthew 1, whom YHWH raised up to become the 14th generation as well, thus completing the list. But let's look a little deeper. Jehoiakim was left out for another, equally important reason. As we will discover in subsequent chapters, this single missing name between the 13th and 14th generations of Yeshua is indeed a key to interpreting the greatest messianic prophecy in the Scripture.

> In the third year of the reign of Jehoiakim king of Judah came Nebuchadnezzar king of Babylon unto Jerusalem, and besieged it . . . And the king spake unto Ashpenaz the master of his eunuchs, that he should bring certain of the children of Israel, and of the king's seed, and of the princes . . . Now among these were of the children of Judah, Daniel, Hananiah, Mishael, and Azariah. (Daniel 1:1–6)

As we read here, a young man named Daniel, really not much older than a boy, was taken captive by Nebuchadnezzar along with the Judean king Jehoiakim. It was nearly 70 years later that this same Judean captive, now a very old man, received the prophecy of 70 weeks.

> In the first year of Darius the son of Ahasuerus, of the seed of the Medes, which was made king over the realm of the Chaldeans; in the first year of his reign I Daniel understood by books the number of the years, whereof the word of YHWH came to Jeremiah the prophet, that he would accomplish seventy years in the desolations of Jerusalem. (Daniel 9:1–2)

Keep in mind that when Daniel read about the 70 years of captivity prophesied by Jeremiah, he knew without any doubt that this period of time was drawing to a close, because his own captivity began those 70 years! It was in this context that Daniel raised his moving intercessory prayer to YHWH for his people and the city of Jerusalem. A short time later, the angel Gabriel came to Daniel and gave him the prophecy of 70 weeks.

In the following pages I'd like to ask you to join me on a thrilling adventure as we explore this wonderful prophecy given to a Judean captive named Daniel. The importance of this prophecy cannot be overstated. Again, it is the only prophecy in the entire Bible that provides a specific, datable timeline for the coming of the Messiah. This prophecy proves that indeed Yeshua was the Messiah promised in the Scripture!

But this prophecy does not come to us without controversy. What if I told you that most of what scholars have told us about Daniel 9 and the prophecy of 70 weeks has been built upon erroneous assumptions that have altered our view of the prophecy so much that we have lost our focus on the Messiah? Did you know that most commentators on Daniel 9 cannot give a single biblical chronological synchronism that clearly defines the starting point for the prophecy of 70 weeks during the Persian era? Did you know that the most widely held measure of time used to calculate Daniel 9 is not even related to a biblical reckoning of time, nor can it be found in the historical record? The uncomfortable truth about Daniel 9 is that it is one of the most widely known but least understood prophecies in the Bible, and the consequences of misunderstanding it are far-reaching—they shape our understanding not only of Yeshua's coming but also of the end of the world and our own place in redemptive history.

Here is the point. Daniel 9 and the prophecy of 70 weeks influences nearly every aspect of how we see the Yeshua's life and ministry. The prophecy helps us date Yeshua's birth, His ministry, and His death. Daniel 9 is also a large part of the framework upon which we have built our view of the consummation of this age and Yeshua's return. That's an incredible weight hanging on just a few verses out of the thousands in the biblical record. Daniel 9 and the prophecy of 70 weeks is without a doubt the most influential prophecy in the Bible. Because of the weight we place on it, it is incumbent upon us to ensure that our understanding is based upon sound biblical fact, not well-intentioned traditions.

So once again, as I asked when we began Book I, *The 13th Enumeration: Key to the Bible's Messianic Symbolism*, let's roll up our sleeves and dig into the words of the living God. Let's search for the treasures He has left for us to find. At the end of this journey I can't promise you that you'll agree with everything I've written about the prophecy of 70 weeks, but I will guarantee that once you've finished this book, you will have a knowledge of the subject, strengthened by sound and reasonable biblical facts, which will serve you well in building a strong contextual foundation for your own understanding of this incredibly influential prophecy.

One final note: You'll find that I quote many passages of Scripture in this book, and it is my hope that you will not gloss over them. They are the real substance of this book. My words in the following pages are but the rough and uneven stitches holding together some of the beautiful pieces of our Creator's grand tapestry, in which He reveals His intention to reconcile all mankind through Yeshua the promised Messiah. So let's begin the adventure . . .

Part I:
Keystone of the Covenant

Chapter 1:
Bridging the Covenants

"Seventy weeks are determined upon thy people and upon thy holy city, to finish the transgression, and to make an end of sins, and to make reconciliation for iniquity, and to bring in everlasting righteousness, and to seal up the vision and prophecy, and to anoint the most Holy."

Daniel 9:24

The book of Genesis tells us of what is arguably the single greatest tragedy in mankind's history. It records mankind's first sin and how, as a result, our ancestors were cursed with death and cast out of Eden. But thankfully, the story doesn't end there. Mankind is not left without hope of a future restoration and reconciliation with our Creator. Before Adam and Eve were cast out of the garden, our Creator, YHWH, promised them that someday their "seed" would triumph over the serpent who had deceived them. Thus began one of the most ancient and important covenants in the Bible, the covenant of the promised seed.

One way to look at the Bible's underlying redemptive message is to see the Old Testament (Covenant) texts as YHWH's promise to reconcile and restore mankind through the promised seed of the Messiah and the record of how that promise was worked out through the descendants of Adam and Eve. The New Testament (Covenant) texts, on the other hand, show how the ancient redemptive promises of the Bible have been and will be fulfilled in the Messiah Yeshua, that promised seed.

What makes the prophecy of 70 weeks so relevant is that it is here, in the ninth chapter of the book of Daniel, that we first find a specific timetable for the fulfillment of the ancient promise made to Adam and Eve and confirmed to subsequent generations through Noah, Abraham, Isaac, Jacob, and David, and finally fulfilled in Yeshua the Messiah. Before we continue, let's briefly trace this covenant through the Scriptures. Please take a moment to read the verses below; they are imperative to establishing the covenantal promise that was to be fulfilled in the future Messiah.

> And I will put enmity between thee [the serpent] and the woman, and between thy seed and her seed; it shall bruise thy head, and thou shalt bruise his heel. (Genesis 3:15)

> And God spake unto Noah, and to his sons with him, saying, And I, behold, I establish my covenant with you, and with your seed after you. (Genesis 9:8–9)

> By myself have I sworn [to Abraham], saith YHWH . . . *And in thy seed shall all the nations of the earth be blessed; because thou hast obeyed my voice.* (Genesis 22:16–18, emphasis mine)

> And YHWH appeared unto him [Isaac], and said . . . And I will make thy seed to multiply as the stars of heaven, and will give unto thy seed all these countries; *and in thy seed shall all the*

nations of the earth be blessed. (Genesis 26:2–4, emphasis mine)

And Jacob went out from Beersheba . . . And, behold, YHWH stood above it, and said, I am YHWH God of Abraham thy father, and the God of Isaac . . . and in thee *and in thy seed shall all the families of the earth be blessed.* (Genesis 28:10–14, emphasis mine)

I have made a covenant with my chosen, I have sworn unto David my servant, Thy seed will I establish for ever, and build up thy throne to all generations. Selah. (Psalm 89:3–4)

Ye are the children of the prophets, and of the covenant which God made with our fathers, saying unto Abraham, *And in thy seed shall all the kindreds of the earth be blessed.* Unto you first God, having raised up his Son Jesus, sent him to bless you, in turning away every one of you from his iniquities. (Acts 3:25–26, emphasis mine)

Blessed be the Lord God of Israel; for he hath *visited and redeemed his people,* and hath raised up an horn of salvation for us in the house of his servant David; as *he spake by the mouth of his holy prophets, which have been since the world began.* (Luke 1:68–70, emphasis mine)

And Mary said [speaking of Yeshua], My soul doth magnify the Lord . . . He hath holpen his servant Israel, in remembrance of his mercy; as he spake to our fathers, to Abraham, and to his seed for ever. (Luke 1:46–55)

And when he had removed him, he raised up unto them David to be their king; to whom also he gave testimony, and said, I have found David the son of Jesse, a man after mine own heart, which shall fulfil all my will. *Of this man's seed hath God according to his promise* raised unto Israel a Saviour, Jesus. (Acts 13:22–23, emphasis mine)

Now to Abraham and his seed were the promises made. He saith not, *And to seeds, as of many; but as of one, And to thy seed, which is Christ.* And this I say, that the covenant, that was confirmed before of God in Christ, the law, which was four hundred and thirty years after, cannot disannul, that it should make the promise of none effect. (Galatians 3:16–17, emphasis mine)

The Promised Seed

We see in the verses above that YHWH confirmed the covenant of the promised seed with Adam, Noah, Abraham, Isaac, Jacob, and David. Luke 1:68–70 goes so far as to say that YHWH promised to raise up a "horn of salvation" for Israel as testified by the "holy prophets" from the very beginning of the world. In Luke 1, Mary acknowledges that indeed her seed, whom the angel Gabriel told her to name Yeshua ("salvation of YHWH"), is a confirmation of the promise made to Abraham. The apostle Paul confirms this in his address to the Jews of Antioch, explaining that Yeshua is the promised seed of David. Finally, in his letter to the Galatians, the apostle Paul further clarifies that the covenant of the promised seed was brought to its fullest expression in the person of Yeshua the Messiah. The New Testament fully explains how the Messiah Yeshua reconciled mankind to YHWH by shedding His blood on our behalf, and in so doing, forever satisfied the legal requirement of the sacrificial law.

    Indeed, Book I of this series, *The 13th Enumeration: Key to the Bible's Messianic Symbolism,* showed that Yeshua is linked with the symbolism of sacrificial atonement and that this symbolism is woven into the very fabric of the biblical record. As we further explore the prophecy of 70 weeks, keep in mind this covenantal thread promised to the fathers. It is the underlying premise upon which many of the Bible's messianic prophecies rest. Although Daniel 9 has come to be seen almost entirely as a prediction of the coming Antichrist, it too is premised upon the thread of the seed covenant. As we turn our attention directly to Daniel 9, it may surprise you to learn that Daniel mentions the covenant of the promised Messiah in the very first verses of the chapter. Let's take a look.

Chapter 2:
The Forgotten Covenant

"And I prayed unto YHWH my God, and made my confession, and said, O Lord, the great and dreadful God, keeping the covenant and mercy to them that love him, and to them that keep his commandments."
Daniel 9:4

Those with an interest in Bible prophecy are likely familiar with the infamous "covenant" mentioned in Daniel 9:27. By far the majority of scholars today believe the covenant found in Daniel 9:27 is to be made or confirmed with Israel by some yet-future evil world leader, and it is this covenant that will set in motion the final seven years of this age— aka "the Great Tribulation"— before the Messiah Yeshua returns to reign on this earth.

But how many of you are familiar with the covenant of Daniel 9:4? Arguably, it is this first covenant mentioned in the chapter that establishes the underlying context for the entire prophecy revealed to Daniel by the angel Gabriel. In fact, a careful reading of Daniel 9:1–23 shows that the prophecy of 70 weeks, given in the last four verses of the chapter, is in part an answer to Daniel's impassioned prayer in those first twenty-three verses.

> And I prayed unto YHWH my God, and made my confession, and said, O Lord, the great and dreadful God, keeping the *covenant and mercy* to them that love him, and to them that keep his commandments. (Daniel 9:4, emphasis mine)

Daniel's prayer was predicated upon a covenant he knew the Lord would keep. What covenant was that, and why does it matter so much to our understanding of the entire prophecy?

Covenants and Controversy

As we look at the covenant of Daniel 9:4, keep in mind that it is almost always ignored by scholars when discussing Daniel 9:24–27 and the prophecy of 70 weeks. As you will see in the following pages, this omission is not trivial. As mentioned above, one of the most well-known aspects of the prophecy of 70 weeks is the covenant of Daniel 9:27, which a majority of scholars believe will be made or confirmed with the yet-future Antichrist. But what if we could prove that the covenant of Daniel 9:4 is inseparably linked to the covenant of Daniel 9:27? What if the covenant of Daniel 9:27 is not a prediction of some yet-future treaty or agreement made by some evil secular world leader but a covenant made by the living God of the Bible? Can you imagine how that would alter our view of the prophecy of 70 weeks?

As I stated earlier, Daniel 9 is one of the most well-known but least understood prophecies in the Bible, and the fourth verse of Daniel 9 proves that point. The reality of the covenant of Daniel 9:4 is that it is the most important covenant mentioned in the Bible, yet far too frequently, it is glossed over in this passage as if it has no relevance to the prophecy at all. Today, let's remedy that oversight.

The Bible's Messianic Message

To me, one of the most wonderful aspects of the Bible is the consistency of its messianic message. Each part adds color and texture to show the love of our Creator, YHWH, for mankind and His plan to reconcile us to Himself. Sometimes the threads of this plan are not obvious while other times they are on bold display, but you can count on the fact that each thread weaves part of the tapestry that shows YHWH's love.

Here in Daniel 9:4 we have a major thread of YHWH's plan to reconcile mankind to Himself. Together, let's trace that thread back in time and see if we can find the origin of this forgotten "covenant and mercy."

Crossing the Jordan

Our first destination takes us back to the final year of Israel's wandering in the wilderness. Israel is just this side of the Jordan River and ready to enter the promised land. Moses is admonishing, instructing, and encouraging the people before he passes leadership to Joshua (Yeshua) the son of Nun, after which Israel will cross over the Jordan.

> And because *he loved thy fathers, therefore he chose their seed after them*, and brought thee out in his sight with his mighty power out of Egypt. (Deuteronomy 4:37, emphasis mine)

For thou art an holy people unto YHWH thy God: YHWH thy God hath chosen thee to be a special people unto himself, above all people that are upon the face of the earth. YHWH did not set his love upon you, nor choose you, because ye were more in number than any people; for ye were the fewest of all people:

But because YHWH loved you, and because *he would keep the oath which he had sworn unto your fathers*, hath YHWH brought you out with a mighty hand, and redeemed you out of the house of bondmen, from the hand of Pharaoh king of Egypt. Know therefore that YHWH thy God, he is God, the faithful God, which keepeth *covenant and mercy* with them that love him and keep his commandments to a thousand generations . . . Wherefore it shall come to pass, if ye hearken to these judgments, and keep, and do them, that YHWH thy God shall keep unto thee the *covenant and the mercy* which he sware unto thy fathers. (Deuteronomy 4:34, 7:6–12, emphasis mine)

Covenant and Mercy

If we need confirmation that Daniel is referring to the same "covenant and mercy" as mentioned by Moses in Deuteronomy, all we need to do is read the next several verses of Daniel's prayer. Daniel 9:5 onward acknowledges that indeed Israel had not kept the words of Moses, and despite that, Daniel pleads with YHWH to remember the exodus and His deliverance of His people from Egypt.

Consider the context of Daniel's words in chapter 9 for a moment. Here we find a very old man who has been a captive in the land of Babylon for nearly 70 years as a result of his people's unfaithfulness. He has just read and understood the prophecy of Jeremiah, in which he learns that his captivity is nearly over. Remember that it was Daniel's captivity, along with that of King Jehoiakim, which began the 70 years prophesied by Jeremiah (Daniel 1:1–6).

Promised to the Fathers

With this realization, Daniel gives one of the most beautiful and impassioned prayers in the Bible. This prayer is the catalyst for the prophecy of 70 weeks which follows. In this context, the very first words out of Daniel's mouth concerning the "covenant and mercy" take on added significance.

So what is the "covenant and mercy" promised to the fathers, mentioned by both Daniel and Moses, and when did this covenant take effect? According to Moses in Deuteronomy 9:5, the "fathers" to whom the "covenant and mercy" were given are none other than Abraham, Isaac, and Jacob. As you read the passage below, remember it is still within the context of Moses's speech to Israel before they were to cross over the Jordan River and take possession of the promised land.

Also keep in mind that the term "mercy" in this passage is the Hebrew word *checed,* and it means goodness, kindness, or faithfulness. The words "covenant" and "mercy" in the Daniel 9:4 are connected by the letter "*waw*," and as such they do not have to describe two separate items or ideas. In grammatical terms it's a hendiadys, which means both words describe a single idea. In other words mercy, kindness, or faithfulness may in part testify to the characteristics of the covenant.

> Not for thy righteousness, or for the uprightness of thine heart, dost thou go to possess their land: but for the wickedness of these nations YHWH thy God doth drive them out from before thee, and *that he may perform the word which YHWH sware unto thy fathers, Abraham, Isaac, and Jacob.* (Deuteronomy 9:5, emphasis mine)

Moses lets us know that the "covenant and mercy" promised to the fathers began with the father of the nation, Abraham. So let's explore the covenant made with Abraham and see why Daniel might bring it to mind when he petitioned YHWH in Daniel 9:4.

The Oath of Sevens

I think it appropriate to mention here that the word "sware" in the passage above is the Hebrew word *shaba.* Shaba is the root from which the Hebrew word *shabuwa,* or sevens, is derived. You and I know shabuwa as "weeks," as it is translated in our English Bibles, as in the 70 weeks of Daniel 9.

Coincidence? Hardly, and here's why. The very first time the word shaba or "sware" is used by YHWH in the Bible, it references the covenant He made with Abraham in Genesis 22. As we will see, this covenant is the promise of the coming Messiah, the very covenant which both Moses and Daniel were referring to.

The Faith of Abraham

To me, one of the most poignant stories in the Bible is when YHWH tests Abraham's faith by asking him to sacrifice his only son. Abraham's response and actions are a testimony to his amazing faith. And it is here in the twenty-second chapter of Genesis, where this story is told, that we find the origins of the covenant which YHWH sware (*shaba*) with Abraham. Take a moment to read a few excerpts of this wonderful story.

> And it came to pass after these things, that God did tempt Abraham, and said unto him, Abraham: and he said, Behold, here I am. And he said, Take now thy son, thine only son Isaac, whom thou lovest, and get thee into the land of Moriah; and offer him there for a burnt offering upon one of the mountains which I will tell thee of. (Genesis 22:1–2)

Abraham obeys YHWH and arrives in the land of Moriah, where he knows he is to sacrifice his son on one of the mountains. But listen to his faith speaking in this next passage:

> And Abraham said unto his young men, Abide ye here with the ass; and I and the lad will go yonder and worship, and come again to you. (Genesis 22:5)

Did you get that? Abraham knew he had to sacrifice his son, but even so he told his young men that both he and Isaac would go and worship *and* "come again." The next passage is one of my favorites. Listen to the words of a father and his young son. These words are both a testimony to Abraham's faith and a prophecy that speaks of the coming Messiah.

> And Isaac spake unto Abraham his father, and said, My father: and he said, Here am I, my son. And he said, Behold the fire and the wood: but where is the lamb for a burnt offering? And Abraham said, My son, *God will provide himself a lamb* for a burnt offering: so they went both of them together. (Genesis 22:7–8, emphasis mine)

As a father of five precious children, this passage nearly brings me to tears when I read it. How innocent Isaac's question, and what faith from Abraham! I can't help but ask myself if I would have that kind of faith. Thankfully Abraham did, because as you will see, it was this act of faith that YHWH used to bring forth the "seed" of the Messiah.

> And the angel of YHWH called unto Abraham out of heaven the second time, and said, *By myself have I sworn* [*shaba*], saith YHWH, for because thou hast done this thing, and hast not withheld thy son, thine only son: that in blessing I will bless thee, and in multiplying I will multiply thy seed as the stars of the heaven, and as the sand which is upon the sea shore; and thy seed shall possess the gate of his enemies; *and in thy seed*

> *shall all the nations of the earth be blessed*; because thou hast obeyed my voice. (Genesis 22:15–18, emphasis mine)

You see, the covenant made with Abraham was not just about a future promised land for his descendants (although that was an important part of it). The primary driving purpose of the Abrahamic covenant was the promise of the coming seed by which all nations of the earth would be blessed. In wonderful biblical symbolism, Abraham didn't have to sacrifice his son because YHWH provided a substitution for Isaac. Over a thousand years later, on that very same mount, Yeshua the Messiah became YHWH's sacrificial substitution on behalf of all mankind. Indeed YHWH, "provided Himself a lamb." The apostle Paul explains this passage more fully in Galatians 3:

> Now to Abraham and his seed were the promises made. *He saith not, And to seeds, as of many; but as of one, And to thy seed, which is Christ.* And this I say, that the covenant, that was confirmed before of God in Christ, the law, which was four hundred and thirty years after, cannot disannul, that it should make the promise of none effect. (Galatians 3:16–17, emphasis mine)

This passage by the apostle Paul brings us full circle in a beautiful show of biblical congruency. The forgotten covenant mentioned by the prophet Daniel in Daniel 9:4 is none other than the promise of the coming Messiah by which all nations of the earth were to be blessed. Even more compelling is that this covenantal promise is the first recorded *shaba* personally made by YHWH in the Bible, and centuries later, this *shaba*, or oath of sevens, would be the basis for the prophecy of 70 weeks (shabuwa) given to Daniel.

How awesome and appropriate is that!

Daniel's first words in chapter 9 are a petition to the living God of the Bible to remember the covenant of the coming Messiah that YHWH swore (shaba) with Abraham. In answer to Daniel's prayer, just twenty verses later, YHWH sends the angel Gabriel with the prophecy of 70 weeks (shabuwa), the defining messianic prophecy in the Scripture.

> At the beginning of thy supplications the commandment came forth, and I am come to shew thee; for thou art greatly beloved: therefore understand the matter, and consider the vision. Seventy weeks [shabuwa] are determined upon thy people and upon thy holy city, to finish the transgression, and to make an end of sins, and to make reconciliation for iniquity, and to bring in everlasting righteousness, and to seal up the vision and prophecy, and to anoint the most Holy. (Daniel 9:23–24)

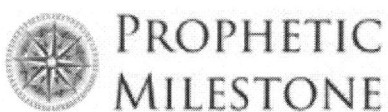
PROPHETIC MILESTONE

Prophetic Milestone: Covenant and Mercy with Abraham

As we explore the prophecy of Daniel 9, I will be highlighting prophetic milestones in YHWH's plan to redeem mankind through the promised Messiah. In Book III of the

Prophecies and Patterns series, *The Jubilee Code: Prophetic Milestones in the Bible,* we will consider these milestones in the overall context of the Bible's chronological record. Keep an eye out for these prophetic milestones, because as you will learn in the next book, they show YHWH's guiding hand in the history of mankind in startling and unmistakable ways.

A Wonderful Plan of Redemption

As I stated at the beginning of this chapter, the consistency of the Bible's messianic message is truly amazing. YHWH has always had a plan to reconcile mankind through Yeshua, the promised seed of Abraham, and this plan of redemption is woven into every aspect of the biblical record. Not surprisingly, this promised reconciliation is the very essence of the prophecy of 70 weeks, from the start of Daniel's prayer to the very last verse.

So next time you are thinking about the "covenant" of Daniel 9:27, before assigning the whole thing to the Antichrist and the Great Tribulation, won't you first consider the forgotten covenant of Daniel 9:4 and the *shaba* YHWH swore with Abraham? Stepping back to look at the bigger context, won't you consider that the story God is telling here is far more powerful, far-reaching, and glorious than we have assumed? As you will see more fully in the coming pages, the promise of the coming Redeemer mentioned in Daniel 9:4 is the contextual bedrock upon which the prophecy of 70 weeks rests. While you thinking about these covenants, consider them in light of the words of Zechariah, the father of John, and Mary, the mother of Yeshua:

Blessed be the Lord God of Israel; for he hath visited and redeemed his people, and hath raised up an horn of salvation for us in the house of his servant David; as he spake by the mouth of his holy prophets, which have been since the world began . . .

To perform the mercy promised to our fathers, and to remember his holy covenant . . . The oath which he sware to our father Abraham . . . To give knowledge of salvation unto his people by the remission of their sins, through the tender mercy of our God; whereby the dayspring from on high hath visited us, to give light to them that sit in darkness and in the shadow of death, to guide our feet into the way of peace. (Luke 1:68–79, emphasis mine—see also Isaiah 42)

And Mary said, My soul doth magnify the Lord, and my spirit hath rejoiced in God my Saviour. For he hath regarded the low estate of his handmaiden: for, behold, from henceforth all generations shall call me blessed . . . He hath holpen his servant Israel, in remembrance of his mercy; *as he spake to our fathers, to Abraham, and to his seed for ever.* (Luke 1:46–55, emphasis mine)

Ye are the children of the prophets, and of the covenant which God made with our fathers, saying unto Abraham, *And in thy seed shall all the kindreds of the earth be blessed.* Unto you first God, having raised up his Son Jesus, sent him to bless you, in turning away every one of you from his iniquities. (Acts 3:25–26, emphasis mine)

Building on the Covenant of Daniel 9

Now that we've established the underlying covenantal context of Daniel 9:4, we are in a much better position to begin building on this foundation a sound interpretation of this wonderful prophecy. In keeping with a construction theme, let's use the blueprints YHWH has given us to begin adding a framework to the foundation of Daniel 9:4. Together, let's continue to build upon what we have learned and see just how grand a prophetic structure YHWH has designed.

In closing, I remind you of the wonderful messianic prophecy found in Zechariah 9, which speaks of the coming Messiah who brings salvation and deliverance from the pit by the "blood of the covenant":

> Rejoice greatly, O daughter of Zion; shout, O daughter of Jerusalem: behold, thy King cometh unto thee: he is just, and having salvation; lowly, and riding upon an ass, and upon a colt the foal of an ass. And I will cut off the chariot from Ephraim, and the horse from Jerusalem, and the battle bow shall be cut off: and he shall speak peace unto the heathen: and his dominion shall be from sea even to sea, and from the river even to the ends of the earth. *As for thee also, by the blood of thy covenant I have sent forth thy prisoners out of the pit* wherein is no water. (Zechariah 9:9–11, emphasis mine)

Remember, a building is only as strong as the foundation which holds it together. Never forget the covenant!

Chapter 3:
Thy Holy Mountain

"O Lord, according to all thy righteousness, I beseech thee, let thine anger and thy fury be turned away from thy city Jerusalem, thy holy mountain: because for our sins, and for the iniquities of our fathers, Jerusalem and thy people are become a reproach to all that are about us. Now therefore, O our God, hear the prayer of thy servant, and his supplications, and cause thy face to shine upon thy sanctuary that is desolate, for the Lord's sake. O my God, incline thine ear, and hear; open thine eyes, and behold our desolations, and the city which is called by thy name: for we do not present our supplications before thee for our righteousnesses, but for thy great mercies. O Lord, hear; O Lord, forgive; O Lord, hearken and do; defer not, for thine own sake, O my God: for thy city and thy people are called by thy name.
Daniel 9:16–19

After Daniel reminds YHWH of His covenant and mercy in Daniel 9:4, he proceeds to list Judah's and Israel's sins and iniquities from the time of the exodus to his present day. Daniel humbly acknowledges that YHWH's wrath and judgments are righteous and deserved and that YHWH must keep His word.

For context's sake, I once again remind you to keep in mind Daniel's personal circumstances. He had been taken captive by Nebuchadnezzar nearly 70 years earlier, beginning the 70 years' captivity prophesied by Jeremiah. We learn in Daniel 9:2 that Daniel had just discovered by reading the words of Jeremiah that this captivity was nearing an end. So we find Daniel petitioning YHWH to turn His anger and fury "away from thy city Jerusalem, thy holy mountain."

Think about that for a moment. Daniel understood YHWH's "anger and fury" as being directed toward Jerusalem, the "holy mountain." To you and me the words "holy mountain" might not call to mind any further biblical idea or story, but to Daniel and the Jewish people, the "holy mountain" reminded them of Genesis 22 and the "covenant and mercy" YHWH promised to Abraham when he was willing to sacrifice his son Isaac. For it was on those very same mountains where Abraham had been called upon to sacrifice Isaac that Solomon built the First Temple, and where hundreds of years later the Son of God would lay down His life as a sacrifice for mankind's sins.

> Then on the third day Abraham lifted up his eyes, and saw the place afar off . . .
>
> And Abraham called the name of that place Jehovahjireh: as it is said to this day, *In the mount of YHWH* it shall be seen. And the angel of YHWH called unto Abraham out of heaven the second time, and said, By myself have I sworn [*shaba*], saith YHWH, for because thou hast done this thing, and hast not withheld thy son, thine only son: that in blessing I will bless thee, and in multiplying I will multiply thy seed as the stars of the heaven, and as the sand which is upon the sea shore; and thy seed shall possess the gate of his enemies,

> *And in thy seed shall all the nations of the earth be blessed;* because thou hast obeyed my voice. (Genesis 22:6–18, emphasis mine)

70 Years of Divine Anger

It is clear from Daniel 9 that YHWH was furious with Israel. We will deal with this more fully in a subsequent chapter, but for context's sake, it is important to further clarify this period of "anger and fury" mentioned in Daniel 9:16. We learn from the prophet Zechariah, in chapter 1 of his own biblical prophecy, that this divine anger mentioned by Daniel ended nearly eighteen years after Daniel's prayer. Eighteen years is a long time to wait, but finally YHWH did return to Jerusalem.

Zechariah 1 records that the 70 years of YHWH's divine anger ended in the second year of Darius 'the Great' Artaxerxes (520 BC). By counting back from the end of YHWH's divine anger, we can ascertain the catalyst for this wrath 70 years earlier as we arrive at 589 BC and the departure of YHWH's shekinah glory from the holy mountain and the temple, as recorded in Ezekiel 8–10. In the following abridged passage we see just how far Israel had descended into sin:

> And he put forth the form of an hand, and took me by a lock of mine head; and the spirit lifted me up between the earth and the heaven, and brought me in the visions of God to Jerusalem, to the door of the inner gate that looketh toward the north; where was the seat of the image of jealousy, which provoketh to jealousy . . .

He said furthermore unto me, Son of man, seest thou what they do? even the great abominations that the house of Israel committeth here, that I should go far off from my sanctuary? but turn thee yet again, and thou shalt see greater abominations . . . So I went in and saw; and behold every form of creeping things, and abominable beasts, and all the idols of the house of Israel, pourtrayed upon the wall round about . . .

He said also unto me, Turn thee yet again, and thou shalt see greater abominations that they do. Then he brought me to the door of the gate of YHWH's house which was toward the north; and, behold, there sat women weeping for Tammuz. Then said he unto me, Hast thou seen this, O son of man? turn thee yet again, and thou shalt see greater abominations than these. And he brought me into the inner court of YHWH's house, and, behold, at the door of the temple of YHWH, between the porch and the altar, were about five and twenty men, with their backs toward the temple of YHWH, and their faces toward the east; and they worshipped the sun toward the east.

Then he said unto me, Hast thou seen this, O son of man? Is it a light thing to the house of Judah that they commit the abominations which they commit here? for they have filled the land with violence, and have returned to provoke me to anger: and, lo, they put the branch to their nose. Therefore will I also deal in fury: mine eye shall not spare, neither will I have pity: and though they cry in mine ears with a loud voice, yet will I not hear them. (Ezekiel 8:3–18)

To really get a sense of how these events relate, I encourage you to peruse the chart below. It shows the period of YHWH's divine anger relative to the 70 years of captivity and the departure of YHWH's presence from Solomon's temple.

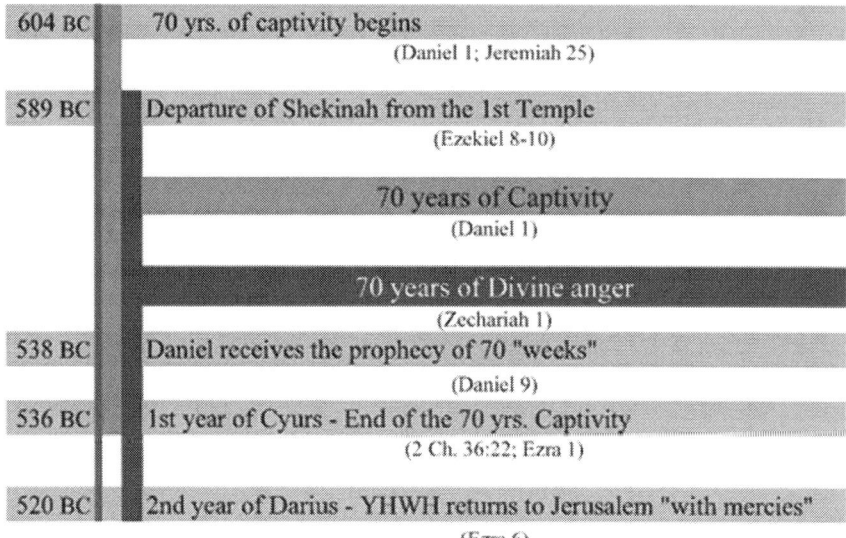

Precise dates will be discussed elsewhere

YHWH Returns to Jerusalem

As you read the following passage, remember it for later, because it is one of the most pivotal events of the Second Temple era—not to mention it has direct bearing on how we interpret Daniel 9 and the prophecy of 70 weeks. Here Zechariah describes the return of YHWH to Jerusalem with "mercies":

> Then the angel of YHWH answered and said, O YHWH of hosts, how long wilt thou not have mercy on Jerusalem and on the cities of Judah, against which thou hast had indignation these *threescore and ten* [70] *years*?
> Therefore thus saith YHWH; I am returned to Jerusalem with mercies: my house shall be built in it, saith YHWH of hosts, and a line shall be stretched forth upon Jerusalem. (Zechariah 1:12–16, emphasis mine)

Let's look at YHWH's departure and return to Jerusalem in the context of Daniel 9. Keep in mind that Daniel, Ezekiel, and Zechariah all emphasize the connection between Jerusalem, the temple, and Israel's sins. Daniel 9:16 connected YHWH's "anger and fury" to Jerusalem and His holy mountain. Zechariah shows that this divine "indignation" began when YHWH's presence left the temple and Jerusalem due to the sins of Israel described in Ezekiel 8–10. The following passages describe the fury of YHWH and His departure from the temple and Jerusalem because of the abominations committed by Israel. Once again, it is the prophet Ezekiel who tells the story:

> And it came to pass in the sixth year, in the sixth month, in the fifth day of the month [589 BC], as I sat in mine house, and the elders of Judah sat before me, that the hand of the Lord YHWH fell there upon me . . .

> And the glory of the God of Israel was gone up from the cherub, whereupon he was, to the threshold of the house . . . And it came to pass, while they were slaying them [those committing the abominations in the temple], and I was left, that I fell upon my face, and cried, and said, Ah Lord YHWH! wilt thou destroy all the residue of Israel in thy pouring out of thy fury upon Jerusalem? . . .
>
> Then the glory of YHWH went up from the cherub, and stood over the threshold of the house; and the house was filled with the cloud, and the court was full of the brightness of the YHWH's glory . . .
>
> Then the glory of YHWH departed from off the threshold of the house, and stood over the cherubims. And the cherubims lifted up their wings, and mounted up from the earth in my sight: when they went out, the wheels also were beside them, and every one stood at the door of the east gate of YHWH's house; and the glory of the God of Israel was over them above. (Ezekiel 8:1, 9:3–8, 10:4, 10:18–19)

Shine Thy Face Upon Thy Sanctuary

In Daniel 9:16, Daniel petitions YHWH to turn away His "anger and fury" from Jerusalem and the "holy mountain." Now, in verse 17, Daniel asks YHWH to let His "face shine upon thy sanctuary that is desolate." This verse confirms that YHWH had turned His face away from Jerusalem and the holy mount, but it further clarifies that what YHWH really left was His "sanctuary." What makes Jerusalem special among all cities of the earth is that it is the one place YHWH, the living God of the Bible, chose to meet with mankind. As Daniel 9:18 describes it, it is the "city which is called by thy name." Daniel finishes,

> And whiles I was speaking, and praying, and confessing my sin and the sin of my people Israel, and presenting my supplication before YHWH my God f*or the holy mountain of my God . . .* (Daniel 9:20, emphasis mine)

The Holy Mountain

Can you see the events described through Daniel's eyes by this point? Because of the prophecy of Jeremiah, he understood that a period of desolation regarding Jerusalem was likely drawing to a close. Daniel acknowledged that it was the sins of his people that had caused YHWH to depart from Jerusalem, His holy mountain, and scattered the people among the nations. He understood that YHWH was still angry with them. But instead of trying to convince YHWH that they deserved His mercy, he acknowledged something else: If YHWH was to remember His covenant and mercy toward the people and the city of Jerusalem, it would have to be because YHWH was merciful and truthful, because YHWH always kept His word. Through the prophet Jeremiah, YHWH had given His word that Israel would return from captivity after 70 years, and now was the time to perform that return, for YHWH's own honor and glory were at stake.

Before we move on to the specifics of the prophecy of 70 weeks, it is important to emphasize that Daniel saw the desolation of Jerusalem and the holy mountain as a result of YHWH's departure from the temple. What made Jerusalem special from Daniel's perspective was the presence of YHWH in His holy temple, and it is this presence that Daniel pleads for in Daniel 9:16–20. Remember, YHWH's house was the very heart of Jerusalem. Its destruction marked the de facto end of Jerusalem, and its reconstruction marked Jerusalem's new beginning.

Strangely enough, when interpreting Daniel 9 and the "commandment to restore and build Jerusalem," many sever the clear biblical relationship between Jerusalem and the house of YHWH. In the coming pages we'll explore the reasons for this separation and the chronological and interpretational errors which have grown out of it.

Chapter 4:
Redemption in 70 Sevens

"Seventy weeks [shabuwa] *are determined upon thy people and upon thy holy city."*
Daniel 9:24a

I have no idea what an angelic visitation would be like, but I can imagine it would be a truly amazing experience. We learn in Daniel 9:23 that at the very beginning of Daniel's supplications to YHWH, the angel Gabriel was dispatched with the prophecy of 70 weeks (*shabuwa*) in part because Daniel was "greatly beloved" of YHWH. Can you imagine what it would be like to hear that? Wow!

In any case, Gabriel begins his explanation of this wonderful prophecy by summarizing a series of events that will transpire during this 70 week period.

> Seventy weeks are determined upon thy people and upon thy holy city, to finish the transgression, and to make an end of sins, and to make reconciliation for iniquity, and to bring in everlasting righteousness, and to seal up the vision and prophecy, and to anoint the most Holy. (Daniel 9:24)

Sevens

Before we look at the prophesied events during this 70 week period, it is important to briefly explain the word "weeks" in a little more detail. As used in the text of Daniel 9 quoted above, the word "weeks" is actually the Hebrew term *shabuwa,* and it literally means seven or a period of seven. As we learned in chapter 2, shabuwa comes from the Hebrew root *shaba,* which means to swear or make an oath. Based upon my studies and my limited knowledge of Hebrew, I understand that shabuwa as it is used in several instances in Daniel 9 is a rather unusual plural masculine form of the word. Later, in our exploration of this prophecy, we will learn the amazing reason the plural masculine form of shabuwa was chosen by YHWH.

At this point, suffice it to say we need to try not to add our own presuppositional biases to our interpretation of the prophecy. Shabuwa simply means seven or a group of seven. By using the English term "week" to translate it, we have inadvertently added a calendric bias to our point of view. To you and me, a week implies a period of seven days of calendric time. Many then extrapolate this "week" to a literal seven-day or seven-year period of time . At this point we have no way to determine whether this is a valid premise, so for the sake of accuracy, just keep in mind that "70 weeks" in the most literal, reasonable sense simply means "70 sevens" (70 x 7). What those 70 sevens are meant to be measured in—days, weeks, years, or some other period of time—is yet to be determined.

For accuracy's sake, as we move forward in our investigation of Daniel 9, I will be gradually replacing the word "weeks" with *sevens* and *shabuwa*, its original Hebrew equivalent. My hope is that by the end of this book you will think of this prophecy in its Hebrew context of shaba (sware) and shabuwa (sevens) or an oath of sevens.

> Seventy weeks [shabuwa] are determined upon thy people and upon thy holy city, to finish the transgression, and to make an end of sins, and to make reconciliation for iniquity, and to bring in everlasting righteousness, and to seal up the vision and prophecy, and to anoint the most Holy. (Daniel 9:24)

An Overview of the 70 Sevens

So our first glimpse of this wonderful prophecy is an overview of the events that would transpire during a period of time described as 70 sevens. This is where our preliminary review of Daniel 9:1–23 really becomes valuable to us, allowing us to understand that this prophecy was given within the context of Daniel's prayers to YHWH on behalf of his people and the holy city. More specifically, Daniel saw the "holy city" in terms of the "holy mountain," where YHWH's "desolate sanctuary" had once been built by a people singled out among all the nations of the earth to serve YHWH in a special way. A central part of that calling was the sacrificial service given to Moses and carried out in the holy mountain located in Jerusalem.

Daniel's perspective here cannot be emphasized enough: without YHWH's presence, Jerusalem and the holy mountain are just a piece of real estate. Don't ever lose sight of that important fact. Daniel saw Jerusalem not primarily in terms of a city for his people to return to, but as a city for YHWH to return to, where Daniel's people had the privilege of serving Him. But in order for YHWH to return to Jerusalem and the holy mountain, the Jewish people had to first return from captivity and rebuild the temple. This goal is in fact the central focus, yes, the driving factor behind the Jewish people's desire to return and build Jerusalem.

Six Milestones that Changed the World

Let's turn our attention to those events which the angel Gabriel tells Daniel will take place within or during the 70 weeks, expressed in six goals set out by YHWH. We will deal more fully with these six goals at the end of this book, but briefly, let's recapitulate each one in light of the context of Daniel 9:1–23.

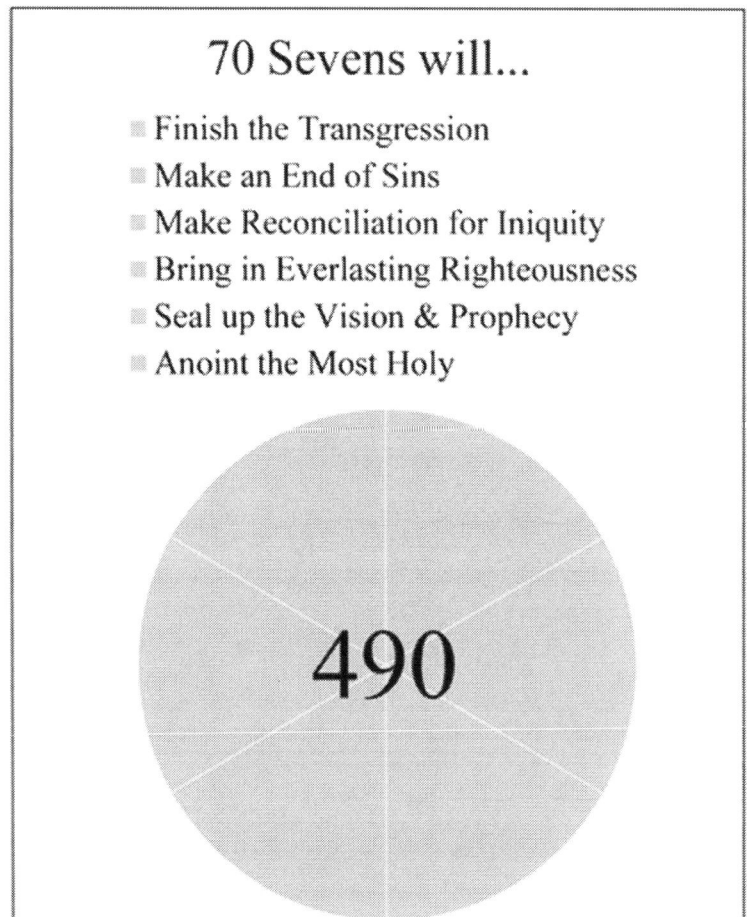

As we explore each of these six goals, I remind you to consider them in light of Daniel's intercessory prayer and the forgotten covenant of Daniel 9:1–23, because they cannot be separated from this context.

> And now, O Lord our God, that hast brought thy people forth out of the land of Egypt with a mighty hand, and hast gotten thee renown, as at this day; *we have sinned*, we have *done wickedly*. O Lord, according to all thy righteousness, I beseech thee, let thine anger and thy fury be turned away from thy city Jerusalem, thy holy mountain: because for *our sins*, and *for the iniquities of our fathers*, Jerusalem and thy people are become a reproach to all that are about us.
>
> Now therefore, O our God, hear the prayer of thy servant, and his supplications, and cause thy face to shine upon thy sanctuary that is desolate, for the Lord's sake. O my God, incline thine ear, and hear; open thine eyes, and behold our desolations, and the city which is called by thy name: for we do not present our supplications before thee for our righteousnesses, but for thy great mercies.
>
> O Lord, hear; *O Lord, forgive*; O Lord, hearken and do; defer not, for thine own sake, O my God: for thy city and thy people are called by thy name.
>
> And whiles I was speaking, and praying, and *confessing my sin and the sin of my people Israel*, and presenting my

> supplication before YHWH my God for the holy mountain of my God . . . (Daniel 9:15–20, emphasis mine)

Do you see the connection between Daniel's prayer and the six messianic goals Daniel was given by the angel Gabriel in reply? Daniel confessed his people's sins, iniquity, and wickedness and pleaded with YHWH to forgive them without delay. Shortly thereafter, the angel Gabriel gave Daniel a vision which explained exactly when that forgiveness and reconciliation would come. In summary, Gabriel showed Daniel that concerning his people and the holy city, from YHWH's perspective, it would take 70 weeks to finish the transgression, make an end of sins, make reconciliation for iniquity, and bring in everlasting righteousness.

> Seventy weeks are determined upon thy people and upon thy holy city, to finish the transgression, and to make an end of sins, and to make reconciliation for iniquity, and to bring in everlasting righteousness, and to seal up the vision and prophecy, and to anoint the most Holy. (Daniel 9:24)

Let's focus in on this a moment. In chapter 2, "The Forgotten Covenant," we saw that the "covenant and mercy" mentioned in Daniel 9:4 is in fact a reference to the covenant made with Abraham that in his seed all nations of the earth would be blessed. We learned earlier that the apostle Paul explained that this covenant made with Abraham was indeed confirmed by YHWH "in Christ" 430 years before the law was given. In Zechariah 9 we learn that this blood covenant brought salvation and deliverance from the pit. And in Acts 3:25–26, it is this covenant of the promised seed, made with Abraham, that confirms that the promised Messiah was brought forth for the purpose of "turning away every one of you from his iniquities":

> Ye are the children of the prophets, and of the covenant which God made with our fathers, saying unto Abraham, *And in thy seed shall all the kindreds of the earth be blessed.* Unto you first God, having raised up his Son Jesus, sent him to bless you, in turning away every one of you from his iniquities. (Acts 3:25–26, emphasis mine)

Whether Daniel or Zechariah fully understood it or not, we now know in hindsight that YHWH became flesh in the person of Yeshua so that He might indeed reconcile the seed of Abraham and in a larger context all the descendants of Adam (all nations of the earth) to Himself by the shedding of His blood on our behalf. A few verses are sufficient to explain this:

> Rejoice greatly, O daughter of Zion; shout, O daughter of Jerusalem: behold, thy King cometh unto thee: he is just, and having salvation; lowly, and riding upon an ass, and upon a colt the foal of an ass. And I will cut off the chariot from Ephraim, and the horse from Jerusalem, and the battle bow shall be cut off: and he shall speak peace unto the heathen: and his dominion shall be from sea even to sea, and from the river even to the ends of the earth. *As for thee also, by the blood of thy*

covenant I have sent forth thy prisoners out of the pit wherein is no water. (Zechariah 9:9–11, emphasis mine)

For Christ also hath once suffered for sins, the just for the unjust, that he might bring us to God, being put to death in the flesh, but quickened by the Spirit. (1 Peter 3:18)

For then must he often have suffered since the foundation of the world: but now once in the end of the world hath he appeared to put away sin by the sacrifice of himself. (Hebrews 9:26)

Wherefore then serveth the law? It was added because of transgressions, till the seed should come to whom the promise was made; and it was ordained by angels in the hand of a mediator. (Galatians 3:19–20)

And she shall bring forth a son, and thou shalt call his name JESUS [Yeshua—Salavation of YHWH]: for he shall save his people from their sins. (Matthew 1:21)

Herein is love, not that we loved God, but that he loved us, and sent his Son to be the propitiation for our sins. (1 John 4:10)

But this man, after he had offered one sacrifice for sins for ever, sat down on the right hand of God. (Hebrews 10:12)

> And ye know that he was manifested to take away our sins; and in him is no sin. Whosoever abideth in him sinneth not: whosoever sinneth hath not seen him, neither known him. (1 John 3:5–6)

> For he hath made him to be sin for us, who knew no sin; that we might be made the righteousness of God in him. (2 Corinthians 5:21)

The sum of the matter is that Yeshua came to redeem Israel (and all mankind) from their sins, just as Daniel prayed for and just as YHWH promised from the very beginning.

> Ye are the children of the prophets, and of the covenant which God made with our fathers, saying unto Abraham, *And in thy seed shall all the kindreds of the earth be blessed.* Unto you first God, having raised up his Son Jesus, sent him to bless you, in turning away every one of you from his iniquities. (Acts 3:25–26, emphasis mine)

It is an indisputable New Testament fact that Yeshua came to reconcile all the world to YHWH. Indeed, it is equally clear that He accomplished His purpose. But where does that leave us in terms of the overreaching redemptive message of the 70 sevens in regards to Daniel's people and the city of Jerusalem? Was this prophecy only a bridge between the Old and New Covenants? Was its only purpose to describe those earth-shattering events of the first century, or does it also span the past two thousand years to a yet-future date when Daniel's people and the city of Jerusalem will be restored, as described in so many other wonderful Old and New Testament passages?

Rest assured YHWH does indeed keep His word, but as we saw in Book I, *The 13th Enumeration: Key to the Bible's Messianic Symbolism,* He doesn't always carry out His purposes in the manner in which we expect. Often our expectations are based upon our limited worldview, and therein lies the problem. YHWH sees the end from the beginning, but we cannot even see tomorrow clearly.

> Let the wicked forsake his way, and the unrighteous man his thoughts: and let him return unto YHWH, and he will have mercy upon him; and to our God, for he will abundantly pardon.
>
> For my thoughts are not your thoughts, neither are your ways my ways, saith YHWH. For as the heavens are higher than the earth, so are my ways higher than your ways, and my thoughts than your thoughts. (Isaiah 55:7–9)

The Jewish believers of Yeshua's day believed He had come to establish the messianic kingdom in their generation. Those of faith were ready, but YHWH was not. You see, they didn't understand the full implications of YHWH's covenant with Abraham. That covenant promised that through Abraham's seed, *all* nations of the earth were to be blessed. That blessing was initialized when Yeshua paid the price for the sins of both Jews and Gentiles. That promise took on new importance when the apostle Paul was commissioned by Yeshua on the road to Damascus.

> I say then, Hath God cast away his people? God forbid. For I also am an Israelite, of the seed of Abraham, of the tribe of Benjamin. God hath not cast away his people which he foreknew . . . I say then, Have they stumbled that they should fall? God forbid: but rather through their fall salvation is come unto the Gentiles, for to provoke them to jealousy. Now if the fall of them be the riches of the world, and the diminishing of them the riches of the Gentiles; how much more their fulness? (Romans 11:1–2, 11–12)

As we turn our attention to a more detailed exploration of the prophecy of 70 weeks in Part II: Countdown to the Messiah, please remember the underlying messianic context of this wonderful prophecy. Daniel 9 is first and foremost a prophecy about the coming of YHWH's anointed Redeemer. As Revelation 19:10 reminds us, it is Yeshua who is the true "spirit of prophecy," and no place in the Bible exemplifies that better than Daniel chapter 9 and the prophecy of 70 sevens.

> *". . . for the testimony of Jesus is the spirit of prophecy."*
> Revelation 19:10

Part II:

The Second Temple Era

Introduction

Part I of this book explored the 70 weeks prophecy within the panoramic context of YHWH's plan to reconcile all mankind to Himself through Yeshua, the Messiah promised in the Scripture. That context included a look at the covenant of Daniel 9:4, which we traced back to Moses, Abraham, and ultimately the garden of Eden and mankind's original sin.

Now, with this foundational perspective firmly fixed in our minds, we will take a closer look at the blueprints for this great prophecy and see if we can get a clearer picture of what YHWH intended when He sent the angel Gabriel with this incredible prophetic message of a coming Messiah.

As a high-school-educated plumber, I don't have the ability or the desire to dazzle you with fancy arguments. What I can offer is what I hope is a reasonable and common-sense look at the passage and the evidence for how we should interpret it that seeks to see the prophecy through its Second Temple era context. This context matters deeply, because this period in biblical history is where the countdown to the Messiah originates. It is the events described in the books of Chronicles, Ezra, Nehemiah, Daniel, Haggai, and Zechariah that provide us with an accurate date in history upon which to calculate the 70 weeks prophecy—and see where (and to whom) it brings us. Without the chronology of the Second Temple era, it is impossible to prove that Yeshua (Jesus) fulfilled the prophecy of 70 sevens.

But I have some unsettling news to share with you related to the Second Temple era and the prophecy of Daniel 9. Even though the Bible is rich in details, this period of time is almost totally ignored by those who write on the prophecy of 70 weeks. In other words, most of the interpretations of Daniel 9 that you and I have read simply don't have any biblical foundation at all! And it doesn't matter whether you believe Yeshua fulfilled the prophecy of 70 weeks at some point in the past or will do so at some point in the future. Without a biblical understanding of Second Temple chronology, the foundation is still missing.

As Christians we often point to the fact that some scientists make unreasonable assumptions about the theory of evolution. I mean come on, we still haven't seen that conclusive "missing link" proving that man evolved from some primal ooze. Yet in the overwhelming majority of the cases, we as Christians cannot provide a single missing link to connect the most important messianic prophecy in the Bible with its own internal biblical and secular chronology. Is it too strong to call this theological hypocrisy? Folks, I don't know about you, but I hate being a hypocrite. So let's remedy that in the following pages. Even if we don't end up agreeing in the end, at the very least, I promise that by the conclusion of this discussion you will have reasonable facts upon which to connect biblical and secular history with the coming of the Messiah. Fair enough?

So let's get to it.

As we investigate this prophecy, the following visual outline might be helpful:

Overview of 70 Sevens

- Commandment to Restore and Build
- 7 Sevens until the Messiah (49)
- 62 Sevens the Plaza & Wall Rebuilt (434)
- Messiah Cut off After 62 Sevens
- 1 Seven the Covenant Confirmed (7)

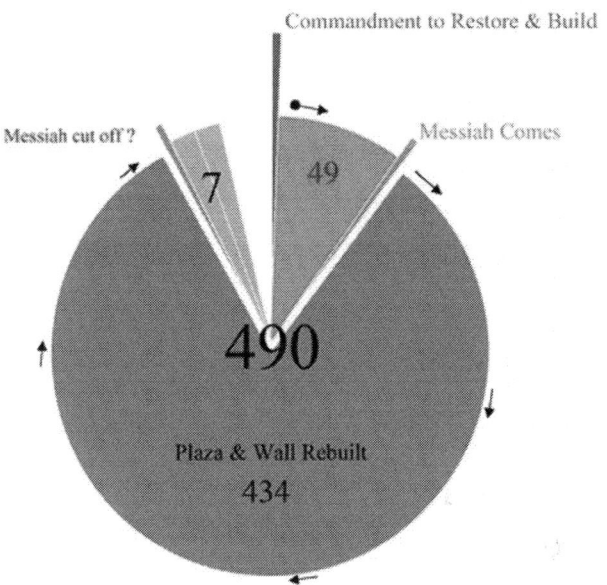

Overview of the 70 Sevens

The text of Daniel 9:24–27 breaks down the prophecy into several important segments, or epochs, if you will. The biblical text starts in verse 24 with a summary of six important goals which are accomplished by the 70 sevens. Keep in mind for future reference that the six goals of Daniel 9:24 all take place *during* these 70 sevens. They don't take place before, after, or in some gap in between. If during our investigation we find that any of these goals have been fulfilled in the course of biblical history, then we know from the context of verse 24 that their fulfillment fell during the 70 sevens. I know this may seem like it's just common sense, but keep this in mind for later—it will become important. The six goals of Daniel 9:24 in the context of the 70 sevens are the very heart of this messianic prophecy.

> Seventy weeks are determined upon thy people and upon thy holy city, to finish the transgression, and to make an end of sins, and to make reconciliation for iniquity, and to bring in everlasting righteousness, and to seal up the vision and prophecy, and to anoint the most Holy. (Daniel 9:24)

In perhaps one of the most surprising aspects of modern scholarship regarding Daniel 9, many unhinge the Messiah Yeshua's death and resurrection from the prophecy of 70 sevens by placing it outside of this 70 sevens time frame. If that makes you just a little uncomfortable, I understand, because it does me as well. This strange disconnect is just one of the many aspects of modern scholarship on the passage that we'll explore in subsequent chapters.

70 Sevens will...

- Finish the Transgression
- Make an End of Sins
- Make Reconciliation for Iniquity
- Bring in Everlasting Righteousness
- Seal up the Vision & Prophecy
- Anoint the Most Holy

490

7 Sevens to the Messiah

I've had a special interest in the prophecy of 70 sevens for most of my life. I've read many books that have interpreted this prophecy in a multitude of different ways, and if you were to ask me what is one of the most ignored parts of the prophecy, I would have to say it is the last part of the following passage:

> Know therefore and understand, that from the going forth of the commandment to restore and to build Jerusalem unto the Messiah the Prince shall be seven weeks. (Daniel 9:25a)

In clear, unequivocal terms, the angel Gabriel explains to Daniel that from the "commandment to restore and build Jerusalem unto the Messiah the Prince" there will be 7 sevens (*shabuwa*). This might seem like a straightforward statement on its own, but it creates an interpretational problem for scholars, because it seems impossible for the same Messiah to arrive after 7 sevens yet still be alive to be "cut off" nearly 62 sevens later as described in Daniel 9:26. A little confusing, isn't it?

Well, the key to this interpretational puzzle is found in the 13th Enumeration. Do you remember in Book I, *The 13th Enumeration: Key to the Bible's Messianic Prophecy,* where we learned that the apostle Matthew represented Yeshua as both the 13th and 14th generation in Matthew 1? Do you remember the name of the missing king who was left out of the list between the 13th and 14th generations? Yes, that king's name was Jehoiakim, "Whom YHWH Raises Up." This gap between the 13th and 14th generations marks in beautiful symbolism the exact start of the 70 years' captivity of Judah, as well as the start of the captivity of the young man named Daniel, who nearly 70 years later was given the very prophecy we are exploring in this book. You will be thrilled to learn in the following pages that this gap in the lineage of Yeshua, this "mistake" so many have pointed to over the past centuries in an attempt to discredit the Scriptures, is in fact the very key to understanding how the Messiah can come after 7 sevens and then nearly 62 sevens later still be alive to be "cut off" for the sins of mankind!

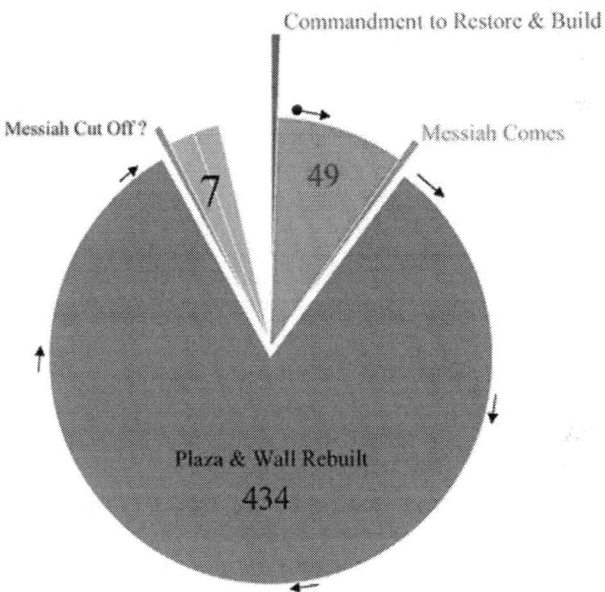

The Wall and Moat During 62 Sevens

The next segment of the prophecy is a period of time when the street (plaza) and wall are rebuilt. This is the longest section of the prophecy and is equal to 62 sevens or 434 periods of time:

> . . . and threescore and two weeks: the street shall be built again, and the wall, even in troublous times. (Daniel 9:25b)

The word "street" used here in the text is the Hebrew word *rechob,* and it means a broad or open place, i.e. a plaza. Many believe this plaza is a reference to the open place of the temple complex proper. We will look at the chronology in more detail later, but briefly, this temple was completed in the sixth year of Darius 'the Great' Artaxerxes (516 BC).

Ezra 7-10 records a gathering of the people to the temple plaza in the seventh year of Artaxerxes. Nehemiah, the governor of Jerusalem, did not complete the wall of Jerusalem until the twentieth or twenty-first year of Artaxerxes. Centuries later, Herod would undertake a massive remodeling effort of the Temple Mount and Jerusalem. As John 2:20 notes, Herod's improvements of the temple complex lasted at least forty-six years. I think it reasonable to conclude that it is this lengthy period of construction and reconstruction from Nehemiah to Herod that is covered by the 62 sevens of Daniel 9.

For accuracy's sake regarding the plaza and wall construction efforts under the "Artaxerxes" of Persia, it should be noted that Artaxerxes was a title that applied to several Persian kings during the Second Temple era. In the coming chapters, we will explore the biblical context of the Second Temple era to determine the identity of this Persian king who was so instrumental in helping the Jewish people rebuild Jerusalem, but for now his identity must remain one of the best-kept secrets of the Bible's Second Temple chronology.

The Messiah Cut Off after 62 Weeks

In Part I of this book we showed how Daniel's prayer for the covenant and mercy of YHWH was in reality a call for the coming Messiah. Daniel further pleaded with YHWH to forgive Israel's sins and return to the desolate sanctuary. With this context in mind, we now turn to one of the greatest interpretational ironies of the Bible's prophetic texts. The prophecy of Daniel 9 is a chronological blueprint for the coming Messiah, yet many scholars today believe the most important event in YHWH's redemptive plan for mankind is not part of the prophecy of 70 weeks.

> And after threescore and two weeks shall Messiah be cut off, but not for himself. (Daniel 9:26)

I'll try to explain. Daniel 9:26 states that the Messiah will be "cut off" after 62 sevens. Take a look at the chart below. After the 62 sevens (62 x 7 = 434) that follow the original 7 sevens, only the final seven is left. This means 69 sevens have run their course. Common sense would indicate that Yeshua's death and resurrection, the most important messianic event in biblical history up to this point, would take place in the final seven or week of the prophecy. Yet many scholars today unhinge the Messiah's redemptive efforts on our behalf from the prophecy of 70 sevens and instead place Yeshua's death and resurrection into the period of a now nearly two-thousand-year gap between the 69th and 70th sevens of Daniel 9.

Think about the implications of that for a moment. The very essence of the six goals of Daniel 9 is the answer to Daniel's desperate plea for forgiveness and reconciliation for his people's sins against

YHWH. Yet, according to many well-meaning and equally well-respected scholars, the very act that defines that forgiveness and reconciliation is missing from the prophecy of 70 weeks.

> O Lord, hear; O Lord, forgive; O Lord, hearken and do; defer not, for thine own sake, O my God: for thy city and thy people are called by thy name. And whiles I was speaking, and praying, and confessing my sin and the sin of my people Israel, and presenting my supplication before YHWH my God for the holy mountain of my God . . . (Daniel 9:19–20)

So what do you think? Is the greatest messianic prophecy in the Bible missing the very events that define and fulfill the Messiah's redemptive purpose as it relates to mankind's sins? Such a scenario would seem improbable, but let's see where the evidence leads. We can rest assured in the knowledge that the Bible's messianic message is congruent even if our own understanding seems clouded sometimes.

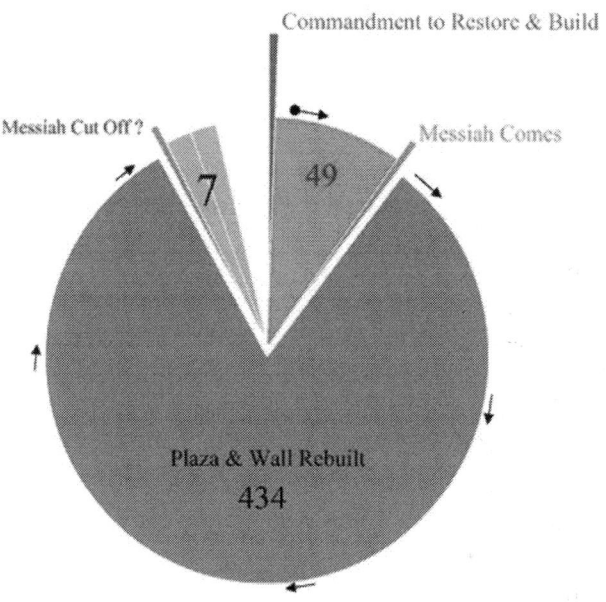

The Final Seven

By far the most controversial aspect of Daniel 9 amongst biblical scholars is the final "week" or seven of the prophecy. Today, the predominant scholarly position is that the final seven is a yet-future time known commonly as the Great Tribulation, a period of cataclysmic upheaval and war that will culminate in the second coming of Yeshua the Messiah. This position holds sway in the general population as well, and there's a good chance that you too hold or have held it. But before we completely prejudice this part of the 70 sevens, let's take a look at what the Scripture says concerning this final period of time in Daniel's prophecy:

> And after threescore and two weeks shall Messiah be cut off, but not for himself: and the people of the prince that shall come shall destroy the city and the sanctuary; and the end thereof shall be with a flood, and unto the end of the war desolations are determined. And he shall confirm the covenant with many for one week: and in the midst of the week he shall cause the sacrifice and the oblation to cease, and for the overspreading of abominations he shall make it desolate, even until the consummation, and that determined shall be poured upon the desolate. (Daniel 9:26–27)

Verse 26 above tells us that the Messiah is cut off after the 62 sevens, the city and the sanctuary (which had not yet been rebuilt as of the time Daniel was given the prophecy) are destroyed, and war and desolations are determined until the consummation. Verse 27 adds further detail by explaining that "he" shall confirm a covenant for the final week, but on the "wings of abomination" he shall make the temple desolated until the consummation.

Intriguing information to be sure, but does the prophecy speak to events past or future? Does Daniel 9:26–27 speak to a coming Messiah or a yet-future Antichrist? These are the questions of the hour, and we will seek to answer them in the coming pages, but first let me introduce you to the heroes and villains of this era in biblical history. For all that it remains vague and shadowy to many a reader, the

Second Temple era is one of the most intriguing in biblical history. It is my privilege to take you on a guided tour.

A Fascinating Cast of Characters

As we explore the biblical history related to the prophecy of 70 sevens, we meet a fascinating cast of characters whose lives are inexorably entwined with the events of this monumental period in Jewish history. Realistically, we can't properly understand the prophecy of 70 sevens if we don't understand the history of the Second Temple era, and the best way to understand this era is to see it through the eyes of those lived it. Here is the biblical cast of heroes we'll learn about as we relive this pivotal era in Jewish history.

- **Daniel.** Beloved prophet of YHWH and recorder of the 70 sevens prophecy.
- **Cyrus the Great.** "King of Babylon" and the only secular ruler whom the Bible calls YHWH's "anointed" (Messiah).
- **Ahasuerus.** A ruler of Persia after Cyrus (Ezra 4:6). "Ahasuerus" was a title held by several other Persian kings as well.
- **Ahasuerus.** A Persian king who chose Hadassah (Esther) as his queen (the book of Esther).
- **Artaxerxes.** A ruler of Persia who stopped construction of the Second Temple (Ezra 4:7).
- **Joshua.** High priest and leader of the repatriated Jewish captives.

- **Zerubbabel.** Governor of Jerusalem, contemporary of Joshua the high priest.
- **Darius 'the Great' Artaxerxes.** The most famous Persian king, ruler over 127 provinces from India to Ethiopia. The Persian king who allowed the temple construction to continue.
- **Hadassah (Esther).** Queen of Persia who delivered the Jewish people from their enemies.
- **Ezra.** Priest and scribe, teacher of the law, and son of the high priest Seraiah.
- **Nehemiah.** Cupbearer to an Artaxerxes of Persia, governor of Jerusalem after Zerubbabel.
- **Artaxerxes.** The unnamed king of Persia who allowed Ezra to beautify the temple and Nehemiah to rebuild the walls and gates of Jerusalem. As already noted, this was a title held by several different Persian rulers.

For those wondering if it is really important to understand what the Bible has to say about this era of biblical history, let me ask you a question. If your professor told you George Washington came to America with Christopher Columbus, what would you think about his grasp of early American history? Wouldn't you have reasonable cause to question his view and any conclusions he'd made based upon that flawed understanding?

Now what if I told you we've made an error of similar magnitude and that this error has completely altered our view of the Bible's Second Temple history? Take a look at the above list once more. Some of the heroes on that list have been moved to another era in biblical history altogether, despite the rich chronological evidence of the Bible that this is where they belong. Impossible, you say! Ask yourself, then, which of the above heroes you can place in their biblical context using the Bible's own internal evidence. I'm not asking what you believe or what you've been told about these people and when they lived, but what you can prove using a reasonable rendering of the biblical record. That's much more difficult, isn't it?

"So what?" you might ask. "So we mixed up a bit of Old Testament chronology that really doesn't matter all that much anyway. What's the big deal?" You couldn't be more wrong. First of all, as I've stated earlier, this era is the basis upon which we build our chronological proof that Yeshua is the Messiah promised in Daniel 9. Second, the prophecy of 70 weeks is one of the major pillars of modern-day eschatology. In other words, Daniel 9 provides a major portion of the framework upon which we build our understanding of the events which will happen during the tribulation and leading up to the second coming of Yeshua. It affects our understanding of our own day and of the future. This is not one of those times when we can say "close is good enough." As good stewards of YHWH's Word, it is our responsibility and privilege to ensure we get this correct.

Let me reassure you: the Bible's chronological record is accurate and congruent. It can be understood. In fact, I personally believe the chronology of the Bible is a key to seeing how YHWH has worked in the past and thus providing a glimpse into the future as well. It doesn't require convoluted arguments and incredible exceptions or a PhD in quantum physics to understand. We simply have to read it in its most natural and reasonable context. I can't promise you that you will agree with all of my conclusions about Daniel 9 and the prophecy of 70 sevens by the time you've finished this book, but I will guarantee you that if you are willing to make just a little effort, you will gain a commanding understanding of the Second Temple era, and you will see the prophecy of 70 sevens from an entirely different perspective. Are you willing to make the effort?

Countdown to the Messiah

Daniel 9 and the 70 weeks prophecy is a biblical promise and countdown to a coming Redeemer. This introduction has given us an idea of some of the beauty and challenges we will face as we explore the specifics of this wonderful prophecy. As with any good investigation, we will start with the information we can determine with reasonable certainty and see what revelations this leads to.

Every countdown has a starting point, and the starting point for the prophecy of 70 sevens is the commandment to restore and build Jerusalem. Let us now turn our attention to the events that begin the Bible's most famous countdown to the Messiah.

Chapter 1:

The Commandment to Restore and Build

"Know therefore and understand, that from the going forth of the commandment to restore and to build Jerusalem unto the Messiah the Prince shall be seven weeks."
Daniel 9:25

In Part I we found an ancient man named Daniel in a passionate prayer for the restoration of Jerusalem and YHWH's desolate sanctuary. Acknowledging his and his people's unrighteousness, Daniel admits the righteousness of YHWH's anger. Nevertheless, he pleads with YHWH to forgive them and remember the covenant He made with Moses and Abraham. In answer to Daniel's prayer, YHWH sends the angel Gabriel to reveal the future of Daniel's people and the city of Jerusalem as it relates to their sins and transgressions, a future that is summarized in the six goals of Daniel 9:24. So begins the great countdown to the Messiah, the Prince.

The Word to Restore and Build

I don't know about you, but if I've read Daniel 9:25 once, I've read it a hundred times. But I never gave much thought to the word "commandment": "from the going forth of the commandment to restore and to build Jerusalem unto the Messiah the Prince shall be seven weeks." As it turns out, I should have!

The English word "commandment," as it comes to us in Daniel 9:25, is a translation of the Hebrew word *dabar*. It means speech, word, speaking, utterance, etc. Of the 1439 times the word *dabar* is used in the KJV of the Bible, it is only translated as "commandment" twenty times. Today most scholars believe that this commandment was a decree issued by a secular Persian ruler during the Second Temple era. I mean, we all know it only makes sense for a commandment to be issued by a king, right? But what if that is only partially correct? What if we aren't thinking big enough?

What is really interesting, when you get into the Bible's use of the word, is that the vast majority of the time dabar is used in the Scripture it references the word, speech, or utterance of YHWH Himself. Did you know dabar is used four times in Daniel 9? It is first used in Daniel 9:2 to describe the word of YHWH that came to Jeremiah concerning the 70 years of Jerusalem's desolation. Here, take a look:

> In the first year of his reign I Daniel understood by books the number of the years, whereof the *word* [dabar] *of YHWH* came to Jeremiah the prophet, that he would accomplish seventy years in the desolations of Jerusalem. (Daniel 9:2, emphasis mine)

Dabar is next used in Daniel 9:12, and once again it references the word of YHWH. The third dabar found in Daniel 9 is in verse 23. Here the angel Gabriel explains to Daniel that at the beginning of his prayer he (Gabriel) was dispatched with the "word" of YHWH concerning the prophecy of 70 sevens.

> And he informed me, and talked with me, and said, O Daniel, I am now come forth to give thee skill and understanding. At the beginning of thy supplications *the commandment* [word/dabar] *came forth*, and I am come to shew thee; for thou art greatly beloved: therefore understand the matter, and consider the vision. (Daniel 9:22–23, emphasis mine)

This brings us to Daniel 9:25 and the "commandment to restore and build Jerusalem." Based upon the context of Daniel 9, the verse might better be read as the "word to restore and build Jerusalem." That kind of changes the perspective, doesn't it? For centuries, scholars have argued about which Persian ruler's commandment begins the prophecy of 70 sevens, but few indeed have ever considered that the countdown might begin with the very words of the living God of the Bible.

Before we search for this "word," whether it be of God or men, it will be valuable to define another word which is critical to the context of Daniel 9. That word is "restore."

> Know therefore and understand, that from the going forth of the commandment [word] to *restore* and to build Jerusalem . . . (Daniel 9:25a, emphasis mine)

Once again we have a Hebrew word that has a great impact on how we view this verse. The word "restore" comes from the Hebrew *shuwb,* and its primary meaning is to return or turn back to something that has already begun. Interestingly, shuwb is also used in Daniel 9:25b, and it is translated as "again":

> . . . and threescore and two weeks: the street shall be built *again* [shuwb], and the wall, even in troublous times. (Daniel 9:25, emphasis mine)

As we explore the events of the Second Temple era and the Jewish people's return to Jerusalem, keep the word *shuwb* in mind. This idea of turning back to something that has already begun just might help us identify the commandment or word that begins this great prophecy.

Let's take one more look at the verse now with the primary meaning of the Hebrew words *dabar* and *shuwb* used in place of the English words "commandment" and "restore":

> Know therefore and understand, that from the going forth of the *word* to *return* and to build Jerusalem unto the Messiah the Prince shall be seven weeks . . . (Daniel 9:25a, emphasis mine)

That kind of adds a new dimension to this verse, doesn't?

If you are still wondering why the starting point of the great prophecy even matters, consider the implications if we get it wrong. Daniel 9 is a prophecy which defines the nature and timing of a major part of YHWH's redemptive plan for mankind. Scholars in the past several centuries have built an entire chronological framework of end-time events upon the prophetic chronology described in Daniel 9. Think about that for a moment. Did you know that the idea of a seven-year tribulation period is based entirely on an interpretation of Daniel 9 with a specific starting point in the Second Temple era? If the starting point of Daniel 9 didn't take place when we believe it did, then how can we have any confidence that we correctly understand its ending point and all its associated eschatological implications? The truth of the matter is we can't.

Like I said, this is really about stewardship. YHWH had a purpose for initiating the prophecy of 70 weeks with a word to return and build. It could be a word given by a man or a word from YHWH Himself, as we have seen, but let's not skip the first and most important step in interpreting this prophecy just because we assume we understand what YHWH meant. Instead, together as Bereans, let's search for the answers He intended for us to find, even if those answers challenge us to look at the whole prophecy in new ways.

With these considerations in mind, let's start by looking at the four potential Persian decrees of Daniel 9:25 and see if they have biblical merit to be considered the "word to return and build Jerusalem."

The Persian Four

If you are at all familiar with the prophecy of Daniel 9, you probably know that scholars have traditionally pointed to four biblical commandments or decrees that potentially meet the criteria of Daniel

9:25. According to Chronicles, Ezra, and Nehemiah, all four of these decrees were given by secular Persian rulers at some point during the Second Temple era. The Persian four are as follows:

1. A decree by Cyrus (the Great) in his first year (2 Chronicles 36:22)
2. A decree by Darius (the Great) Artaxerxes in his second year (Ezra 6:7–14)
3. A decree by "Artaxerxes" (Longimanus?) in his seventh year (Ezra 7)
4. A decree by "Artaxerxes" (Longimanus?) in his twentieth year (Nehemiah 2)

To get the chronological context of these four decrees, let's take a moment to review the chart below. The biblical decrees are listed in green relative to where they fall in the secular chronological timeline, dated according to the most widely held understanding chronology of biblical scholars today. (Whether these dates are correct or not is one of the questions we will explore in the pages to come.) Understanding their context in the Second Temple era will helps us determine whether these four decrees are valid candidates for the "word to return and build Jerusalem."

Never lose sight of the fact that these decrees are the foundation upon which many respected scholars build their interpretation of Daniel 9 as well as their related eschatological worldview. In fact, many scholars are so dependent on these Persian decrees for their interpretation of Daniel 9 and the 70 weeks that they have modified biblical and secular history to make them fit the prophecy of 70 weeks. Don't get me wrong, I don't believe this has been done intentionally. It just shows how influential well-meaning assumptions can be when they have no foundation in biblical fact. That is why we must, as good stewards of YHWH's Word, take the time to make sure our foundation is set upon rock-solid biblical truth.

Persian Decrees to Restore and Build

604 BC	70 yrs. of captivity begins (Daniel 1; Jeremiah 25)
589 BC	Departure of Shekinah from the 1st Temple (Ezekiel 8-10)
	70 years Captivity (Daniel 1)
	70 years of Divine anger (Zechariah 1)
538 BC	Daniel receives the prophecy of 70 "weeks" (Daniel 9)
#1 536 BC	Decree of Cyrus to rebuild the Temple - End of the 70 yrs. Captivity (2 Ch. 36:22; Ezra 1)
520 BC	YHWH returns to Jerusalem "with mercies" (Zechariah 1)
#2 520 BC	Decree of Darius - Construction on the Temple continues (Ezra 6:7-14)
#3 458 BC	Decree by "Artaxerxes" Longimanus given to Ezra the Priest and Scribe (Ezra 7)
#4 445 BC	Decree by "Artaxerxes" Longimanus given to Nehemiah to rebuild the wall (Nehemiah 2)

Precise dates will be discussed elsewhere

Clearly, we don't yet have enough biblical contextual information to determine which, if any, of these decrees are the decree YHWH had in mind when He sent the prophecy to Daniel though the angel Gabriel, but in the following chapters we will look more closely at each one and see what biblical evidence we can gather that might help us make that determination. As our search proceeds, keep the following questions in mind:

- Could this decree be considered a dabar or word to return and build Jerusalem?
- Did this decree cause the Jewish people to shuwb (return or turn back) and build Jerusalem?
- Was this event of enough relevance to constitute "building Jerusalem"?
- Can the date of this decree be firmly established in both the biblical and secular record?

As a final thought, it essential to remember that the 70 weeks prophecy is the most important messianic prophecy in the Scripture. As such, it is only reasonable to believe that the word, decree, or commandment that begins it is of a special significance in the biblical record.

Our search for the start to the countdown to the Messiah begins with Cyrus of Persia in 536 BC. To this great biblical hero we now turn our attention.

Chapter 2:

Cyrus the Great:
A Decree to Rebuild the Temple and Jerusalem

"That saith of Cyrus, He is my shepherd, and shall perform all my pleasure: even saying to Jerusalem, Thou shalt be built; and to the temple, Thy foundation shall be laid."
Isaiah 44:28

We begin our search for the "commandment" of Daniel 9:25 with Cyrus the Great of Persia, founder of the Achaemenid Empire. It is believed by some scholars that it was Cyrus's viceroy or general, Darius the Median, who is mentioned in Daniel 5:31. If you recall, this Darius conquered Babylon on that infamous night when Belshazzar, king of Babylon, asked Daniel to read the "handwriting on the wall."

Although Cyrus ruled his empire for nearly twenty years before conquering Babylon, Ezra 5 counts Cyrus's first year from the point when he became "king of Babylon" in approximately 536 BC. This type of provincial reckoning of secular kings is quite common in the Bible. Cyrus died about seven years later in 530 BC. His son Cambyses II ruled in his place. Some scholars place Cyrus's first year as king of Babylon in 538 BC. For the purpose of our investigation of Daniel 9, either date will suffice.

Historians consider Cyrus an especially notable figure in ancient history. One of his greatest achievements was organizing his empire into satrapies, which allowed him to rule efficiently. Cyrus was well respected by those he conquered and ruled, and in many cases his subjects did not consider him their enemy but instead extolled him as a great leader. During his reign Cyrus encouraged religious diversity in his kingdom by allowing those he ruled to worship as they chose, even to the point of helping them restore their religious monuments. As is recorded in the Bible, Cyrus encouraged the Jewish people to build their temple to YHWH. Cyrus is the only secular ruler in the Bible to be called YHWH's "anointed" or messiah (Isaiah 45:1).

Cyrus's decree allowing the Jewish people to return and build Jerusalem and the temple ended the 70 years of Babylonian captivity. Here is the biblical record of that event:

> Now in the first year of Cyrus king of Persia, that the word of YHWH spoken by the mouth of Jeremiah might be accomplished, YHWH stirred up the spirit of Cyrus king of Persia, that he made a proclamation throughout all his kingdom, and put it also in writing, saying, Thus saith Cyrus king of Persia, All the kingdoms of the earth hath YHWH God of heaven given me; and he hath charged me to build him an house in Jerusalem, which is in Judah. Who is there among you of all his people? YHWH his God be with him, and let him go up. (2 Chronicles 36:22–23)

> But in the first year of *Cyrus the king of Babylon* the same king Cyrus made a decree to build this house of God. (Ezra 5:13, emphasis mine)

That saith of Cyrus, He is my shepherd, and shall perform all my pleasure: even saying to Jerusalem, Thou shalt be built; and to the temple, Thy foundation shall be laid. Thus saith YHWH to his *anointed*, to Cyrus, whose right hand I have holden, to subdue nations before him; and I will loose the loins of kings, to open before him the two leaved gates; and the gates shall not be shut. (Isaiah 44:28–45:1, emphasis mine)

There are several things about this proclamation or decree that are worth mentioning. First, the term "proclamation" used in 2 Chronicles 36:22 is the Hebrew word *qol-abar*, which comes from sound or voice (*qol*) and pass over (*abar*), hence "proclamation." In Ezra 5:13, this proclamation is called a decree, which comes from the Aramaic *te'em* for decree, judgment, or command. This does not have quite the same essence as *dabar,* or word.

Second, as many scholars are quick to point out, the decree by Cyrus primarily concerned rebuilding the temple, as found in 2 Chronicles 36 and Ezra 5. Only in Isaiah 44 is the city of Jerusalem mentioned in the context of building the temple. I think it only fair to counter that some event had to mark the de facto event of rebuilding Jerusalem. If reconstruction of the temple does not qualify as such an event, I can think of few others that would! A close reading of Isaiah 44:28–45 above does indeed indicate that building the temple was equated with "building Jerusalem."

Third, not to be overlooked is that Cyrus's decree is the only one of the four decrees given while the Jewish people were still under a cloud of divine anger. In the chart above you can see that YHWH's divine anger did not end until the second year of Darius 'the Great', a full sixteen years after 536 BC.

There are several points that make this decree worth considering as a fulfillment of Daniel 9:25 and several that do not.

Testing the First Decree

How does this commandment or decree given by Cyrus to the Jewish people stand in light of our four questions regarding the prophecy of Daniel 9:25?

- Could this commandment be considered a dabar or word to return and build Jerusalem?
- Did this commandment cause the Jewish people to shuwb (return or turn back) and build Jerusalem?
- Was this building event of enough relevance to constitute building Jerusalem?
- Can the date of this commandment be firmly established in the biblical and secular record?

Positives:
1. This was a decree to rebuild the temple and Jerusalem.
2. The decree comes at a pivotal point in biblical history.
3. Cyrus is one of the most respected secular leaders in the Bible.
4. The date for Cyrus's decree is given in the Bible.

Negatives:

1. The Jewish people were still under YHWH's divine anger when Cyrus's decree was given.
2. A decree or proclamation doesn't have the same essence as a dabar or word.
3. This decree does not fully satisfy the essence of the word *shuwb*, to return or turn back to something already begun.
4. Cyrus's decree was given in 536 BC and makes a reasonable first-century messianic fulfillment of the prophecy using the 70 sevens difficult if not impossible, because it is hard to see how 70 sevens or 490 periods of time can be stretched from 536 BC to most commonly accepted dates for Christ's birth (4–1 BC), and especially so for His death and resurrection (29–33 AD). It's a difference of some forty to eighty years, a little too far for comfort.

As you can see, there are some good reasons to consider Cyrus's decree as a fulfillment of Daniel 9:25, but there are also some difficulties with this position—most notably the misalignment with the first century. For the moment, let's consider it a draw and move on to the next candidate for the decree that begins our countdown to the Messiah. To the auspicious year of 520 BC and the Persian Darius 'the Great', son of Hystaspes, we now turn our attention.

Chapter 3:

Darius 'the Great' Artaxerxes:
A Decree to Continue Construction on the Temple

"And the God that hath caused his name to dwell there destroy all kings and people, that shall put to their hand to alter and to destroy this house of God which is at Jerusalem. I Darius have made a decree; let it be done with speed."

Ezra 6:12

It could be argued that Persia's power and influence reached its zenith during the reign of Darius 'the Great' Artaxerxes. Darius played a central role in the Jewish people's reestablishment of Jerusalem and the temple service. By his sixth year of rule the Second Temple, the very heart of Jerusalem, was completed, nearly sixteen years after permission to build it had first been given by Cyrus.

Darius was the third Persian ruler after Cyrus the Great. Cyrus died in 530 BC, and his son Cambyses II ruled for eight years. For a short period after Cambyses's death, Bardis the Magian usurper (aka Smerdis) ruled. This imposter, by some accounts, was a double for Cambyses II's murdered brother. When Cambyses died, Bardis, who was already impersonating the brother of Cambyses II, took the game to a whole new level and assumed the throne as Artaxerxes of Persia. After ruling for less than a year, he was deposed by Darius 'the Great', son of Hystaspes, also known historically as Artaxerxes (Ezra 6:14. See also Ussher, *Annals of the World,* page 126, section 1015.)

Trouble in the Promised Land

To understand the decree given by Darius 'the Great', we need to back up a bit and give a little history of the Jewish people's efforts to rebuild the temple after the decree of Cyrus. Believe it or not, after the Jewish people returned to Jerusalem in 536 BC, for the next sixteen years they didn't get much further than making an altar and laying some foundation stones for the temple. There were two causes for this.

First, the inhabitants of the land harassed their building efforts. They saw the temple as the essence of a reestablished Jewish nation-state, and they understood how this threatened their power and influence in the region. One only has to read today's headlines to understand how this same dynamic is once again in play today. A few verses are sufficient to illustrate what happened.

> Now in the second year of their coming unto the house of God at Jerusalem, in the second month, began Zerubbabel the son of Shealtiel, and Jeshua the son of Jozadak, and the remnant of their brethren . . . to set forward the work of the house of YHWH. (Ezra 3:8)

> Now when the adversaries of Judah and Benjamin heard that the children of the captivity builded the temple unto YHWH God of Israel . . . Then the people of the land weakened the hands of the people of Judah, and troubled them in building, and hired counsellors against them, to frustrate their purpose,

> all the days of Cyrus king of Persia, even until the reign of Darius king of Persia. (Ezra 4:1–5)

Here's how it went down: Cyrus made the initial decree that allowed the Jewish people to rebuild the temple. In the second year of their return, they began work on the temple, but they only got part of the foundation laid before Bishlam, Mithredath, Tabeel, and the "rest of their companions" started harassing their building efforts. This harassment continued all the way to the reign of Darius 'the Great'.

Many biblical scholars have a hard time with Persian era chronology because they have refused to take the biblical account at face value. In secular Persian history, we have the following four kings from Cyrus to Darius:

1. Cyrus (king over Babylon) for seven years (536–530 BC)
2. Cambyses II (his son) for eight years (529–522 BC)
3. Bardis (aka Smerdis) the usurper for part of a year (522 BC)
4. Darius 'the Great' Artaxerxes for thirty-six years (521–486 BC)

Now compare this to what the Bible says in Ezra chapters 1–6. We already know that Cyrus gave the initial decree that allowed construction to commence on the temple in 536 BC. In Ezra 4, we learn that the enemies of the Jews in the beginning of the reign of Ahasuerus petitioned him with accusations against the Jewish people's building efforts. This Ahasuerus is likely Cambyses II, the son of Cyrus. That being the case, it is likely the efforts to stop construction fell on unsympathetic ears. From what we know historically,

Cambyses II mostly continued in his father's footsteps until his unexpected death during his Egyptian campaign. It is worth noting that one of the Elephantine Papyri published by Professor Sachau of Berlin in 1911 records that while Cambyses tore down temples of the Egyptian gods at Elephantine, he preserved the temple of YHWH that had been constructed there.

> And in the reign of Ahasuerus, in the beginning of his reign, wrote they unto him an accusation against the inhabitants of Judah and Jerusalem. (Ezra 4:6)

With their petition to stop construction having no effect, the enemies of the Jewish people continued their harassment. It wasn't until a new king came to power in Persia, one whom Ezra 4:7 identifies only as "Artaxerxes," that the enemies of the Jewish people were able to officially stop construction of the temple. This new king was likely the Magian imposter who assumed the throne on Cambyses's death. This imposter is known historically as Bardis, Smerdis, or Gaumata. Notice especially in the passage below that the building of the "city" is described in the context of building the temple.

> And in the days of Artaxerxes wrote Bishlam, Mithredath, Tabeel, and the rest of their companions, unto Artaxerxes king of Persia . . . This is the copy of the letter that they sent unto him, even unto Artaxerxes the king; Thy servants the men on this side the river, and at such a time. Be it known unto the

king, that the Jews which came up from thee to us are come unto Jerusalem, building the rebellious and the bad city, and have set up the walls thereof, and joined the foundations . . .

We certify the king that, if this city be builded again, and the walls thereof set up, by this means thou shalt have no portion on this side the river. Then sent the king an answer unto Rehum the chancellor, and to Shimshai the scribe, and to the rest of their companions that dwell in Samaria, and unto the rest beyond the river, Peace, and at such a time . . .

Give ye now commandment to cause these men to cease, *and that this city be not builded, until another commandment shall be given from me . . . Then ceased the work of the house of God which is at Jerusalem.* So it ceased unto the second year of the reign of Darius king of Persia. (Ezra 4:7–24, emphasis mine)

As the ancient Athenian author Xenophon records in his *Cyropaedia* (8.3.11 and 3.1.23), the Magians were polytheistic sun worshipers. If this imposter was the Artaxerxes of Ezra 4:7–24 as a chronological reading of Ezra would suggest, then as a Magian he would not have shared the same religious or political worldview as Cyrus and Cambyses. In light of the Jewish monotheistic worldview, this might, in part, explain his desire to see construction on the temple stopped.

Historically, there were only two Persian kings between Cyrus the Great and Darius 'the Great'. The biblical account confirms this by identifying them as Ahasuerus and Artaxerxes (Ezra 4).

Now that we have a better idea of the events that transpired between the reign of Cyrus and Darius, let's look at the decree of Darius 'the Great' Artaxerxes.

A Decree to Restart Construction of Jerusalem

To briefly recap, we have learned that Cyrus gave the initial decree that allowed the Jewish people to return and build Jerusalem and the temple. The enemies of the Jewish people tried to stop construction of the temple at the start of the reign of Ahasuerus (Cambyses II) with little success. When Cambyses II died, they approached Artaxerxes (Bardis, aka Smerdis, the Magian usurper), who granted them permission to stop construction. After just a few months, Darius 'the Great' Artaxerxes deposed the usurper and assumed the throne as king of Persia.

Shortly thereafter, a game-changing event took place in the affairs of the Jewish people. Ezra 5 gives us the details:

> Then the prophets, Haggai the prophet, and Zechariah the son of Iddo, prophesied unto the Jews that were in Judah and Jerusalem in the name of the God of Israel, even unto them. Then rose up Zerubbabel the son of Shealtiel, and Jeshua the son of Jozadak, and began to build the house of God which is at Jerusalem: and with them were the prophets of God helping them. (Ezra 5:1–2)

At this point we are in the second year of Darius 'the Great' of Persia. Haggai and Zechariah, the prophets, prophesied to Zerubbabel the governor and Joshua ("Jeshua" here in Ezra) the high priest to restart construction of the temple after the Artaxerxes of Ezra 4:7 had stopped it. The Jewish people listened to the prophets and once again started working on the temple. This caused the enemies of the Jews to freak out. They immediately sent letters to Darius in protest, thinking he would support their cause and stop construction. Darius decreed that a search should be made for the original decree of Cyrus which allowed the Jews to return and build. The decree was found, and Darius, to the consternation of the Jews' enemies, allowed construction to proceed. Not only that, but Darius helped the construction efforts along by providing resources from his royal treasury.

> Then Darius the king made a decree, and search was made in the house of the rolls, where the treasures were laid up in Babylon. And there was found at Achmetha, in the palace that is in the province of the Medes, a roll, and therein was a record thus written: In the first year of Cyrus the king the same Cyrus the king made a decree concerning the house of God at Jerusalem, Let the house be builded, the place where they offered sacrifices, and let the foundations thereof be strongly laid. (Ezra 6:1–3)

> Now therefore, Tatnai, governor beyond the river, Shetharboznai, and your companions the Apharsachites, which are beyond the river, be ye far from thence: Let the work of this house of God alone; let the governor of the Jews and the elders of the Jews build this house of God in his place. Moreover I

make a decree what ye shall do to the elders of these Jews for the building of this house of God: that of the king's goods, even of the tribute beyond the river, forthwith expenses be given unto these men, that they be not hindered. (Ezra 6:6–8)

Also I have made a decree, that whosoever shall alter this word, let timber be pulled down from his house, and being set up, let him be hanged thereon; and let his house be made a dunghill for this. And the God that hath caused his name to dwell there destroy all kings and people, that shall put to their hand to alter and to destroy this house of God which is at Jerusalem. I Darius have made a decree; let it be done with speed. Then Tatnai, governor on this side the river, Shetharboznai, and their companions, according to that which Darius the king had sent, so they did speedily. (Ezra 6:11–13)

Ouch! Reminiscent of Esther and Haman, isn't it? I'll bet the enemies of the Jewish people didn't see that coming! Darius, the king of Persia, made it clear that anyone hindering the efforts of the Jewish people to rebuild the temple was to be put to death. He further decreed that resources from his own royal treasury were to be used to help the building efforts. Just four years later the temple, the very heart of Jerusalem's religious system, and the city itself were finished and dedicated. Thanks in part to this decree by Darius 'the Great', the Second Temple era of the Jewish people officially began.

Testing the Second Decree

So how does this commandment or decree given by Darius 'the Great' Artaxerxes to the Jewish people stand in light of our four questions?

- Could this decree be considered a dabar or word to return and build Jerusalem?
- Did this decree cause the Jewish people to shuwb (return or turn back) and build Jerusalem?
- Was this building event of enough relevance to constitute building Jerusalem?
- Can the date of this decree be firmly established in the biblical and secular record?

Positives:

1. This decree came the same year YHWH's divine anger ended.
2. The date for this decree (520 BC) is well established in the historical and biblical record.
3. Based upon Isaiah 44, Ezra 4, and Daniel 9:1–23, we can see that building the temple was in fact the focal point in rebuilding Jerusalem.

Negatives:

1. Only in the loosest sense could this decree by Darius be considered a "word" or dabar to restore and build.

2. Darius's decree did not instruct the Israelites to "return and build" because they were already working on the temple in obedience to the prophesying of Zechariah and Haggai. His decree simply allowed what had already begun to continue.
3. It would seem difficult if not impossible to stretch the 70 sevens from the second year of Darius (520 BC) until the coming of Yeshua the Messiah. Although it's getting closer, it's still a difference of some thirty years to Yeshua's birth and sixty to His death.

Once again we have reached an impasse. Though this decree by Darius 'the Great' Artaxerxes has some attractive aspects to it as a candidate for the prophecy's fulfillment, it also has many challenges that seem to disqualify it from consideration. Again, let us withhold judgment until we have weighed all the evidence.

To further that pursuit, we now turn our attention to the third decree given by a Persian ruler, one whom the Bible identifies simply by the title of Artaxerxes. This is where the biblical record gets truly fascinating—and complicated.

Chapter 4:

The Seventh Year of Artaxerxes:
A Decree for Ezra to Beautify the Temple

"Now after these things, in the reign of Artaxerxes king of Persia, Ezra the son of Seraiah . . . This Ezra went up from Babylon; and he was a ready scribe in the law of Moses, which YHWH God of Israel had given: and the king granted him all his request, according to the hand of YHWH his God upon him . . . And he came to Jerusalem in the fifth month, which was in the seventh year of the king."

Ezra 7:1–7

So far we've looked at two of the four decrees that scholars have postulated might be the "commandment" of Daniel 9:25. Now we turn our attention to the last two. This, unfortunately, is where modern scholarship takes a detour from a reasonable reading of the biblical chronological record. I'll do my best to explain, but first, let's take a look at the verses used as the basis for this next decree to be considered the "commandment" of Daniel 9:25. I've abridged parts of this passage for clarity's sake. It's well worth your time to read the passage in its entirety, for it is the basis for one of the biggest and most influential chronological errors scholars have made about the biblical record.

> Now this is the copy of the letter that the king Artaxerxes gave unto Ezra the priest, the scribe, even a scribe of the words of

the commandments of YHWH, and of his statutes to Israel. Artaxerxes, king of kings, unto Ezra the priest, a scribe of the law of the God of heaven, perfect peace, and at such a time. I make a decree, that all they of the people of Israel, and of his priests and Levites, in my realm, which are minded of their own freewill to go up to Jerusalem, go with thee . . . And to carry the silver and gold, which the king and his counsellors have freely offered unto the God of Israel . . . That thou mayest buy speedily with this money bullocks, rams, lambs, with their meat offerings and their drink offerings, and offer them upon the altar of the house of your God which is in Jerusalem.

And whatsoever shall seem good to thee, and to thy brethren, to do with the rest of the silver and the gold, that do after the will of your God. The vessels also that are given thee for the service of the house of thy God, those deliver thou before the God of Jerusalem. And whatsoever more shall be needful for the house of thy God, which thou shalt have occasion to bestow, bestow it out of the king's treasure house. And I, even I Artaxerxes the king, do make a decree to all the treasurers which are beyond the river, that whatsoever Ezra the priest, the scribe of the law of the God of heaven, shall require of you, it be done speedily, unto an hundred talents of silver, and to an hundred measures of wheat, and to an hundred baths of wine, and to an hundred baths of oil, and salt without prescribing how much.

Whatsoever is commanded by the God of heaven, let it be diligently done for the house of the God of heaven: for why should there be wrath against the realm of the king and his sons? . . . And thou, Ezra, after the wisdom of thy God, that is in thine hand, set magistrates and judges, which may judge all the people that are beyond the river, all such as know the laws of thy God; and teach ye them that know them not. And whosoever will not do the law of thy God, and the law of the king, let judgment be executed speedily upon him, whether it be unto death, or to banishment, or to confiscation of goods, or to imprisonment.

Blessed be YHWH God of our fathers, which hath put such a thing as this in the king's heart, to beautify the house of YHWH which is in Jerusalem . . . And I was strengthened as the hand of YHWH my God was upon me, and I gathered together out of Israel chief men to go up with me. (Ezra 7:11–28)

This sure sounds similar to the decree of Darius 'the Great' from the previous chapter, doesn't it? In any case, from the verses above, we can safely say that this decree by "Artaxerxes" is a decree to beautify the temple at Jerusalem. It also gives Ezra special powers to ensure that the law of YHWH is taught and followed by the repatriated children of Israel.

A few things stand out about this decree. First, the text does not tell us when the decree was given. It does tell us that Ezra went up to Jerusalem in the seventh year of Artaxerxes, but we are left to guess when this Artaxerxes gave this decree.

Second, the text does not identify this Persian Artaxerxes. It is important to understand that the term *Artaxerxes* is not a name; it is merely a title given to Persian kings, much like "Caesar" in Rome centuries later. In Ezra 4:7, the Persian Artaxerxes who ordered construction of the temple to stop was likely Smerdis, the Magian usurper, with his decree given at some point between the first year of Cyrus and the second year of Darius. But he is not necessarily the only Artaxerxes named in Scripture. As we will explore more fully in the coming pages, Darius 'the Great' was also known historically as Artaxerxes. For the present, just keep in mind that Artaxerxes is a *title*. We must allow the Bible's chronological context to identify him.

The third and final fact I would like to bring to your attention is the context of this passage in Ezra 7. Ezra 6 finished with the completion of the temple in the sixth year of Darius 'the Great'. Now that the temple is completed, Ezra, the priest and scribe, feels compelled to go up to Jerusalem and teach the people the law. Ezra 7:7 fixes these events to the seventh year of Artaxerxes. Modern scholarship ignores the possibility that the Artaxerxes of Ezra 7 is one and the same as Darius 'the Great' Artaxerxes in Ezra 6—though that seems to be the most reasonable conclusion given the dates! Instead, a gap of nearly sixty years is inserted into the chronology between Ezra 6 and 7 with very little contextual justification, during which another Artaxerxes is supposed to have arisen.

Although we have enough information to identify the decree of Ezra 7, we cannot be totally certain of its chronological context. In other words, we cannot yet date this decree from a biblical context, thus we do not have enough information to answer our four questions.

So let's dig a little deeper into the life and times of Ezra, the priest and scribe. If we can determine his place in the Second Temple era, we can then confidently date the decree which was given to him by this Persian "Artaxerxes." I think you'll find Ezra was truly a fascinating player in these events.

Chapter 5:

Ezra, the Priest and Scribe:
His History and Lineage Relative to the Second Temple Era

"Now after these things, in the reign of Artaxerxes king of Persia, Ezra the son of Seraiah . . . This Ezra went up from Babylon; and he was a ready scribe in the law of Moses, which YHWH God of Israel had given: and the king granted him all his request, according to the hand of YHWH his God upon him."

Ezra 7:1–6

During the Second Temple period, few Old Testament characters hold a more prominent position than Ezra. The Bible identifies him as a priest and scribe. It is believed that he was the author of the book of Ezra as well as Chronicles. Both of these accounts provide valuable insights into the triumphs and tragedies of the Judean captives' efforts in rebuilding the Second Temple and Jerusalem.

As we learned in the previous chapter, after the completion of the temple in the sixth year of Darius, Ezra in the seventh year of the reign of a Persian "Artaxerxes" desired to return to Jerusalem and teach the people the law of YHWH. What is unclear from the text is the precise identity of this Persian Artaxerxes. For well over two centuries, biblical scholars have identified this Artaxerxes as the Persian king Longimanus, circa 464–424 BC. It's a handy identification, allowing Daniel's 70 sevens, interpreted as 490 years, to take us straight to the life of Yeshua. Considering the importance of

Ezra's history to our understanding of Daniel 9, you might assume this Old Testament chronology would be well established upon a reasonable biblical basis. Surprisingly, this is not the case. If you find that hard to believe, all you have to do is pick up any commentary on the prophecy of Daniel 9 or the Second Temple era. You'll be hard-pressed to find a single biblical chronological reference for Ezra or Nehemiah's place in that time period.

To me the most disconcerting fact about this is that the Bible is rich in chronological details concerning Ezra and Nehemiah. If in fact the 70 sevens countdown to the Messiah begins with a decree given to Ezra or Nehemiah during the reign of a Persian Artaxerxes, then it is only reasonable to establish Ezra's and Nehemiah's place in the Second Temple era relative to secular Persian chronology so that we can date the decree of this unnamed Persian Artaxerxes. That is the purpose of this chapter. So let's see just how much biblical evidence there is for the life and times of Ezra the priest and scribe.

Son of the High Priest

What does the Bible say about Ezra? Who was this mysterious teacher of the Torah who was compelled to return to Jerusalem and teach his people the law of YHWH?

One of the best ways to learn about someone is by meeting his or her parents. In Ezra's case, you'll not find a more influential father than the last high priest of Solomon's temple. Let me introduce you:

> Now after these things, in the reign of Artaxerxes king of
> Persia, Ezra the son of Seraiah, the son of Azariah, the son of

Hilkiah, the son of Shallum, the son of Zadok, the son of Ahitub, the son of Amariah, the son of Azariah, the son of Meraioth, the son of Zerahiah, the son of Uzzi, the son of Bukki, the son of Abishua, the son of Phinehas, the son of Eleazar, the son of Aaron the chief priest . . . (Ezra 7:1–5)

Lineage of **Seraiah** last high priest of the 1st Temple		Lineage of **Ezra** son of Seraiah Priest and Scribe
I Chron. 6:3-15		Ezra 7
(Ezra)	24	Ezra
Seraiah	23	Seraiah
Azariah	22	Azariah
Hilkiah	21	Hilkiah
Shallum	20	Shallum
Zadok	18	Zadok
Ahitub	17	Ahitub
Amariah	16	Amariah
Azariah	15	Azariah
Johanan	14	
Azariah	13	
Ahimaaz	12	Names left out
Zadok	11	of Ezra's Lineage
Ahitub	10	
Amariah	9	
Meraioth	8	Meraioth
Zerahiah	7	Zerahiah
Uzzi	6	Uzzi
Bukki	5	Bukki
Abishua	4	Abishua
Phinehas	3	Phinehas
Eleazar	2	Eleazar
Aaron	1	Aaron

The verse above says that Ezra was the son of Seraiah. What's fascinating about this statement is that Seraiah, son of Azariah, was the last high priest of Solomon's temple. Second Kings 25:8–21 tells us that Seraiah was taken by Nebuzaradan to Riblah in the nineteenth year of Nebuchadnezzar and was killed there.

> And in the fifth month, on the seventh day of the month, which is the nineteenth year of king Nebuchadnezzar king of Babylon, came Nebuzaradan, captain of the guard, a servant of the king of Babylon, unto Jerusalem: and he burnt the house of YHWH, and the king's house, and all the houses of Jerusalem, and every great man's house burnt he with fire. And all the army of the Chaldees, that were with the captain of the guard, brake down the walls of Jerusalem round about.
>
> Now the rest of the people that were left in the city, and the fugitives that fell away to the king of Babylon, with the remnant of the multitude, did Nebuzaradan the captain of the guard carry away . . . And the captain of the guard took Seraiah the chief priest, and Zephaniah the second priest, and the three keepers of the door . . . And Nebuzaradan captain of the guard took these, and brought them to the king of Babylon to Riblah:
>
> And the king of Babylon smote them, and slew them at Riblah in the land of Hamath. So Judah was carried away out of their land. (2 Kings 25:1–21)

I think most everyone would agree that it's reasonable to assume Ezra could not have been conceived after the death of his father, Seraiah. Let's further assume, for the sake of argument, that Ezra was born the year his father was killed. (Not really a reasonable assumption considering the events that took place in Jerusalem, but it's the latest he could have been born, so let's go with it—we'll need this to determine a reasonable age for him relative to the events of the Second Temple era.) The nineteenth year of Nebuchadnezzar by many accounts was 584 BC, so we will take that as Ezra's year of birth.

The following verse places Ezra in the seventh year of a Persian Artaxerxes.

> Now after these things . . . This Ezra went up from Babylon . . . unto Jerusalem, in the seventh year of Artaxerxes the king. And he came to Jerusalem in the fifth month, which was in the seventh year of the king. (Ezra 7:1–8)

In order to establish Ezra's place in the chronology of the Second Temple era, all we now need to do is determine the date for the seventh year of Artaxerxes. Again, the term "Artaxerxes" is simply a title which was applied to several Persian kings. For the sake of brevity, I will not list all the bearers of this title, only those relevant to this period of the Second Temple era and whose reign lasted at least thirty-two years, as required by Nehemiah 5:14. Remember, Ezra and Nehemiah were contemporaries, so the "thirty-second year of Artaxerxes" below gives us a minimum criteria when searching for the identity of our biblical Artaxerxes.

> Moreover from the time that I was appointed to be their governor in the land of Judah, from the twentieth year even unto the two and thirtieth year of Artaxerxes the king, that is,

twelve years, I and my brethren have not eaten the bread of the governor. (Nehemiah 5:14)

Those Persian kings who qualify with reigns of thirty-two years or more are Darius 'the Great' Artaxerxes, Artaxerxes Longimanus, and Artaxerxes Memnon. With the above information, it is a simple matter to calculate Ezra's minimum age during the reign of his "Artaxerxes." In the table below, you will see the youngest Ezra could have been in the seventh year of each Artaxerxes known to Second Temple history. That bears repeating: the dates below are the *absolutele youngest* Ezra could have been during the reign of each potential ruler. Keep in mind that Ezra was also alive fourteen years later at the dedication of the wall in Jerusalem and took an *active* part in those ceremonies.

	7th yr Persian King	Ezra's Minimum age	Ezra's Minimum age at dedication of wall
7th yr. Darius "the Great" Artaxerxes	515 BC	69 yrs. old	83 yrs. old
7th yr. Artaxerxes (Longimanus)	458 BC	126 yrs. old	140 yrs. old
7th yr. Artaxerxes (Memnon)	398 BC	186 yrs. old	200 yrs. old

The question is simple and the answer obvious: which of the above Persian kings most reasonably qualifies as a contemporary of Ezra? For those who follow the dictum "when the plain sense of the text makes sense, seek no other sense" but still wish to claim (as most do) that Ezra and Artaxerxes Longimanus were contemporaries, Ezra's age creates an interpretational problem. By no reasonable comparative measure can it be said that Ezra was a contemporary of the Persian king Longimanus, nor is there any credibility to the claim that he lived to be, at the very least, two whole decades older than Moses!

What the above chronology reasonably demonstrates is that Ezra was in fact a contemporary of Darius 'the Great'. For those who would see Ezra as being over two times the age of any of his biblical or secular contemporaries, I remind you of the words of King David, who lived five hundred years before Ezra:

> For all our days are passed away in thy wrath: we spend our years as a tale that is told. The days of our years are threescore years and ten; and if by reason of strength they be fourscore years, yet is their strength labour and sorrow; for it is soon cut off, and we fly away. (Psalm 90:9–10)

Ezra's age Relative to Secular Chronology

Nebuchadnezzar (sole rule) - 43 yrs	43
19th yr Nebuchadnezzar - Ezra's *minimum* age >>	
Evil-Merodach - 2 yrs	2
Nergal-sherezer - 4 yrs	4
Nabonidos - 17 yrs	17
Cyrus - 7 yrs	7
Cambyses - 8 yrs	8
Darius (the Great) Artaxerxes - 36 yrs	36
Xerxes I - 21 yrs	21
Artabanus - 7mths Ignored	
Artaxerxes I (Longimanus) - 41 yrs	41
Darius II (Nothus) - 19 yrs	19

Totals: 83, 57

Cyrus to Artaxerxes

If indeed the life and times of Ezra took place during the reign of Darius 'the Great' Artaxerxes, what other evidence might there be to support this straightforward reading of Ezra's chronology? Again, biblical scholarship for centuries has placed Ezra some time later, making this a question worth considering.

To keep us on point, let me recap the chronology of the Second Temple era to really nail down the context. In 536 BC, Cyrus gave a decree which allowed the Judean captives to return and build the temple in Jerusalem. Ezra 1:1–3 tells of these events:

> Now in the first year of Cyrus king of Persia, that the word of YHWH by the mouth of Jeremiah might be fulfilled, YHWH stirred up the spirit of Cyrus king of Persia . . . Thus saith Cyrus king of Persia, YHWH God of heaven . . . he hath charged me to build him an house at Jerusalem . . . Who is there among you of all his people? his God be with him, and let him go up to Jerusalem, which is in Judah, and build the house of YHWH God of Israel, (he is the God,) which is in Jerusalem. (Ezra 1:1–3)

As I explained in a previous chapter, for the next sixteen years the enemies of the Jewish people harassed them in their efforts to build the temple. In fact, the Jewish people did not get much further than laying the altar and the foundation of the temple during that time. Ezra

4:7 then tells us construction was stopped by the decree of an Artaxerxes of Persia between the reigns of Cyrus and Darius.

In 520 BC, the second year of Darius, YHWH, through the prophets Haggai and Zechariah, told the people to restart construction. Joshua the high priest, Zerubbabel the governor, and the people of Judea listened to the words of YHWH through the prophets, and construction on the temple resumed (Ezra 6:14). Four years later, the temple was finished in the sixth year of Darius, and in answer to Daniel's prayer, YHWH, the living God of the Bible, once more had a dwelling place to meet with mankind.

The Persian Chronology

The chart below is a summary of Persian rulers from Cyrus to Artaxerxes II. Going forward, it will provide a handy reference for those trying to figure out how the Persian kings we know from secular history relate to the Second Temple era chronology we see in the Bible.

Persian Rulers	Secular Dates	# yrs.	Biblical Name	Reference
Cyrus	536-530 BC	7 yrs.	Cyrus	Ezra 1
Cambyses (son of Cyrus)	529-522 BC	8 yrs.	Ahasuerus	Ezra 4:6
Bardis (Magian imposter)	522 BC	.058 yrs.	Artaxerxes	Ezra 4:7
Darius 'the Great' Artaxerxes	521-486 BC	36 yrs.	Darius & Artaxerxes	Ezra 6:1; 6:14; 7:1
Xerxes I	485-465 BC	21 yrs.	Not mentioned	Not mentioned
Artabanus (ignored)	465 BC	.06 yrs.	Not mentioned	Not mentioned
Artaxerxes I (Longimanus)	464-424 BC	41 yrs.	???	???
Darius II (Nothus)	423-405 BC	19 yrs.	Not mentioned	Not mentioned
Artaxerxes II (Memnon)	404-359 BC	46 yrs.	Not mentioned	Not mentioned

The Seventh Year of Artaxerxes

The next stop in our search for Ezra's place in the Second Temple era leads us to Ezra 7 and "the seventh year of Artaxerxes." Once again, I remind you of the curious way many well-meaning biblical scholars take the most natural reading of the text and make it more complicated. I'll try to explain the problem. Ezra 6 ends with the completion of the Second Temple in the sixth year of Darius (516 BC). Ezra 7 starts with Ezra, the priest and scribe, setting off on his journey to Jerusalem in the seventh year of Artaxerxes. Most biblical scholars have assumed that this "Artaxerxes" is a reference to Artaxerxes I (Longimanus). But this requires them to insert a gap of about fifty-eight years between Ezra 6 and Ezra 7. They do this despite the fact that the Bible identifies the Persian king Darius 'the Great' as an Artaxerxes:

> And the elders of the Jews builded, and they prospered through the prophesying of Haggai the prophet and Zechariah the son of Iddo. And they builded, and finished it, according to the commandment of the God of Israel, and according to the commandment of Cyrus, and Darius, and Artaxerxes king of Persia. And this house was finished on the third day of the month Adar, which was in the sixth year of the reign of Darius the king. (Ezra 6:14–15)

It is imperative to note that the verses above clearly state that the Jewish people "builded and finished" the temple according to the "commandments" of the God of Israel, Cyrus, Darius, and Artaxerxes king of Persia. Yet, notice that it also states unequivocally that the temple was *finished* by the sixth year of Darius, and it lists those responsible for completing it by that sixth year. That means, according to the most natural and plain reading of Ezra 6:14, that all the secular rulers mentioned in the text must have ruled at some point previous to the sixth year of Darius.

Who then is the "and Artaxerxes" mentioned in Ezra 6:14? It's unlikely to be the Artaxerxes of Ezra 4:7, because that Artaxerxes *stopped* construction of the temple. Who then could it be? Many biblical scholars have assumed, contrary to the clear context of the verse, that this is a reference to Artaxerxes I—Longimanus, who reigned almost sixty years after the temple was completed. What is going on here?

The error is actually found in the English translation of the passage. It stems from presuppositional bias and the erroneous use of the Hebrew letter *waw*. In order to show that Ezra lived during the reign of Artaxerxes Longimanus, as they presupposed, the translators used the letter *waw* to form a conjunction instead of a hendiadys (two words with one meaning), as the context would dictate. In Hebrew, the letter *waw* is often used as a regular conjunction, but as most Hebrew lexicons explain, it also has a much wider, though less common, use as well. Below is the TWOT Hebrew lexicon explaining the use of *waw*:

519.0 – w (wa) . . . **and, so, then, when, now, or, but, that** and many others.

(ASV and RSV similar.) The vocalization varies.

This is an inseparable prefix which is used as a conjunction or introductory particle which can usually be translated "and."

The fundamental use of the prefix is that of a simple conjunction "and," connecting words ("days and years," Gen. 1:14), phrases ("and to divide" Gen. 1:18) and complete sentences (connecting Gen. 2:11 with verse 12). However it is used more often and for a greater variety of construction than is the English connector "and."

It is often used at the beginning of sentences, for which reason the KJV begins many sentences with an unexplained "and." This use may be explained as a mild introductory particle and is often translated "now" as in Exo 1:1 where it begins the book (KJV, ASV; the RSV ignores it completely; cf. Gen 3:1; Gen 4:1).

The item following the prefix is not always an additional item, different from that which preceded: "Judah and Jerusalem" (Isa. 1:1), pointing out Jerusalem especially as an important and representative part of Judah; "in Ramah, and his own city" (1 Sam 28:3), the two being the same place, hence the translation "even" as explanatory.

When the second word specifies the first the construction is called a "hendiadys," i.e., two words with one meaning. For example, "a tent and dwelling" in 2 Sam 7:6 means "a dwelling tent."

(TWOT 519.0, emphasis mine)

Considering that use of *waw* to form a hendiadys, take a look at the little chart below. It shows *waw* as it appears in the Hebrew text of Ezra 6:14:

Ezra 6:14	
"Even" Artaxerxes	
Hebrew	**English translation**
ארתחששתא	Artaxerxes
ו	and, therefore, also then, even, yet, now
וארתחששתא	"even" Artaxerxes

And the elders of the Jews builded, and they prospered through the prophesying of Haggai the prophet and Zechariah the son of Iddo. And they builded, and finished it, according to the commandment of the God of Israel, and according to the commandment of Cyrus, and Darius, [even] Artaxerxes king of Persia. (Ezra 6:14–15)

Since there is no reasonable contextual basis to assume that the Artaxerxes of Ezra 6:14 was another Persian king who helped finish the temple by the sixth year of Darius—especially a future one!—the translators should have used *waw* to form a hendiadys, not to denote two different people. Their decision to use the *waw* in this way was premised upon the necessity to show that Ezra was a contemporary of Artaxerxes Longimanus so that their messianic expectations concerning Daniel 9 could be satisfied. There is simply no other reason to add another Persian king to the chronology of Ezra 6:14–15, especially one who lived nearly sixty years after the events described were completed.

Darius, Even Artaxerxes

Now take a look at the Ezra 6 and 7 in this context. In the sixth year of Darius "even" Artaxerxes, the Second Temple is completed. Just a few verses later in chapter 7, Ezra the priest and scribe requests permission to go up to Jerusalem and teach the people the Torah. Ezra 7 explains that Darius, aka Artaxerxes, granted Ezra his request, and thus begins Ezra's journey to Jerusalem in the seventh year of king Darius 'the Great' Artaxerxes of Persia.

In summary, by every reasonable measure of biblical interpretation, Ezra was a contemporary of Darius 'the Great', and in fact the most reasonable reading of Ezra 6:13–15 supports this. Trying to stretch Ezra's chronology to the reign of Artaxerxes Longimanus hopelessly tortures the text and creates numerous interpretational inconsistencies which cannot be overcome with any reasonable rendering of the Bible's chronological record.

With this chronology established, we are now able to look again at the decree to beautify the temple found in Ezra 7—our third option for a prophetic fulfillment of Daniel 9:25.

Testing the Third Decree

How does this commandment or decree given by Artaxerxes to Ezra stand in light of our four questions?

- Could this decree be considered a dabar or word to return and build Jerusalem?
- Did this decree cause the Jewish people to shuwb (return or turn back) and build Jerusalem?
- Was this building event of enough relevance to constitute building Jerusalem?
- Can the date of this decree be firmly established in the biblical and secular record?

Positives:
1. Hard-pressed to find any, as the list of negatives will demonstrate.

Negatives:
1. It is difficult to see this permission granted to Ezra as a word or even a "commandment" to return and build Jerusalem.
2. Ezra's building efforts were limited to beautifying the temple. This is hardly a defining moment in the Second Temple era and certainly does not constitute building Jerusalem.
3. The text does not provide us the ability to date Artaxerxes's decree, even though we are able to establish Ezra's place in the chronology.

4. While the date of this decree can be fixed in the biblical record, this is ultimately still a negative because it leaves us considerably short of the arrival of Yeshua. Most scholars have argued that the countdown should begin in the days of Longimanus, but by all reasonable biblical evidence, Ezra was not a contemporary of Artaxerxes Longimanus.

Our look at the third decree regarding the restoration of Jerusalem and the temple has provided us with very little biblical evidence to confidently claim it is the "commandment" of Daniel 9:25 and thus the starting point of our messianic countdown—even though many scholars have claimed it is. In fact, by looking closely at the Bible's chronological evidence, we can reasonably say that Ezra has been misplaced in the Second Temple era! This startling fact has major repercussions for our view of not only the Second Temple era but of the prophecy of 70 sevens itself. With this new perspective, let's now investigate the fourth and final Persian commandment to restore and build Jerusalem.

Chapter 6:

The Twentieth Year of Artaxerxes: A Decree to Rebuild the Walls and Gates of Jerusalem

"Then I told them of the hand of my God which was good upon me; as also the king's words [dabar] *that he had spoken unto me. And they said, Let us rise up and build. So they strengthened their hands for this good work."*
Nehemiah 2:18

Nearly thirteen years after Ezra went up to Jerusalem during the reign of Artaxerxes, we learn that Nehemiah, the cupbearer to that same Artaxerxes, received permission to travel to Jerusalem and rebuild the walls of the city, which were in disrepair. Here is the biblical account:

> And it came to pass in the month Nisan, in the twentieth year of Artaxerxes the king, that wine was before him: and I took up the wine, and gave it unto the king. Now I had not been beforetime sad in his presence. (Nehemiah 2:1)

> And I said unto the king, If it please the king, and if thy servant have found favour in thy sight, that thou wouldest send me unto Judah, unto the city of my fathers' sepulchres, that I may build it. And the king said unto me, (the queen also sitting by him,) For how long shall thy journey be? and when wilt thou return?

> So it pleased the king to send me; and I set him a time. Moreover I said unto the king, If it please the king, let letters be given me to the governors beyond the river, that they may convey me over till I come into Judah; and a letter unto Asaph the keeper of the king's forest, that he may give me timber to make beams for the gates of the palace which appertained to the house, and for the wall of the city, and for the house that I shall enter into. And the king granted me, according to the good hand of my God upon me. (Nehemiah 2:5–8)

By far, the decree by this unnamed Persian Artaxerxes—once again presumed to be Longimanus, known to history as Artaxerxes I—is the most popular choice when scholars look for the commandment to restore and build Jerusalem prophesied by Daniel. Sir Robert Anderson, the great Christian writer, popularized this theory in his influential book *The Coming Prince*. Anderson does indeed make an impressive case, but surprisingly, he fails to address the scriptural basis for his belief that Ezra and Nehemiah were contemporaries of Longimanus. Instead, Anderson, in one of the most far-reaching eschatological errors of the past two centuries, simply defers to the judgment of the great historian Rawlinson. I quote Rawlinson as found on p. 71 of Anderson's *The Coming Prince*:

> "Artaxerxes I reigned forty years, from 465 to 425. He is mentioned by Herodotus once (6. 98), by Thucydides frequently. Both writers were his contemporaries. There is every reason to believe that he was the king who sent Ezra and

Nehemiah to Jerusalem, and sanctioned the restoration of the fortifications."—RAWLINSON, *Herodotus*, vol. 4, p. 217.

Did you catch that? "There is every reason to believe" is the sum of Rawlinson's and Anderson's evidence for Ezra and Nehemiah's place in the Second Temple era! Not a single reference to Ezra's age or the natural chronological flow of Ezra 6 and 7 is mentioned. Anderson, out of a well-intentioned necessity to prove his interpretation of Daniel 9, simply ignored the biblical evidence, instead relying on unsubstantiated claims by another respected historian.

Unfortunately, historians and Bible scholars of the past two centuries have followed in Anderson's footsteps. I encourage you to see for yourself. Take any popular book on the Second Temple era or the prophecy of Daniel 9, and you'll find virtually no biblical chronological evidence for Ezra and Nehemiah's place in the Second Temple era. What you will find instead are various forms of what I call the "Artaxerxes assumption."

Lest you think I overstate my case, let's look closer at this decree given by Artaxerxes to Nehemiah and see what the Bible's own internal chronological evidence can tell us about it.

The Twentieth Year

First let's look at the starting point of the decree given to Nehemiah. The chronology for this decree begins in the ninth month (Chisleu) of the twentieth year of Artaxerxes, when Nehemiah learned of the terrible conditions in Jerusalem. Hanani, one of Nehemiah's brethren, brought news that the repatriated Jews in Jerusalem were being harassed by their enemies, due in part to the fact that the walls and gates of Jerusalem were broken down.

Nehemiah then petitions YHWH in a prayer reminiscent of Daniel's wonderful pleadings for YHWH's mercy found in Daniel 9:1–23. After Nehemiah's prayer, in the first month (Nisan) in the twentieth year of Artaxerxes, Nehemiah makes his case to the king. (If you're noticing a date discrepancy there, bear with me—we're getting to it.) The king allows Nehemiah to leave his service as a cupbearer and gives a decree that Nehemiah may return to Jerusalem and repair its breaches. This repair of the walls of Jerusalem is what Anderson and many others after him have claimed to be the "commandment to restore and build" prophesied by Daniel.

The first obvious problem with this is the fact that Nehemiah learns of the news in the ninth month of twentieth year of Artaxerxes, but then approaches the king in the first month of the same year. Obviously, it makes no sense for Nehemiah to approach the king eight months before he even learned of the plight of his brethren in Jerusalem.

> The words of Nehemiah the son of Hachaliah. And it came to pass in the month Chisleu, in the twentieth year, as I was in Shushan the palace . . . (Nehemiah 1:1)

> And it came to pass in the month Nisan, in the twentieth year of Artaxerxes the king, that wine was before him: and I took up the wine, and gave it unto the king. Now I had not been beforetime sad in his presence. (Nehemiah 2:1)

Anderson tries to deal with this chronological difficulty by saying the reference in Nehemiah 1 refers to the ascension year of Artaxerxes, while Nehemiah 2 refers to his first year of sole rule. This may be one way to explain it, but my question is, why would the only prophecy in the Bible that requires a specific secular date for its starting point be based upon a secular date that cannot be determined with any degree of certainty? I mean, we are talking about the countdown to the Messiah, and the best the Bible can do is give us a decree with a confusing starting point?

Personally, I don't believe the Bible shows us that YHWH works that way. To my way of looking at the congruency of the biblical record, the most important prophecy in the Bible—a prophecy specifically given as a chronological countdown—must have a clearly definable starting point commensurate with its importance.

So what does that mean? If none of the four options before us can be held with any certainty, what are we to conclude? Simply put, there must be another decree we are missing.

But before we look for such a decree, let's first ensure we understand Nehemiah's place in the Second Temple era, independent of Ezra. After all, we've already learned the peril of making assumptions! Does the Bible provide us any evidence as to the identity of Nehemiah's mysterious Persian king Artaxerxes and thus the starting point of our countdown to the Messiah? Let's look and see.

Chapter 7:

Nehemiah the Governor

"The words of Nehemiah the son of Hachaliah. And it came to pass in the month Chisleu, in the twentieth year, as I was in Shushan the palace . . ."
Nehemiah 1:1

In 520 BC, nearly sixteen years after permission to build the temple had been given, the house of YHWH still lay in the initial stages of construction, with only some of the foundation stones to show for over a decade of effort. Seeing this neglect, YHWH stirred up the prophets Haggai and Zechariah to tell the people to return and build the temple. Four years later the temple in Jerusalem was completed, but very little progress had been made in building the walls of the ancient citadel. The remnant of people who dwelt there were still being harassed by their enemies.

Years later, back in Shushan, the winter palace of the Persian kings, our hero Nehemiah is the cupbearer to King "Artaxerxes." Nehemiah hears of the plight of his brethren in Jerusalem and sets out to do something about it. After pouring his heart out to YHWH in prayer, Nehemiah petitions Artaxerxes to allow him to go up and repair the walls of Jerusalem. Artaxerxes grants his request, and we learn later that Nehemiah also becomes governor (Tirshatha) of Jerusalem for twelve years (Nehemiah 5:14).

As we saw in the previous chapter, many scholars today identify the Persian Artaxerxes in both the books of Ezra and Nehemiah as Artaxerxes Longimanus. But if you've taken a serious look at the information I've provided in the previous chapters on Ezra's place in the Second Temple era, you have a better perspective on why I say such a conclusion is based upon virtually no biblical evidence. But what about the book of Nehemiah? Where does it stand in terms of the chronological evidence related to Ezra and Nehemiah's place in the Second Temple era? I think the answer will surprise you.

Governor of Jerusalem for Twelve Years

In Nehemiah 5:14, we read that Nehemiah was appointed governor from the twentieth to the thirty-second year of Artaxerxes. As we learned in chapter 5, this information is really helpful in our search for the Persian Artaxerxes of Nehemiah, because few Persian kings ruled for thirty-two years or longer. In fact, this chronological gem allows us to limit our search for Nehemiah's Artaxerxes to just three Persian kings. Those kings are Darius 'the Great', Longimanus, and Memnon (see chart below).

> Moreover from the time that I was appointed to be their governor in the land of Judah, from the twentieth year even unto the two and thirtieth year of Artaxerxes the king, that is, twelve years, I and my brethren have not eaten the bread of the governor. (Nehemiah 5:14)

Persian Rulers	Secular Dates	# yrs.	Biblical Name	Reference
Cyrus	536-530 BC	7 yrs.	Cyrus	Ezra 1
Cambyses (son of Cyrus)	529-522 BC	8 yrs.	Ahasuerus	Ezra 4:6
Bardis (Magian imposter)	522 BC	.058 yrs.	Artaxerxes	Ezra 4:7
Darius 'the Great' Artaxerxes	521-486 BC	36 yrs.	Darius & Artaxerxes	Ezra 6:1; 6:14; 7:1
Xerxes I	485-465 BC	21 yrs.	Not mentioned	Not mentioned
Artabanus (ignored)	465 BC	.06 yrs.	Not mentioned	Not mentioned
Artaxerxes I (Longimanus)	464-424 BC	41 yrs.	???	???
Darius II (Nothus)	423-405 BC	19 yrs.	Not mentioned	Not mentioned
Artaxerxes II (Memnon)	404-359 BC	46 yrs.	Not mentioned	Not mentioned

So which of the above Persian kings could reasonably be seen as the Artaxerxes of Nehemiah? Again, most Bible scholars for centuries have placed these key stories in the reign of Longimanus, in 464–424 BC. But there are several additional pieces of evidence in the book of Nehemiah that build a totally different picture of Ezra and Nehemiah's place in the Second Temple era than what is commonly supposed. Let's take a look at this evidence.

Shushan, the Palace of the Kings of Persia

To set the stage in Nehemiah 1:1, we find Nehemiah in Shushan, the winter palace of Persia. For those familiar with the book of Esther, you know that Shushan was the palace of Esther's King Ahasuerus. Keep this pertinent fact in mind, because it is very relevant to understanding the dynamics of why a Jewish man held the very important position of cupbearer to the king of Persia. In the next chapter, we will look at how an often overlooked piece of biblical evidence in the book of Nehemiah will alter our view of the Second Temple era and explain in part why the Jewish people had such a powerful presence in the affairs of Persia.

The Porter of the Gates

Our first substantial piece of chronological evidence related to Nehemiah comes from Nehemiah 12:25–26. This passage tells us that five porters of the gates of Jerusalem were contemporaries with Joiakim (the son of Joshua the high priest), Ezra, and Nehemiah.

> Mattaniah, and Bakbukiah, Obadiah, Meshullam, Talmon, Akkub, were porters keeping the ward at the thresholds of the gates. These were in the days of Joiakim the son of Jeshua, the son of Jozadak, and in the days of Nehemiah the governor, and of Ezra the priest, the scribe. (Nehemiah 12:25–26)

High Priests	Time / Event
Seraiah	killed in 584 BC
Jehozadak	Brother of Ezra Taken into captivity 584 BC
Joshua	returned to Jerusalem in 536 BC
Joiakim	Contemparary of Nehemiah & Ezra (Neh. 12:26)
Eliashib	Contemparary of Ezra (Ezra 10:6)
Joiada	Contemparary of Ezra (Ezra 10:6)
Jonathan	Contemparary of Ezra (Ezra 10:6)
Jaddua	

This reference provides several helpful chronological synchronisms. First, it tells us plainly that Nehemiah and Ezra were contemporaries. The text goes even further by linking Ezra and Nehemiah with Joiakim the son of Joshua, the high priest, and five named porters. In 1 Chronicles 9:7 we find that two of these porters were among the repatriated Babylonian captives who returned to the land of Israel by the decree of Cyrus in 536 BC:

> So all Israel were reckoned by genealogies; and, behold, they were written in the book of the kings of Israel and Judah, who

were carried away to Babylon for their transgression. Now the first inhabitants that dwelt in their possessions in their cities were, the Israelites, the priests, Levites, and the Nethinims . . . And the porters were, Shallum, and Akkub, and Talmon, and Ahiman, and their brethren: Shallum was the chief. (1 Chronicles 9:1–2, 17)

And the rulers of the people dwelt at Jerusalem: the rest of the people also cast lots, to bring one of ten to dwell in Jerusalem the holy city, and nine parts to dwell in other cities . . . Now these are the chief of the province that dwelt in Jerusalem: . . . Moreover the porters, Akkub, Talmon, and their brethren that kept the gates, were an hundred seventy and two. (Nehemiah 11:1–3, 19)

Notice that in 1 Chronicles above, we are told that Shallum was the chief porter. In Ezra 10 we learn that Shallum the porter was one of the men of Jerusalem who had taken a non-Hebrew wife from among the inhabitants of the land. Shallum, along with the rest of the inhabitants of the land, agreed to put away their strange wives at the prompting of Ezra. According to the text, this all took place in the seventh and eighth years of Artaxerxes.

And Ezra the priest, with certain chief of the fathers, after the house of their fathers, and all of them by their names, were separated, and sat down in the first day of the tenth month to examine the matter. And they made an end with all the men

> that had taken strange wives by the first day of the first month. (Ezra 10:16–17)

What this means chronologically is that the same Shallum the chief porter, Akkub, and Talmon who came up to Jerusalem in 536 BC were still alive in the seventh year of a Persian Artaxerxes. Subsequently, Shallum is missing from the lists by the twentieth year of Artaxerxes. It is reasonable to assume that he had either died because of his obvious old age or was demoted because he had taken a wife of non-Hebrew origin. In any case, the above verses show that Shallum, Akkub, and Talmon most reasonably fit in the chronological context of the Second Temple as contemporaries of Darius 'the Great' Artaxerxes. By no reasonable biblical criteria could they have been alive by the seventh year of Artaxerxes Longimanus, or for that matter, nearly fourteen years later in the twenty-first year of Artaxerxes at the dedication of the wall.

Zerubbabel and Nehemiah, the Governors of Jerusalem

Next, let's look at Nehemiah 12:47. This passage links the governorships of Zerubbabel and Nehemiah and the ministrations to the singers and porters.

> And all Israel in the days of Zerubbabel, and in the days of Nehemiah, gave the portions of the singers and the porters, every day his portion: and they sanctified holy things unto the Levites; and the Levites sanctified them unto the children of Aaron. (Nehemiah 12:47)

Nehemiah 12 begins by listing the priests and Levites who came up out of captivity with Joshua and Zerubbabel in the first year of Cyrus. Then, in Nehemiah 12:27, it recounts the dedication of the finished wall of Jerusalem. Finally the chapter closes with the above verses, which clearly imply continuity in the temple service under the leadership of Zerubbabel and Nehemiah. This passage makes much more sense if we see Zerubbabel and Nehemiah as consecutive governors of Jerusalem from the days of Cyrus through to the days of Darius 'the Great', rather than inserting a gap of sixty-plus years between Zerubbabel and Nehemiah to account for the reign of Longimanus.

The First Sukkoth

Nehemiah 8 makes a fascinating statement regarding Israel's observance of the biblical holy day of Sukkoth as it relates to the repatriated captives:

> And all the congregation of them that were come again out of the captivity made booths, and sat under the booths: for since the days of Jeshua the son of Nun unto that day had not the children of Israel done so. And there was very great gladness. (Nehemiah 8:17)

Notice that it describes these people as "them that were come again [returned/shuwb] out of the captivity." The most reasonable reading implies these people were the same generation as those who came up with Joshua and Zerubbabel in 536 BC. This places them as contemporaries of Darius 'the Great', also known as Artaxerxes. Indeed, this confirms the other chronological evidence we have found concerning Nehemiah and Ezra: namely, that they were first-generation contemporaries of those Jewish captives who returned to Jerusalem at the end of the 70 years of Babylonian captivity. Any other reading of the text strains the credibility of sound biblical interpretation.

The Lists of Nehemiah 10 and 12

Our final piece of evidence—and the one that really ties up the chronology of Ezra and Nehemiah—is the lists of Nehemiah 10 and 12. Nehemiah 12 lists the priests and Levites, "chiefs of their fathers" ("ancient men" in Ezra 3:12), who came up out of the captivity with Joshua and Zerubbabel by the decree of Cyrus in 536 BC. In Nehemiah 10, at the dedication of the wall in Jerusalem in the twenty-first year of our mystery king Artaxerxes, we find many of these same priests and Levites alive and active. Take a look at a side-by-side comparison of Nehemiah 10 and 12 in the charts below. The names and their order are reproduced as given in the Scripture.

The Priests & Levites of Nehemiah 10 & 12
1st year of Cyrus - 536 BC Basis

Nehemiah 12	Nehemiah 10	*Nehemiah 10*
Returned with Joshua & Zerubbabel	Sealed with Nehemiah	*Sealed with Nehemiah*
1st year Cyrus	21st year Darius	*21st "Artaxerxes"*
"Chief of their Fathers" (Ezra 3:12)	"even" Artaxerxes	*(if "Artaxerxes" = Longimanus)*
536 BC	501 BC	*444 BC*
Minimum age in 536 BC	Minimum age in 501 BC	*Minimum age in 444 BC*
30-40+ yrs. old?	65-75+ yrs. old?	*122-132+ yrs. old?*

Priests	Priests	*Priests*
	Nehemiah	*Nehemiah*
	Zidkijah	*Zidkijah*
Seraiah	Seraiah	*Seraiah*
	Azariah	*Azariah*
Jeremiah	Jeremiah	*Jeremiah*
Ezra	Pashur	*Pashur*
Amariah	Amariah	*Amariah*
	Malchijah	*Malchijah*
Malluch	Hattush	*Hattush*
Hattush	Shebaniah	*Shebaniah*
Shechaniah	Malluch	*Malluch*
Rehum	Harim	*Harim*
Meremoth	Meremoth	*Meremoth*
Iddo	Obadiah	*Obadiah*
	Daniel	*Daniel*
Ginnetho	Ginnethon	*Ginnethon*
	Baruch	*Baruch*
	Meshullam	*Meshullam*
Abijah	Abijah	*Abijah*
Miamin	Mijamin	*Mijamin*
Maadiah?	Maaziah?	*Maaziah?*
Bilgah	Bilgai	*Bilgai*
Shemaiah	Shemaiah	*Shemaiah*
Joiarib		
Jedaiah		
Sallu		
Amok		
Hilkiah		
Jedaiah		

The Priests & Levites of Nehemiah 10 & 12
1st year of Cyrus - 536 BC Basis

Nehemiah 12	Nehemiah 10	Nehemiah 10
Returned with Joshua & Zerubbabel	Sealed with Nehemiah	*Sealed with Nehemiah*
1st year Cyrus	21st year Darius	*21st "Artaxerxes"*
"Chief of their Fathers" (Ezra 3:12)	"even" Artaxerxes	*(if "Artaxerxes" = Longimanus)*
536 BC	501 BC	*444 BC*
Minimum age in 536 BC	Minimum age in 501 BC	*Minimum age in 444 BC*
30-40+ yrs. old?	65-75+ yrs. old?	*122-132+ yrs. old?*
Levites	**Levites**	*Levites*
Jeshua	Jeshua	*Jeshua*
Binnui	Binnui	*Binnui*
Kadmiel	Kadmiel	*Kadmiel*
Sherebiah	Shebaniah	*Shebaniah*
Judah	Hodijah	*Hodijah*
Mattaniah	Kelita	*Kelita*
Bakbukiah	Pelaiah	*Pelaiah*
Unni	Hanan	*Hanan*
	Micha	*Micha*
	Rehob	*Rehob*
	Hashabiah	*Hashabiah*
	Zaccur	*Zaccur*
	Sherebiah	*Sherebiah*
	Shebaniah	*Shebaniah*
	Hodijah	*Hodijah*
	Bani	*Bani*
	Beninu	*Beninu*
Porters	Porters	*Porters*
(Neh. 12; 1 Ch. 9:1)	(Nehm. 11)	*(Nehm. 11)*
Mattaniah	Akkub	*Akkub*
Bakbukiah	Talmon	*Talmon*
Obadiah		
Meshuallam		
Talmon		
Akkub		

Which is the more reasonable explanation? These "chief men" were most reasonably sixty-five to seventy-five years old during the reign of Darius 'the Great' Artaxerxes or these men would have been at their youngest 122–132 years old during the reign of Artaxerxes Longimanus. Pretty compelling, isn't it?

Please see the chart below for a relative perspective on the age of the priests and Levites in comparison to the secular chronology of Babylon and Persia. As you peruse the chart, keep Ezra 3:12 in mind.

Some of these "chief men" were already "ancient" by the first year of Cyrus when the temple foundation was laid by Joshua and Zerubbabel.

> But many of the priests and Levites and chief of the fathers, who were ancient men, that had seen the first house, when the foundation of this house was laid before their eyes, wept with a loud voice; and many shouted aloud for joy. (Ezra 3:12)

In summary, the most reasonable explanation of the evidence given in this chapter shows that Nehemiah and Ezra were contemporaries of Darius 'the Great', also known as Artaxerxes. Any other rendering of the chronology requires one to ignore the most reasonable and natural reading of the books of Nehemiah, Ezra, and Chronicles.

Priests & Levites Age
Relative to Secular Chronology

Nebuchadnezzar (sole rule) - 43 yrs	43
Evil-Merodach - 2 yrs	2
Mergal-sherezer - 4 yrs	4
Nabonidos - 17 yrs	17

1 yr Cyrus - Priests & Levites (*Chief of their Fathers*) age + >>

Cyrus - 7 yrs	7	
Cambyses - 8 yrs	8	35
Darius (the Great) Artaxerxes - 36 yrs	36	
Xerxes I - 21 yrs	21	57
Artabanus - 7mths Ignored		
Artaxerxes I (Longimanus) - 41 yrs	41	
Darius II (Nothus) - 19 yrs	19	

Testing the Fourth Decree

How does this commandment or decree given by Artaxerxes to Nehemiah stand in light of our four questions?

- Could this decree be considered a dabar or word to return and build Jerusalem?
- Did this decree cause the Jewish people to shuwb (return or turn back) and build Jerusalem?
- Was this building event of enough contextual relevance to constitute building Jerusalem?
- Can the date of this decree be firmly established in the Biblical and secular record?

Positives:
1. In a general sense, rebuilding the walls of Jerusalem could be considered "building Jerusalem."
2. Nehemiah 2:18 does mention dabar in the context of Artaxerxes's "words" to Nehemiah.

Negatives:
1. Nehemiah, based upon the all available biblical evidence, was not a contemporary of Artaxerxes Longimanus. The Bible places him as a contemporary of Darius 'the Great' Artaxerxes. The date of this decree can be roughly placed in biblical

chronology, but it leaves us short of Yeshua's birth in a way we should consider troubling if this is indeed our starting point.
2. Nehemiah was given permission to repair the walls and gates of Jerusalem, but Daniel 9:25 indicates that rebuilding the plaza and walls was to take place during the sixty-two weeks as part of the ongoing construction efforts, not as the initiating event.
3. This decree by Artaxerxes in its most literal sense was not a word (*dabar*) for the Jewish people to return (shuwb) or turn back to the building efforts. This decree was given specifically to Nehemiah to build the walls of Jerusalem.
4. There is some reasonable uncertainty about the exact date of this decree given by Artaxerxes.

In Closing

The Bible's internal chronological evidence does not provide a reasonable basis upon which to claim Nehemiah was a contemporary of Artaxerxes Longimanus. Instead, it makes a compelling case that Nehemiah was in fact a contemporary of Darius 'the Great' Artaxerxes of Persia. Thus any interpretation of Daniel 9 which uses as its starting point a decree in the reign of the Longimanus can no longer claim its fulfillment in Yeshua. Further, because many today see Daniel 9 and the 70 weeks prophecy as part of a future eschatological framework, this erroneous Artaxerxes assumption has troubling implications for much of today's popular eschatological thought.

By this time, our study may have radically challenged your understanding of this whole era. But what if I told you we were still missing a pivotal piece of evidence related to the Second Temple era and Nehemiah's efforts to rebuild the walls of Jerusalem? Indeed, this is the case. In the next chapter we will learn how a young Jewish maiden's courage changed the history of the Jewish people and influenced the very events we have been discussing in the past several chapters.

Chapter 8:
Queen of 127 Provinces

"Now it came to pass in the days of Ahasuerus, (this is Ahasuerus which reigned, from India even unto Ethiopia, over an hundred and seven and twenty provinces:) . . ."
Esther 1:1

To me one of the coolest statements in the book of Nehemiah is an often overlooked mention of the queen of Persia. It's a statement that frankly seems out of place unless you understand the chronological context of the Persian era. In the past few chapters, we've learned that the Jewish people were shown amazing favor during the reign of Darius 'the Great' Artaxerxes. This king over 127 provinces went out of his way to financially support and encourage the construction of the temple of Jerusalem as well as the city itself. It turns out there is more to the story than most of us have realized, and the book of Nehemiah gives us a clue:

> And it came to pass in the month Nisan, in the twentieth year of Artaxerxes the king, that wine was before him: and I took up the wine, and gave it unto the king . . . And the king said unto me, *(the queen also sitting by him,)* For how long shall thy journey be? and when wilt thou return? So it pleased the king to send me; and I set him a time. (Nehemiah 2:1–6, emphasis mine)

Kind of curious, isn't it? Why do you think Nehemiah saw fit to include this seemingly irrelevant information about the queen of Persia? Why would his Jewish readers care about Artaxerxes's Gentile queen? Well, this apparently trivial fact gives us a glimpse into the internal affairs of Darius 'the Great' Artaxerxes during the early years of his reign. The most likely reason the queen of Persia would be mentioned by Nehemiah is that his audience understood who he was referring to. As we will see, Nehemiah mentioned the queen of Persia because this was none other than the Jewish heroine Hadassah, or as she is commonly known, Esther. If you are skeptical, that's understandable—many respected biblical scholars have claimed that Esther was the queen of the Persian king Xerxes I, Darius the Great's successor. In the book of Esther itself he is merely called "Ahasuerus." But what does the biblical record say?

As we learned in the past several chapters, the Bible provides reasonable if not conclusive evidence that Darius 'the Great' was also called Artaxerxes and that it was during his reign that the events of Ezra and Nehemiah took place. So here we find Nehemiah, cupbearer to Darius 'the Great' Artaxerxes, asking the king for permission to return to Jerusalem and rebuild its walls. The text also informs us that the queen was present at this audience.

Artaxerxes = Ahasuerus?

Some might understandably challenge the notion that the Artaxerxes of Nehemiah is the same as the Ahasuerus of the book of Esther, but let's withhold judgment until we've looked at all of the evidence.

First, it is important to once again note that "Ahasuerus" is a title given to Persian kings, much like the title "Artaxerxes." As we saw in chapter 3, the Bible identifies Cyrus's son Cambyses with the title of Ahasuerus, and Daniel 9 identifies a Darius "of the seed of the Medes" as the son of an Ahasuerus. Including the reference in Daniel 9, we have at least three Medes or Persians whom the Bible identifies with this title. The ISBE Bible Dictionary entry 297 explains:

> 297 Ahasuerus or Asseurus
> <a-haz-u-e'-rus>, (Septuagint Grk: *Assoueros*, but in Tobit 14:15 Asueros; the Latin form of the Hebrew Heb: *'achashwerosh*, a name better known in its ordinary Greek form of Xerxes): It was the name of two, or perhaps of three kings mentioned in the canonical, or apocryphal, books of the Old Testament.

With this evidence in mind, neither Artaxerxes nor Ahasuerus should be understood as proper names, and as such they provide us little basis upon which to determine the identity of the Persian kings being mentioned in the biblical passages. As we have done with Ezra and Nehemiah, we will rely on the Bible's internal chronological evidence as well as other circumstantial details to make our determinations.

Back to Shushan the Palace

In our efforts to determine the identity of the Persian Ahasuerus spoken of here in Nehemiah, let's turn our attention to the location of these events. Nehemiah 1:1 and Esther 1:1–2 provide the details on Shushan, the palace of the Persian kings.

> The words of Nehemiah the son of Hachaliah. And it came to pass in the month Chisleu, in the twentieth year, as I was in *Shushan the palace* . . . (Nehemiah 1:1, emphasis mine)

> Now it came to pass in the days of Ahasuerus, (this is Ahasuerus which reigned, from India even unto Ethiopia, over an hundred and seven and twenty provinces:) that in those days, when the king Ahasuerus sat on the throne of his kingdom, which was in *Shushan the palace* . . . (Esther 1:1–2, emphasis mine)

The above verses allow us to conclude that both events took place in the same location. But is the Artaxerxes of Nehemiah the same as the Ahasuerus of Esther? Take a look at the following biblical and secular sources and see what you think:

> Now it came to pass in the days of Ahasuerus, (this is Ahasuerus which reigned, from *India even unto Ethiopia, over an hundred and seven and twenty provinces*:) . . . (Esther 1:1 LXE, emphasis mine)

> Now when Darius reigned, he made a great feast unto all his subjects, and unto all his household, and unto all the princes of Media and Persia, and to all the governors and captains and

lieutenants that were under him, from *India unto Ethiopia, of an hundred twenty and seven provinces*. (1 Esdras 3:1 KJA, emphasis mine)

The great king *Artexerxes unto the princes and governors of an hundred and seven and twenty provinces from India unto Ethiopia*, and unto all our faithful subjects, greeting. (Ester 16:1 KJA (Greek), emphasis mine)

In the second year of the *reign of Artaxerxes the great king*, on the first day of Nisan, *Mardochaeus* the son of Jairus, the son of Semeias, the son of Chisaeus, of the tribe of Benjamin, a Jew dwelling in the city Susa, a grat [sic] man, serving in the king's palace, saw a vision. Now he was of the captivity which Nabuchodonosor king of Babylon had carried captive from Jerusalem, with Jechonias the king of Judea. (Esther 1:1 LXE, emphasis mine)

In the fourth year of the reign of Ptolemeus and Cleopatra, Dositheus, who said he was a priest and Levite, and Ptolemeus his son, brought this epistle of Phurim, which they said was the same, and that Lysimachus the son of Ptolemeus, that was in Jerusalem, had interpreted it. In the second year of the reign of *Artexerxes the great*, in the first day of the month Nisan, *Mardocheus* the son of Jairus, the son of Semei, the son of Cisai, of the tribe of Benjamin, had a dream. (Ester 1:1–2 KJA (Greek), emphasis mine)

And the king levied a tax upon his kingdom both by land and sea. And as for his strength and valour, and the wealth and glory of his kingdom, behold they are written in the book of the Persians and Medes, for a memorial. And *Mardochaeus was vicery to king Artaxerxes* and was a great man in the kingdom, and honored by the Jews, and passed his life beloved of his nation. (Esther 10:1 LXE , emphasis mine)

Now, in the first year of the king's reign, Darius feasted those who were about him, and those born in his house, with the rulers of the Medes, and princes of the Persians, and the toparches of India and Ethiopia, and the generals of the armies, of his *hundred and twenty-seven provinces* (*Antiquities of the Jews* 11:33, emphasis mine)

Mordecai, the Jew, in the Greek edition of Esther {Apc Est 11:1-12}, is said to have had a dream on the first day of the month of Nisan, in the second year of the reign of *Artaxerxes the Great (or Ahasuerus or Darius, the son of Hystaspes)*, concerning a river signifying Esther and two dragons portending himself and Haman. 3484c AM, 4194 JP, 520 BC (Ussher, *Annals of the World*, p. 126 , section 1015, emphasis mine)

The first part of the celebration was given over to the hundred and twenty seven rulers of the hundred and twenty-seven provinces of his empire. (Louis Ginzberg, *Legends of the Jews*, XII "Esther—The Feast for the Grandees")

And the elders of the Jews builded, and they prospered through the prophesying of Haggai the prophet and Zechariah the son of Iddo. And they builded, and finished it, according to the commandment of the God of Israel, and according to the commandment of Cyrus, and *Darius,* ~~and~~ *[even] Artaxerxes king of Persia*. (Ezra 6:14, emphasis and strikethrough mine)

Now after these things, *in the reign of Artaxerxes king of Persia,* Ezra the son of Seraiah . . . This Ezra went up from Babylon; and he was a ready scribe in the law of Moses, which YHWH God of Israel had given: and the king granted him all his request, according to the hand of YHWH his God upon him. (Ezra 7:1–6, emphasis mine)

The common thread of all the above references is that Darius 'the Great', also known as Artaxerxes or Ahasuerus, was the Persian king who ruled over 127 provinces from India to Ethiopia. This further strengthens the connection between the events at Shushan the palace as described in the book of Nehemiah and those described in the book of Esther.

But as fascinating as the above circumstantial evidence might be, we still have not provided a solid chronological basis for it. For this evidence we turn to the lineage of Mordecai as found in Esther 2:5–6:

Now in Shushan the palace there was a certain Jew, whose name was Mordecai, the son of Jair, the son of Shimei, the son of Kish, a Benjamite; who had been carried away from Jerusalem with the captivity which had been carried away with Jeconiah king of Judah, whom Nebuchadnezzar the king of Babylon had carried away. (Esther 2:5–6)

Mordecai and Hadassah

Esther 2:5–6 gives the lineage of Mordecai through his great-great-grandfather Kish. The most reasonable reading of this passage shows that Kish, the great-great grandfather of Mordecai and Esther, was taken captive by Nebuchadnezzar at the same time as King Jeconiah of Judah in approximately the eighth or ninth year of Nebuchadnezzar (see 2 Kings 24:12–16, 2 Chronicles 36:10). Chronologically, this means there were eighty years between the start of Kish's captivity (in the ninth year of Nebuchadnezzar) and the seventh year of Darius, 115 years between the ninth year of Nebuchadnezzar and the seventh year of Xerxes I, and 136 years to the seventh year of Artaxerxes I—Longimanus. Using the most reasonable metrics, we find that in order for Esther to be a young girl or damsel (*na'arah,* as she is called in the Hebrew text) in the seventh year of a Persian king, the most reasonable conclusion once again points us in the direction of Darius 'the Great' Artaxerxes.

Lineage of Mordecai & Hadassah (Esther)

Kish	
Shimei	
Abihail	Jair
Hadassah	Mordecai

Some historians claim that it is Mordecai's captivity, not Kish's, that is in view in Esther 2:5–6, but this is not biblically plausible. As the chart above shows, Hadassah and Mordecai were of the same generation. Even if there was a great disparity in their ages, by no reasonable means could Hadassah have still been a na'arah by the reign of Darius 'the Great', and definitely not so by the eras of Xerxes I or Longimanus, if it was Mordecai's captivity which was in view in the passage above. The chronology of the captivity leaves little doubt that Darius 'the Great' was Esther's king.

A Generational Comparative

For visual people like myself, the following chart may help you wrap your mind around the contemporaneous relationships of Esther, Nehemiah, and Ezra and the kings of Persia, Media, Babylon, and

Judah. This chart is based upon the work of Richard Edmund Tyrwhitt in his 1868 book *Esther and Ahasuerus*. I have modified it to include Ezra and Nehemiah as well as the high priests of Judah. For those interested in the subject of Esther and her king, I heartily recommend Tyrwhitt's two-volume work on the subject.

The following chart is too large to fully reproduce on this page, so the following link will take you to a higher resolution PDF image you can view or print:

http://www.danielsseventyweeks.com/Daniels70Weeks%20ChartsPicturesTables.pdf

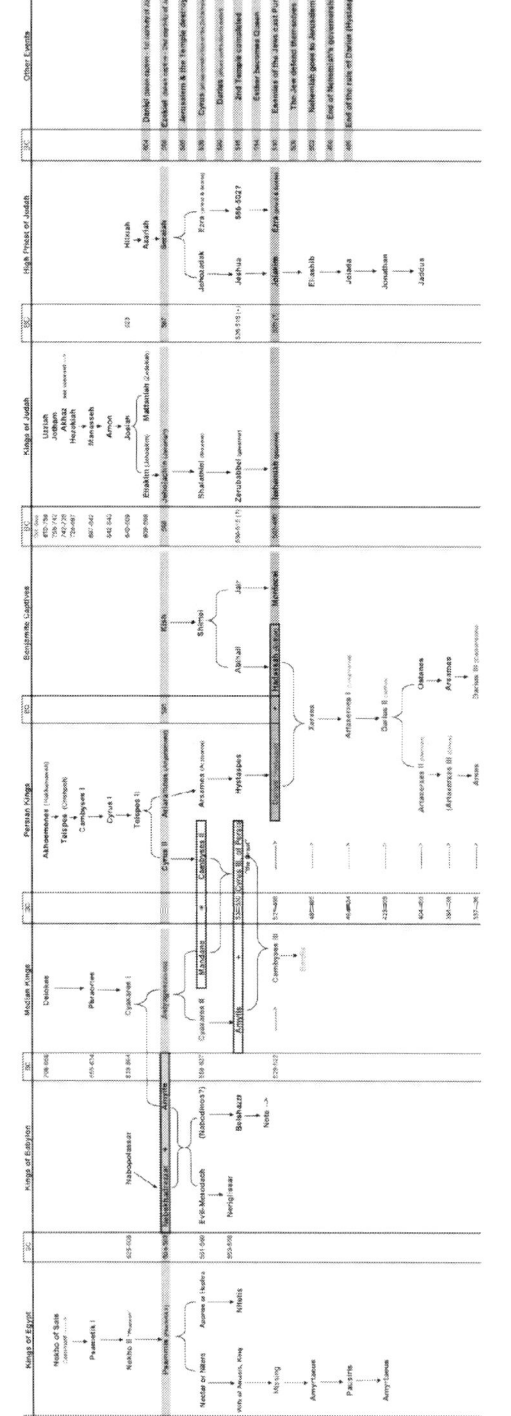

Darius the Huckster

A final piece of evidence regarding Darius's place in the Second Temple era comes from the historian Herodotus, who records that Darius established a revolutionary form of tribute that allowed his subjects to provide goods or commodities in lieu of gold and silver (Herodotus iii:89). This earned Darius the somewhat ignoble title of "Huckster" from Herodotus. It is fascinating to see this confirmed in the books of Esther, Ezra, and Nehemiah. The Darius of Ezra 6 and the Darius "even" Artaxerxes of Ezra 7 did indeed provide material support to the Jewish people from the king's treasure house in the form of commodities, not just money:

> And the king Ahasuerus laid a tribute upon the land, and upon the isles of the sea. (Esther 10:1)

> Then Darius the king made a decree . . . Moreover I make a decree what ye shall do to the elders of these Jews for the building of this house of God: *that of the king's goods, even* of the tribute beyond the river, forthwith expenses be given unto these men . . . And that which they have need of, both *young bullocks, and rams, and lambs,* for the burnt offerings of the God of heaven, *wheat, salt, wine, and oil*, according to the appointment of the priests which are at Jerusalem, let it be given them day by day without fail. (Ezra 6:1–9, emphasis mine)

Now after these things, in the reign of Artaxerxes king of Persia, Ezra the son of Seraiah . . . This Ezra went up from Babylon . . . *And whatsoever more shall be needful for the house of thy God, which thou shalt have occasion to bestow, bestow it out of the king's treasure house.* And I, even I Artaxerxes the king, do make a decree to all the treasurers which are beyond the river, that whatsoever Ezra the priest, the scribe of the law of the God of heaven, shall require of you, it be done speedily, *unto an hundred talents of silver, and to an hundred measures of wheat, and to an hundred baths of wine, and to an hundred baths of oil, and salt without prescribing how much.* (Ezra 7:1–6, 7:20–22, emphasis mine)

The Power of Persia

At the height of Persian power and influence, Darius 'the Great' Artaxerxes ruled over 127 provinces, and Hadassah (Esther) became his queen. Think about the implications of this information! During the reign of Darius 'the Great', a young Jewish woman was queen. Mordecai, Hadassah's cousin, was the second most powerful man in Persia. Nehemiah was cupbearer. Josephus even notes that Zerubbabel, who preceded Nehemiah as governor of Jerusalem, was a bodyguard to the king. This whole picture explains in part the magnanimity of Darius toward the Judean captives' efforts in rebuilding their temple and city. These very same people were some of his most trusted and loyal subjects.

As a side note, Haman's Agagite lineage—a people group with a history of bad blood with the Jews—is often pointed to when explaining his seemingly unjustified hatred of the Jewish people. Now you know the rest of the story. Haman was a power-hungry man, and the Jewish people were clearly a threat to his plans during the rise of Darius 'the Great' to the pinnacle of Persian power and influence.

The following chart provides a chronological timeline of the events found in the books of Ezra, Nehemiah, and Esther as we've explored in the past few chapters. As you look at the timeline, consider the impact Hadassah's efforts had in protecting her brethren throughout the Persian empire. Had she not acted as she did, Ezra, the Judean repatriates, and the very Second Temple itself might have become victims of Haman's evil machinations.

Renal yr.	Events during the reign of Darius 'the Great' Artaxerxes	BC
1st	Darius became king of the Medes & Persians	521
2nd	Darius allowed the temple construction to be continued	520
3rd	Darius made a feast for the rulers of 127 provinces	519
6th	The 2nd Temple was completed	516
7th	The 2nd Temple was dedicated	515
7th	Ezra goes up to Jerusalem	515
7th	Hadassah becomes Queen of Persia	515
12th	Haman casts pur to destroy the Jewish people	510
13th	The Jewish people defend themselves	509
21st	Nehemiah goes up to Jerusalem	501
21st	The wall of Jerusalem completed in 52 days	501
21st	Ezra reads the Law to his people	501
32nd	End of Nehemiah's governorship	490
36th	End of the rule of Darius 'the Great' Artaxerxes	486

Persia and the Coming Messiah

It's fascinating to me to see how YHWH used a secular nation like Persia to play such an important role in the history of the Jewish people. Persia at the height of its power was used by YHWH to restore His people to the land of Israel and rebuild His desolate sanctuary. It is intriguing to note that Britain was the world power of our generation which brought about the return of the Jewish people to the land of Israel after nearly two thousand years of desolations. Even more fascinating, it is the US (once a subject of British rule) that has now taken the mantle of leadership on the world stage, and indeed, our very own government has inserted itself into the current affairs concerning the Jewish people and Jerusalem. Watch in coming years for the world powers involving themselves in the affairs of the Jewish people, Jerusalem, and the Third Temple. As Mark Twain is quoted as saying, "History doesn't repeat itself, but it does rhyme."

Though the events described in the past few chapters were incredibly important to understanding the four Persian commandments to restore and build Jerusalem, our quest to find the starting point to the countdown to the Messiah is not finished. None of those four Persian decrees totally satisfied the contextual criteria of the "word to return and build Jerusalem" of Daniel 9:25. As I have said, there must be a decree we are overlooking—and indeed, there is. The final decree or commandment we will look at is in fact the focal point of all these events, and yet it has been all but ignored by biblical scholars. What I'm talking about is the little known fifth decree to return and restore.

Chapter 9:

The Fifth Decree:
The Word to Return and Build Jerusalem

"Therefore thus saith the LORD; I am returned to Jerusalem with mercies: my house shall be built in it, saith the LORD of hosts, and a line shall be stretched forth upon Jerusalem."

Zechariah 1:16

We started our investigation of Daniel 9:25 and the "commandment to restore and build" in chapter 1 by looking at the Hebrew words *dabar* and *shuwb*. These two words offered a different perspective on the verse and allowed us to consider the possibility that this so-called "commandment" might in fact be a dabar or word from YHWH, the living God of the Bible. In the subsequent chapters we looked at Persian chronology in the context of the four Persian decrees that scholars have at various times claimed represented the "commandment" of Daniel 9:25—ultimately concluding that none of these four decrees qualifies to begin our countdown to the Messiah. This review of Persian chronology has been invaluable to our understanding of the events that led to resettlement of Jerusalem and the reestablishment of the temple service. One last time let's look at these events, but this time let's consider them with the words of YHWH, the living God of the Bible, as our focus.

YHWH, Nebuchadnezzar, and the 70 Years' Captivity

I have studied the prophecy of Daniel 9 for years. To this day I'm still struck by how single-mindedly I looked for a secular decree or commandment as the fulfillment of Daniel 9:25 without any consideration for what impact YHWH's own actions might have in the equation. I still shake my head in wonder at how I ignored the evidence.

Remember, these events all started in the third year of King Jehoiakim of Judah when YHWH caused Nebuchadnezzar to take the people of Judah captive, thus beginning the 70 years prophesied by Jeremiah. Daniel 1:1–6 informs us that a young man named Daniel was taken captive at this time as well. This very same young man, nearly 70 years later, would record the prophecy of 70 sevens, the most important messianic prophecy in the Bible.

> In the third year of the reign of Jehoiakim king of Judah came Nebuchadnezzar king of Babylon unto Jerusalem, and besieged it. And the Lord gave Jehoiakim king of Judah into his hand, with part of the vessels of the house of God: which he carried into the land of Shinar to the house of his god; and he brought the vessels into the treasure house of his god . . . Now among these were of the children of Judah, *Daniel*, Hananiah, Mishael, and Azariah. (Daniel 1:1–6, emphasis mine)

Notice in this next passage how YHWH makes it clear that the people's sins had polluted His house which He had set apart in Jerusalem, and because of this sin His righteous anger was come upon them. Indeed, the next several verses show that as a result of that sin, YHWH caused Solomon's temple to be destroyed and the walls of Jerusalem to be broken down. As you read the following passage from 2 Chronicles 36, keep in mind Daniel 9:1–23 and how Daniel's prayer to YHWH came out of this very context.

> Moreover all the chief of the priests, and the people, transgressed very much after all the abominations of the heathen; *and polluted the house of YHWH which he had hallowed in Jerusalem.*
>
> And YHWH God of their fathers sent to them by his messengers, rising up betimes, and sending; because *he had compassion on his people, and on his dwelling place*: but they mocked the messengers of God, and despised his words, and misused his prophets, *until the wrath of YHWH arose against his people*, till there was no remedy.
>
> Therefore he brought upon them the king of the Chaldees, who slew their young men with the sword in the house of their sanctuary, and had no compassion upon young man or maiden, old man, or him that stooped for age: he gave them all into his hand. And all the vessels of the house of God, great and small, and the treasures of the house of YHWH, and the treasures of the king, and of his princes; all these he brought to Babylon. *And they burnt the house of God, and brake down the wall of Jerusalem,* and burnt all the palaces thereof with fire, and destroyed all the goodly vessels thereof.

> And them [i.e. Jehoiakim, Daniel, Ezekiel, etc,] that had escaped from the sword carried he away to Babylon; where they were servants to him and his sons until the reign of the kingdom of Persia: to fulfil the word of YHWH by the mouth of Jeremiah, until the land had enjoyed her sabbaths: for as long as she lay desolate she kept sabbath, to fulfil threescore and ten years.
>
> Now in the first year of Cyrus king of Persia, that the word of YHWH spoken by the mouth of Jeremiah might be accomplished, YHWH stirred up the spirit of Cyrus king of Persia, that he made a proclamation throughout all his kingdom. (2 Chronicles 36:14–22, emphasis mine)

Israel's Sin Caused the Destruction of the Temple and Jerusalem

It was because of Israel's sins and transgressions that the people of Judah and Jerusalem were carried away captive, the temple was destroyed, and the walls of Jerusalem were broken down. Now, let's fast-forward nearly 70 years to the point when the prophecy of 70 sevens was given. Let's read this passage one last time with our perspective sharpened by what we've learned in the preceding chapters.

> In the first year of Darius the son of Ahasuerus, of the seed of the Medes, which was made king over the realm of the Chaldeans; in the first year of his reign I Daniel understood by books the number of the years, whereof the word of YHWH

came to Jeremiah the prophet, that he would accomplish seventy years in the desolations of Jerusalem.

And I set my face unto the Lord God, to seek by prayer and supplications, with fasting, and sackcloth, and ashes: and I prayed unto YHWH my God, and made my confession, and said, O YHWH, the great and dreadful God, keeping the *covenant and mercy* to them that love him, and to them that keep his commandments; we have sinned, and have committed iniquity, and have done wickedly, and have rebelled, even by departing from thy precepts and from thy judgments: neither have we hearkened unto thy servants the prophets, which spake in thy name to our kings, our princes, and our fathers, and to all the people of the land.

O Lord, righteousness belongeth unto thee, but unto us confusion of faces, as at this day; to the men of Judah, and to the inhabitants of Jerusalem, and unto all Israel, that are near, and that are far off, through all the countries whither thou hast driven them, because of their trespass that they have trespassed against thee. O Lord, to us belongeth confusion of face, to our kings, to our princes, and to our fathers, because we have sinned against thee. To the Lord our God belong mercies and forgivenesses, though we have rebelled against him; neither have we obeyed the voice of YHWH our God, to walk in his laws, which he set before us by his servants the prophets.

Yea, all Israel have transgressed thy law, even by departing, that they might not obey thy voice; therefore the curse is poured upon us, and the oath that is written in the law of Moses the servant of God, because we have sinned against him. And he hath confirmed his words, which he spake against us, and against our judges that judged us, by bringing upon us a great evil: for under the whole heaven hath not been done as hath been done upon Jerusalem . . .

O Lord, according to all thy righteousness, I beseech thee, *let thine anger and thy fury be turned away from thy city Jerusalem, thy holy mountain: because for our sins*, and for the iniquities of our fathers, Jerusalem and thy people are become a reproach to all that are about us. Now therefore,

O our God, hear the prayer of thy servant, and his supplications, and cause thy face to shine upon thy sanctuary that is desolate, for the Lord's sake.

O my God, incline thine ear, and hear; open thine eyes, and behold our desolations, and the city which is called by thy name: for we do not present our supplications before thee for our righteousnesses, but for thy great mercies. O Lord, hear; O Lord, forgive; O Lord, hearken and do; defer not, for thine own sake, O my God: for thy city and thy people are called by thy name. (Daniel 9:1–20 emphasis mine)

Desolation Because of Sin

Daniel 9:1–20 confirms exactly the cause of Judah's captivity and the destruction of Jerusalem as described in 2 Chronicles 36. By both accounts, the defining evidence of YHWH's anger was His desolate sanctuary. The bottom line was that YHWH would not or could not dwell among His people because of their sins, and without YHWH's house and His presence within it, Jerusalem was just a hollow shell.

So we find Daniel in chapter 9, an ancient man, a man beloved of YHWH, in prayer for his people and the desolate sanctuary of his God. In answer to Daniel's prayer, a prayer that finds its genesis in the events described in 2 Chronicles 36, the angel Gabriel is dispatched with a prophecy that lays out the future of Daniel's people and the city of Jerusalem, the one place on this earth where YHWH chose to meet with mankind.

The message of YHWH sent through the angel Gabriel, that famous prophecy of 70 sevens, reassures Daniel that reconciliation, redemption, and righteousness are coming and that Jerusalem will once again be restored. By many accounts it was just a couple of years after Daniel was given this prophecy that YHWH began to set in motion His plan by first raising up Cyrus as "king of Babylon" and then by prompting him to allow the children of Israel to return to Jerusalem and rebuild YHWH's desolate sanctuary.

> Now in the first year of Cyrus king of Persia, that the word of YHWH by the mouth of Jeremiah might be fulfilled, YHWH stirred up the spirit of Cyrus king of Persia, that he made a proclamation throughout all his kingdom, and put it also in writing, saying, Thus saith Cyrus king of Persia, YHWH God of heaven hath given me all the kingdoms of the earth; and he hath charged me to build him an house at Jerusalem, which is

in Judah. Who is there among you of all his people? his God be with him, and let him go up to Jerusalem, which is in Judah, and build the house of YHWH God of Israel, (he is the God,) which is in Jerusalem. (Ezra 1:1–3)

Thus saith YHWH, thy redeemer . . . that confirmeth the word of his servant, and performeth the counsel of his messengers; that saith to Jerusalem, Thou shalt be inhabited; and to the cities of Judah, Ye shall be built . . . that saith of Cyrus, He is my shepherd, and shall perform all my pleasure: even saying to Jerusalem, Thou shalt be built; and to the temple, Thy foundation shall be laid. (Isaiah 44:24–28)

Events Are Reversed

Notice the focus and order of the events described in the above passages. Israel's sins brought about the captivity of Daniel's people. Shortly thereafter, YHWH departed from His sanctuary, and this departure brought about the destruction of the temple and finally the destruction of the city of Jerusalem and its defenses. Keep in mind that it was the destruction of the temple that marked the de facto destruction of Jerusalem.

Now, 70 years later, the events are reversed. Cyrus's decree allowed Israel to return to Jerusalem and rebuild the city. Initially those rebuilding efforts focused on the very heart of the city, that is, YHWH's desolate sanctuary. The entire context of these passages makes it clear that in the eyes of YHWH, the returning Israelites, and the surrounding nations, rebuilding YHWH's house was rebuilding Jerusalem.

Short-Lived Enthusiasm

Unfortunately the enthusiasm of Joshua the high priest, Zerubbabel the governor, and the other repatriated Israelite captives for building the temple didn't last long. As we learned in the previous chapters, the harassment of their enemies and their own personal interests caused them to abandon their efforts to rebuild the temple. For the next sixteen years Israel neglected the house of YHWH and instead expended their efforts on their own dwellings and on intermingling with the women of the surrounding nations.

YHWH Intervenes

Doesn't it seem that YHWH often intervenes in the affairs of men just when all other options are exhausted, when all hope is lost and we have nothing but Him to look to? Well, I think this is what happened at this point in Israel's history. After such glorious beginnings under the decree of Cyrus, the dreams of the early Jewish repatriates were all but squelched. It had been nearly two decades and the temple was still not built, Jerusalem was defenseless, and the people lived scattered amongst their enemies in their own land.

Then something changed. YHWH's divine anger had run its course. In the fullness of His eternal plan, He set events in motion once again. At this pivotal point in Israel's history, the word of YHWH went forth, and He commanded the people to "return and build Jerusalem":

In the second year of Darius the king, in the sixth month, in the first day of the month, came the word [dabar] of YHWH by Haggai the prophet unto Zerubbabel the son of Shealtiel, governor of Judah, and to Joshua the son of Josedech, the high priest, saying, Thus speaketh YHWH of hosts, saying, This people say, The time is not come, the time that YHWH's house should be built.

Then came the word [dabar] of YHWH by Haggai the prophet, saying, Is it time for you, O ye, to dwell in your cieled houses, and this house lie waste? Now therefore thus saith YHWH of hosts; Consider your ways. Ye have sown much, and bring in little; ye eat, but ye have not enough; ye drink, but ye are not filled with drink; ye clothe you, but there is none warm; and he that earneth wages earneth wages to put it into a bag with holes. Thus saith YHWH of hosts; Consider your ways. Go up to the mountain, and bring wood, and build the house; and I will take pleasure in it, and I will be glorified, saith YHWH.

Ye looked for much, and, lo, it came to little; and when ye brought it home, I did blow upon it. Why? saith YHWH of hosts. Because of mine house that is waste, and ye run every man unto his own house . . .

Then Zerubbabel the son of Shealtiel, and Joshua the son of Josedech, the high priest, with all the remnant of the people, obeyed the voice of YHWH their God, and the words [dabar] of Haggai the prophet, as YHWH their God had sent him, and the people did fear before YHWH. Then spake Haggai YHWH's messenger in YHWH's message unto the people, saying,

I am with you, saith YHWH.

And YHWH stirred up the spirit of Zerubbabel the son of Shealtiel, governor of Judah, and the spirit of Joshua the son of Josedech, the high priest, and the spirit of all the remnant of the people; and they came and did work in the house of YHWH of hosts, their God, in the four and twentieth day of the sixth month, in the second year of Darius the king. (Haggai 1:1–15)

Do we understand what we are reading? This is YHWH's own commandment to return and build—clearly given and precisely dated! Thus begins one of the most important events in the history of the world. YHWH begins His countdown to the coming Messiah and mankind's reconciliation to Himself. Here Haggai the prophet witnesses the "word" or dabar of YHWH, the living God of the Bible, commanding Israel to shuwb, to return (turn back) and build His sanctuary, the very heart of the city of Jerusalem. But YHWH wasn't satisfied with giving His word to only one Old Testament prophet. Out of the mouth of two witnesses He confirmed his word.

In the eighth month, in the second year of Darius, came the word [dabar] of YHWH unto Zechariah, the son of Berechiah, the son of Iddo the prophet, saying, YHWH hath been sore displeased with your fathers. Therefore say thou unto them, Thus saith YHWH of hosts; Turn ye unto me, saith YHWH of hosts, and I will turn unto you, saith YHWH of hosts . . .

Upon the four and twentieth day of the eleventh month, which is the month Sebat, in the second year of Darius, came the word [dabar] of YHWH unto Zechariah . . .

Then the angel of YHWH answered and said, O YHWH of hosts, how long wilt thou not have mercy on Jerusalem and on the cities of Judah, against which thou hast had indignation these threescore and ten [70] years? And YHWH answered the angel that talked with me with good words [dabar] and comfortable words [dabar]. So the angel that communed with me said unto me, Cry thou, saying, Thus saith YHWH of hosts; I am jealous for Jerusalem and for Zion with a great jealousy. And I am very sore displeased with the heathen that are at ease: for I was but a little displeased, and they helped forward the affliction.

Therefore thus saith YHWH; I am returned to Jerusalem with mercies: my house shall be built in it, saith YHWH of hosts, and a line shall be stretched forth upon Jerusalem.

Cry yet, saying, Thus saith YHWH of hosts; My cities through prosperity shall yet be spread abroad; and YHWH shall yet comfort Zion, and shall yet choose Jerusalem. (Zechariah 1:1–17, emphasis mine)

PROPHETIC MILESTONE

Prophetic Milestone: The Word of YHWH to Return and Build Jerusalem

The beauty of these two passages is that they both witness to YHWH's "word to return and build Jerusalem." Not only do they fulfill the very contextual essence of Daniel 9:25, but they also both specify the second year of Darius 'the Great' Artaxerxes as the starting point for this dabar or word. In beautiful congruency, the passage above shows that YHWH did indeed hear Daniel's pleadings to remember the covenant and mercy promised to the fathers. What could be more reassuring than to know that YHWH, the living God of the Bible, had returned (shuwb) to Jerusalem with mercies?

And the elders of the Jews builded, and they prospered through the prophesying of Haggai the prophet and Zechariah the son of Iddo. And they builded, and finished it, according to the commandment of the God of Israel, and according to the commandment of Cyrus, and Darius, ~~and~~ [even] Artaxerxes king of Persia. And this house was finished on the third day of the month Adar, which was in the sixth year of the reign of Darius the king. (Ezra 6:14–15)

Take a moment to review the chart below. It shows the divine word given by YHWH as it relates chronologically to the events described in the previous chapters. Also note that I have corrected the timing of the four Persian decrees to reflect the biblical evidence that Darius 'the Great' is the Artaxerxes of Ezra and Nehemiah. It is also worth noting in light of the previous chapter that Hadassah became queen of Persia the very year the temple was dedicated and the year Ezra went up to Jerusalem.

The Decrees of Darius & the 70 Years

604 BC	70 yrs. of captivity begins - start of Daniel's captivity (Daniel 1; Jeremiah 25)
589 BC	Departure of Shekinah from the 1st Temple - 70 years of Divine anger (Ezekiel 8-10)
584 BC	Destruction of Jerusalem and the Temple - 70 years without a Temple (2 Kings 25)
	70 years Captivity (Daniel 1)
	70 years of Divine anger (Zechariah 1)
	70 Years of the Temple's Desolation
538 BC	Daniel receives the prophecy of 70 "weeks" (Daniel 9)
#1 536 BC	Decree of Cyrus to rebuild the Temple - End of the 70 yrs. Captivity (2 Ch. 36:22; Ezra 1)
520 BC	YHWH's Divine Word [*dabar*] to Return and Build Jerusalem (Zechariah 1; Haggai 1; Ezra 6)
#2 520 BC	Decree of Darius - Construction on the Temple continues (Ezra 6:7-14)
515/516 BC	Temple Completed & Dedicated in the 6-7th year of Darius *even* Artaxerxes (Ezra 6 & 7)
#3 515 BC	Decree by Darius 'the Great' Artaxerxes given to Ezra the Priest and Scribe (Ezra 7)
#4 501 BC	Decree by Darius 'the Great' Artaxerxes given to Nehemiah to rebuild the wall (Nehemiah 2)

From This Day Forward

Now, within the context of the second year of Darius, YHWH's return to Jerusalem, and the completion of the temple, consider these intriguing words of Haggai.

> And now, I pray you, consider [*suwm* = set, appoint] from this day and upward, from before a stone was laid upon a stone in the temple of YHWH: Since those days were, when one came to an heap of twenty measures, there were but ten: when one came to the pressfat for to draw out fifty vessels out of the press, there were but twenty. I smote you with blasting and with mildew and with hail in all the labours of your hands; yet ye turned not to me, saith YHWH.
>
> Consider [*suwm* = set, appoint] now from this day and upward, from the four and twentieth day of the ninth month, even from the day that the foundation of YHWH'S temple was laid, consider it. Is the seed yet in the barn? yea, as yet the vine, and the fig tree, and the pomegranate, and the olive tree, hath not brought forth:
>
> *from this day will I bless you.*
>
> And again the word of YHWH came unto Haggai in the four and twentieth day of the month, saying, Speak to Zerubbabel, governor of Judah, saying, I will shake the heavens and the earth; and I will overthrow the throne of kingdoms, and I will destroy the strength of the kingdoms of the heathen; and I

will overthrow the chariots, and those that ride in them; and the horses and their riders shall come down, every one by the sword of his brother. In that day, saith YHWH of hosts, will I take thee, O Zerubbabel, my servant, the son of Shealtiel, saith YHWH, and will make thee as a signet: for I have chosen thee, saith YHWH of hosts. (Haggai 2:15–23, emphasis mine)

A Dwelling Place for YHWH

I don't know that specifying a specific day or month during the second year of Darius is a necessity to begin the countdown to the Messiah, but if one had to be chosen, the twenty-fourth day of the ninth month is a fascinating candidate. As Haggai tells us, the date marks the day the foundation was completed for the place YHWH chose to meet with mankind. The text tells us to consider or count "from this day forward," so let's do that. Nearly 350 years after the second year of Darius, a very important event was celebrated in the twenty-fifth day of the ninth month. It was upon this day that Judas Maccabeus cleansed the temple from the abomination made by Antiochus Epiphanes. Jewish tradition celebrates this event with the festival of Hanukkah, also known as the Feast of Dedication or Festival of Lights.

Now, fast-forward another 160 years to the birth of Yeshua. What is fascinating to me is that if in fact Yeshua the Messiah was born during the Feast of Tabernacles as the New Testament biblical evidence suggests (see Book I in the Prophecies and Patterns series for more on this), then His conception—or the point when He actually became flesh—occurred nine months earlier during the festival of

Hanukkah. In a symbolic sense, you could say His conception marked the point when the foundation for YHWH's new dwelling place with mankind was laid. Nine months later that dwelling place, His body, was born, and Yeshua dwelt or tabernacled with mankind. To me anyway, this brings new meaning to the words of Yeshua during the final years of His ministry as recorded in the gospel of John during the Festival of Lights (Hanukkah) nearly 546 years after YHWH, through the prophet Haggai, told the Jewish people to consider or count from this day forward:

> Jesus answered, Neither hath this man sinned, nor his parents: but that the works of God should be made manifest in him. I must work the works of him that sent me, while it is day: the night cometh, when no man can work. As long as I am in the world,
>
> *I am the light of the world.*
>
> When he had thus spoken, he spat on the ground, and made clay of the spittle, and he anointed the eyes of the blind man with the clay . . .
> And many of them said, He hath a devil, and is mad; why hear ye him? Others said, These are not the words of him that hath a devil. Can a devil open the eyes of the blind? *And it was at Jerusalem the feast of the dedication, and it was winter.* (John 9:3–10:22, emphasis mine)

Opening the eyes of the blind indeed! Fascinating, isn't it, that YHWH connects the construction of the Second Temple with a reminder to consider or count from the day its foundations are laid forward? He marks that day with a very special promise:

> Consider now from this day and upward, from the four and twentieth day of the ninth month, even from the day that the foundation of YHWH's temple was laid, consider it . . . from this day will I bless you. (Haggai 2:18–19)

Then, on nearly the exact same date 515 years later, that promised blessing becomes a reality when Yeshua the son of YHWH becomes flesh.

> Ye are the children of the prophets, and of the covenant which God made with our fathers, saying unto Abraham, And in thy seed shall all the kindreds of the earth be blessed.
> *Unto you first God, having raised up his Son Jesus, sent him to bless you*, in turning away every one of you from his iniquities. (Acts 3:25–26, emphasis mine)

How awesome to realize it was the very words of the living God of the Bible which began the 70 sevens countdown to the Messiah!

Testing the Fifth Decree

So what do you think? How does this commandment or word [dabar] given by YHWH, the living God of the Bible, stand in light of our four questions?

- Could this decree be considered a dabar or word to return and build Jerusalem?
- Did this decree cause the Jewish people to shuwb (return or turn back) and build Jerusalem?
- Was this building event of enough contextual relevance to constitute building Jerusalem?
- Can the date of this decree be firmly established in the biblical and secular record?

Positives:

1. Both literally and symbolically this decree given by YHWH was indeed a "word" or dabar to build Jerusalem. This word was witnessed by Haggai, Zechariah, and Ezra.
2. YHWH's word was a commandment or decree to shuwb (return) and build His sanctuary, the very heart of the city of Jerusalem.
3. YHWH's decree was the very focal point of Israel's efforts to rebuild Jerusalem during the Second Temple era. No single building event was more central to Jerusalem's reestablishment than building YHWH's temple. Its earlier destruction marked the final act in the period of Jerusalem's destruction, and its

reconstruction marked a new beginning. Rebuilding the temple was building Jerusalem, as Daniel 9:1–23, Zechariah 1, and Ezra 4 confirm.

4. The commandment or decree given by YHWH in the second year of Darius 'the Great' Artaxerxes is one of the most well-established dates in the Bible. The second year of Darius 'the Great' is also a well-established date in the history of Persia. This date is mentioned in Ezra 4, Haggai 1, and Zechariah 1. A summary of this decree and the date for it can also be ascertained from Ezra 6:14–15.

5. YHWH's divine word to return and build Jerusalem came the same year His divine anger ended.

Negatives:

1. The second year of Darius 'the Great' Artaxerxes was 520 BC. It would seem difficult if not impossible to make 70 sevens stretch all the way to the birth of Yeshua in 4 BC, or for that matter, to His ministry nearly thirty years later in 27 AD. This is why Bible scholars have tried so hard to make the decree fit the reign of Longimanus.

Making the Impossible Possible

For those of you who have read Book I in this series, *The 13th Enumeration: Key to the Bible's Messianic Symbolism,* you may recall that YHWH often does things in ways that seem impossible from our limited human perspective. We learned how Zerubbabel, a man cursed through all his generations, brought forth the "headstone" of the

Messiah; how Hadassah, a young Jewish maiden, became queen of Persia and delivered her people; how a young shepherd boy defeated a giant; and how YHWH became the son of a carpenter (or builder) so that He might deliver the world from eternal demise.

Daniel 9 and the prophecy of 70 sevens is no exception to YHWH's way of confounding man's estimation of what is possible and what is not. In Book I, we saw how the numbers 13 and 14 are woven into the very fabric of the Bible's messianic symbolism. From the cycles of our Creator's heavenly Rolex to the biblical holy days, the numbers 13 and 14 identify only one hero in biblical history as the promised Messiah. That person is Yeshua ("the salvation of YHWH"), the Messiah promised in the Scripture.

Now, as we turn our attention to the messianic timing aspect of Daniel 9, keep in mind the wonderful symbolism of the numbers 13 and 14, or as I like to call them, the Messiah factors. Daniel 9 and the prophecy of 70 weeks is where the symbolism of these numbers really shines, because these numbers and a biblical reckoning of time make it possible for Daniel 9 and the 70 sevens to bridge the centuries between the Old and New Testaments, starting with the divine word to return and build Jerusalem in 520 BC.

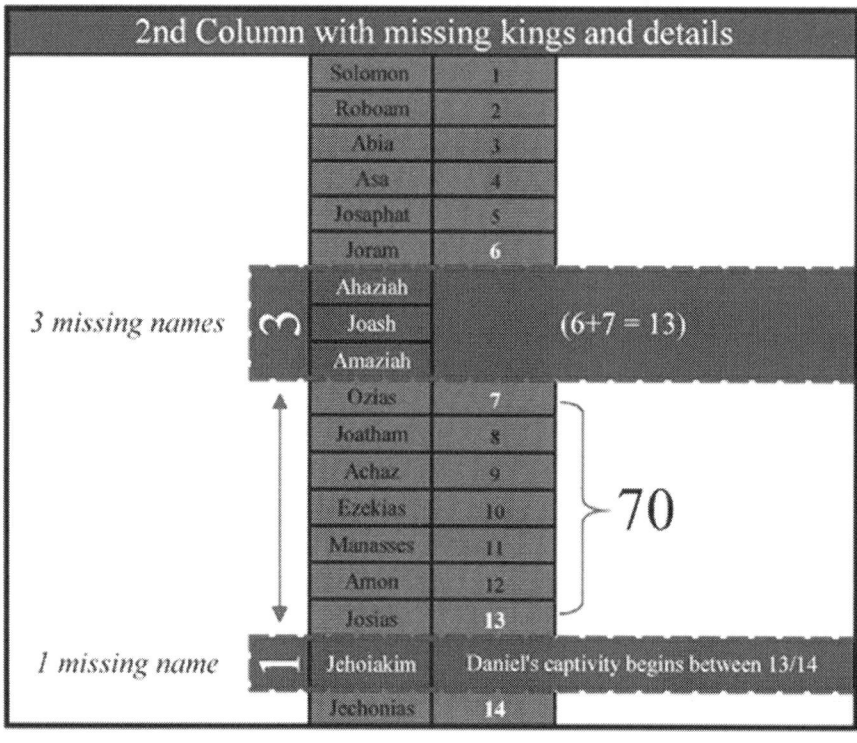

Part III:

Countdown to the Messiah

Introduction

If you've made it this far, you've realized by now that no interpretation of Daniel 9:25 using any of the four Persian decrees as its starting point has a strong scriptural basis. I found myself in a similar position many years ago when I decided to work out the chronology of the Second Temple era as it relates to Ezra and Nehemiah. It was with no little consternation that I realized the case made by Sir Robert Anderson and others—a case upon which we could confidently proclaim the messiahship of Jesus—was flawed, and fatally so at that. As I sifted through many interpretations of Daniel 9 looking for anyone who addressed the Second Temple era chronology, I remembered a book I had read in my late teens that discussed the prophecy at length. Back then the interpretation made no sense to me, but now I decided to revisit that old book in the hopes that it might shed light on the impasse I had reached in my own research of Daniel 9.

I should mention how I came to be a researcher of questions like these in the first place. To say I had a difficult time learning to read would be an understatement. But thanks to my mother's patience and love, by my early teenage years I was finally able to accomplish the task. As if to make up for lost time, I became a voracious reader. I especially loved reading about biblical history and Bible prophecy. Stories of Noah and the flood, Abraham and Egypt, Yeshua and the Romans captivated my imagination and provided many wonderful hours of exploration and discovery.

One very special day in my late teens, I was exploring a dark, dusty corner of the ancient history section of a used book store in our town. If I remember correctly, the store was called Livingstone's. I still remember picking up a small reddish hardcover with faded golden letters that read *The Great Pyramid: Proof of God* by George Riffert. My curiosity overruled my skepticism, and I picked up the book and thumbed through the pages. I purchased the book that day, and it began a wonderful adventure into the history of the Great Pyramid of Giza, one of the ancient wonders of the world.

I soon learned that during the late 1800s and early 1900s there were a great number of books written about the Great Pyramid, many of which proposed that it was a sort of ancient chronograph in stone which, in a mathematical manner, proved the Bible to be the inspired Word of God. For a young kid who loved any topic related to the Bible or Bible prophecy, this was a really fascinating subject to me. To make a long story short, I learned over the subsequent years that any truth to the claims made by these Great Pyramid enthusiasts was mixed with a great deal of conjecture and in some case outright nonsense. But amongst the wild, incredulous claims and fascinating facts was buried a most unusual and fascinating perspective on the prophecy of Daniel 9.

Riffert's book on the Great Pyramid led to another called *The Great Pyramid: Its Divine Message* by Davidson and Aldersmith. It was in this massive, one-hundred-year-old tome on Egyptian history, Bible chronology, the Great Pyramid, and ancient geometry that I first read about a theory of Daniel 9 that was based upon a biblical reckoning of time. Davidson and Aldersmith's theory, which I fully understood only decades later, was based in part upon the Persian chronology of Sir Isaac Newton and Josephus and their explanations of failed first-century Jewish messianic expectations. In short, Davidson and Aldersmith showed that Newton discovered that nearly 240 years of missing Jewish Rabbinic chronology were directly related to the failed Jewish messianic expectations of the Second Temple era and a divine command to restore and build Jerusalem. Davidson and Aldersmith, upon calculating each of the failed messianic attempts, realized that amongst all the different time elements used by the early Jewish messianic expectants, a biblical lunar cycle of 14 was missing. They had tried solar years, lunar years, and 6-, 9-, and 16-cycle lunar "years," but the one number ignored just happened to show that a Jewish man named Yeshua fit the prophecy of 70 sevens perfectly. (In Book III, *The Jubilee Code: Prophetic Milestones in the Bible,* we will look at these failed nationalistic expectations of the Second Temple era messianic expectants and the missing 240 years of the Persian era in the context of Bible's chronology. This line of investigation will shed new light on traditional Rabbinic chronology and the profound influence Daniel 9 has had on past, present, and future Jewish messianic expectations.)

In any case, it wasn't until the day over a decade later when I was investigating the prophecy of Daniel 9 and found myself unable to reconcile the biblical chronology with what many respected Bible scholars claimed regarding Ezra and Nehemiah that I remembered Davidson and Aldersmith's unusual theory. By that time I had a better understanding of biblical time, and Davidson and Aldersmith's theory made a little more sense to me. As you read the following pages, I want to make sure I give credit where it is due. As far as I know David Davidson and Adlersmith basing their research upon the work of Josephus and Newton, were the first to propose a 14-lunar-cycle year reckoning of time as it relates to Daniel 9 and a divine command to restore and build. Over the years I've modified their theory, adding the biblical symbolism related to the 13th Enumeration as well as much of the information you'll read in the following pages.

I think it only fitting to end this introduction with a famous messianic passage from Isaiah 19, which many, like Davidson and Aldersmith, believed referred to the Great Pyramid and its messianic witness—a witness much like the prophecy of Daniel 9, which speaks of the coming of the promised Messiah:

> In that day shall there be an altar to YHWH in the midst of the land of Egypt, and a pillar at the border thereof to YHWH. And it shall be for a sign and for a witness unto YHWH of hosts in the land of Egypt: for they shall cry unto YHWH because of the oppressors, and he shall send them a saviour, and a great one, and he shall deliver them. (Isaiah 19:19–20)

Chapter 1:

Timing the 70 Weeks

"At the beginning of thy supplications the commandment [dabar] *came forth, and I am come to shew thee; for thou art greatly beloved: therefore understand the matter, and consider the vision."*
Daniel 9:23

Our exploration of the Second Temple era left few stones unturned. That examination has given us the means to reasonably ascertain that Ezra and Nehemiah were contemporaries of Darius 'the Great' Artaxerxes according to the Bible's own internal chronology. This has allowed us to see the real contextual relevance of YHWH's "word" to return and rebuild Jerusalem as recorded in the prophets. We know now that it was this command to return and build YHWH's desolate sanctuary, by nature of its pivotal importance, that was the de facto event in rebuilding Jerusalem. Now, with our feet firmly resting on the Bible's own chronological foundation, we have the starting point from which to begin our countdown to the Messiah.

Why No Year?

A starting point for the prophecy of Daniel 9 is an important first step, but in order to reach the correct destination, we must now determine the time scale intended by YHWH when He sent this prophecy to Daniel. Do you remember in Book I, *The 13th*

Enumeration: Key to the Bible's Messianic Symbolism, how I described what would happen if I, as a plumber, did not use the correct measurement scale when reading my customer's blueprints? Yes, even though there might be some functionality to the plumbing system, it would not work as intended by its designer. Well, that is what has happened with Daniel 9 and the prophecy of 70 weeks. Scholars, with good intentions, have been using measurements of time not intended by YHWH.

    Let me ask you a serious question. Have you ever wondered why YHWH did not simply give us the exact number of years for the prophecy of Daniel 9 when he sent the angel Gabriel to Daniel? Why did He veil the prophecy in mysterious periods of time called *shabuwa* or sevens? I mean, come on—why tell us 70 sevens and not just say 490 years?

    If there is one fact evidenced by the biblical record, it is that YHWH, the living God of the Bible, has order and purpose for every one of His actions as they relate to mankind's affairs. Granted we may not always see His purpose in the beginning, but eventually that purpose and order shine through in wonderful ways. Regarding the timing of Daniel 9 and the 70 weeks, then, the only logical conclusion is that YHWH did not want to associate a "year" with the prophecy. YHWH is not the author of confusion or misdirection, so He must have had a greater purpose in framing the prophecy the way He did—a purpose that, once understood, would remove any doubt or uncertainty in identifying the Bible's promised Messiah. As we pursue this new line of investigation, let's keep in mind the words of the wise king Solomon:

> It is the glory of God to conceal a thing: but the honour of kings is to search out a matter. (Proverbs 25:2)

Seven, Sevens, and Seventy

If YHWH purposely did *not* associate solar or even lunar "years"—the measures used by Bible scholars who try to trace the prophecy's fulfillment—with the prophecy of 70 sevens, then what measurement are we to use to interpret this prophetic blueprint?

Let's start by looking more closely at the word most Bibles translates as "weeks" and most scholars interpret as "years." This is the Hebrew word *shabuwa*. Its most basic meaning is simply seven—a period of seven or a heptad. Shabuwa, as we learned earlier, comes from the Hebrew root *shaba,* which means to swear or take an oath.

> Know therefore and understand, that from the going forth of the commandment to restore and to build Jerusalem unto the Messiah the Prince shall be *seven weeks*, and threescore and two weeks: the street shall be built again, and the wall, even in troublous times. (Daniel 9:25, emphasis mine)

But it gets a little more complicated. Scholars have long been challenged by the unusual plural masculine form of the Hebrew word shabuwa used in the text of Daniel 9. As I will explain in a moment, by using this form of shabuwa, the text uses the idiosyncrasies of Hebrew grammar to really draw our attention.

The respected Bible scholar John F. Walvoord, in his book *Daniel: The Key to Prophetic Revelation,* makes the following comments on the subject:

> The conservative interpretation of Daniel 9:24-27 usually regards the time units as years. The decision is, by no means unanimous. Some amillenarians, like Young, who have trouble with fitting this into their system of eschatology consider this an indefinite period of time. Actually, the passage does not say "years"; and because it is indefinite they consider the question somewhat open. Further, as Young points out, the word *sevens* is in the masculine plural instead of the usual feminine plural. No clear explanation is given except that Young feels "it was for the deliberate purpose of calling attention to the fact that the word sevens is employed in an unusual sense" . . .
>
> In the Christological interpretation of Daniel 9:24–27, it is generally assumed that the time units indicated are years. The English word "weeks" is misleading as the Hebrew is actually the plural of the word for seven, without specifying whether it is days, months, or years. (John F. Walvoord, *Daniel: The Key to Prophetic Revelation,* 217, 219)

As exemplified by Walvoord's quote above, scholars understand the word shabuwa as seven or sevens with no contextually implied time measurement associated with it. As we can also see in the quote, there has never been a conclusive reason given for why the text uses the plural masculine form of shabuwa in Daniel 9:25.

Here is what makes the plural masculine form so intriguing from an interpretational perspective. In its normal form, shabuwa is spelled *(shin-beth-waw-ayin)*, but the plural masculine form changes the spelling to *(shin-beth-ayin-yod-mem)*. Minus its vowel pointings, this form has exactly the same phonetic spelling as the Hebrew word *shib'iym* or seventy *(shin-beth-ayin-yod-mem)*.

Shabuwa / Shib'iym

Hebrew	Hebrew (pronunciation)	English
שָׁבוּעַ	shabuwa	sevens
שָׁבֻעִים	shabuwa (plural masculine)	sevens
שִׁבְעִים	shib'iym	seventy
Shabuwa / Shib'iym without vowel pointings		
שבעים	shabuwa / shib'iym	sevens seventy

So was Edward Young, as quoted by Walvoord, correct when he speculated that the word *sevens* is "employed in an unusual sense" in Daniel 9? I think so. What about you? Take a look at Daniel 9:25a as written in Hebrew. Keep in mind that Hebrew is read from right to left. The final two words in Daniel 9:25a are shabuwa (7s) and sheba (7).

וְתֵדַ֨ע וְתַשְׂכֵּ֜ל מִן־מֹצָ֣א דָבָ֗ר לְהָשִׁיב֙ וְלִבְנ֤וֹת יְרֽוּשָׁלִַ֙ם֙ עַד־מָשִׁ֣יחַ נָגִ֔יד שָׁבֻעִ֖ים שִׁבְעָ֑ה

(Daniel 9:25a)

Adding further mystery to the subject is the fact that vowel pointings (the dots and lines over and under Hebrew letters) were not added until sometime in the Middle Ages. This means that when the book of Daniel was written, the "sevens" of Daniel 9:25a could have been read as either *shabuwa* (sevens) or *shib'iym* (seventy). So you see, only by looking at the fuller context of Daniel 9:25–27 could one have possibly determined that the text was referring to the plural masculine form of shabuwa *instead of the Hebrew word shib'iym, which means seventy.* Take a look at how Daniel 9:25 might have read if translated into English without the help of vowel pointings, and following the Hebrew word order rather than the English::

> Know therefore and understand, that from the going forth of the commandment to restore and to build Jerusalem unto the Messiah the Prince shall be *seventy* [shib'yim] *seven* [sheba]. (Daniel 9:25a)

This is how it reads as given in the KJV. Keep in mind the order of the numbers are reversed in the English translation:

> Know therefore and understand, that from the going forth of the commandment to restore and to build Jerusalem unto the Messiah the Prince shall be *seven* [sheba] *weeks* [shabuwa]. (Daniel 9:25a)

This raises an interesting question. Could Yeshua's advice about forgiving one's brother in Matthew 18:21–22 have been a clever reference to Daniel 9:25 and the Hebrew play on words of *shabuwa* (sevens) and *shab'iym* (seventy)? Keep in mind that it was only a short time later that Yeshua put this advice into practice when He died to forgive the sins of His brethren in fulfillment of Daniel 9:24–27.

> Then came Peter to him, and said, Lord, how oft shall my brother sin against me, and I forgive him? till seven times? Jesus saith unto him, I say not unto thee, *Until seven times: but, Until seventy times seven.* (Matthew 18:21–22, emphasis mine)

This is how the prophecy could have read without vowel pointings:

> Know therefore and understand, that from the going forth of the commandment to restore and to build Jerusalem unto the Messiah the Prince shall be seventy (*shib'iym*) seven (*sheba*). (Daniel 9:25a)

Goosebumps, anyone?

A Prophetic Word Puzzle

So exactly what did YHWH intend when He used the word shabuwa in the text of Daniel 9:25, and how does this relate to the timing element of the prophecy of 70 sevens—or "70 seven," as we should perhaps read it? Most scholars simply ignore the separate character of Daniel 9:25a, instead opting to add the 7 weeks until the coming of the Messiah to the 62 weeks during which the wall and plaza are built to arrive at the point after which the Messiah is "cut off" (Daniel 9:26). Obviously, the wording of Daniel 9:25a was intentional, but why? Could this homograph of "70 seven" be a lost key to the prophecy of Daniel 9? Could YHWH have hidden in the text of Daniel 9:25 coded proof that Yeshua is the Messiah?

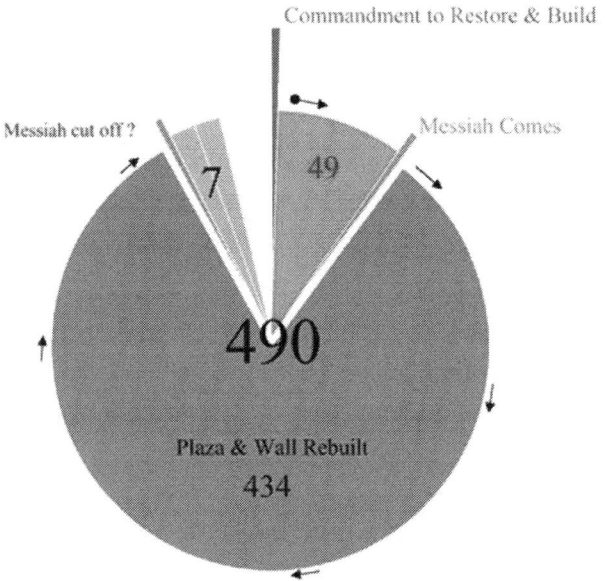

Overview of 70 Sevens

- Commandment to Restore and Build
- 7 Sevens until the Messiah (49)
- 62 Sevens the Plaza & Wall Rebuilt (434)
- Messiah Cut off After 62 Sevens
- 1 Seven the Covenant Confirmed (7)

Believe it or not, the answer to this question is found in our mysterious list of Matthew 1 and the 13th Enumeration of the Messiah. Take another look at this list of Yeshua's generations. You've seen it many times throughout Books I and II, but ponder it now within the context of Daniel 9:25a and the numerical wordplay of 70 seven. See if anything stands out to you in this amazing list. In the next few chapters, we will once again look at the lineage of Yeshua and its significance to a biblical reckoning of time with an intent to figure out this amazing prophetic puzzle.

Lineage of Yeshua (Jesus)
As <u>Summarized</u> in Matthew 1

14 Generations From Abraham to David		14 Generations From David to the captivity		14 Generations From the captivity to Yeshua/Jesus	

As <u>Given</u> in Matthew 1

Abraham	1	Solomon	1	Salathiel	1
Isaac	2	Reaboam	2	Zorobabel	2
Jacob	3	Abia	3	Abiud	3
Judas	4	Asa	4	Eliakim	4
Phares	5	Josaphat	5	Azor	5
Esrom	6	Joram	6	Sadoc	6
Aram	7	Ozias	7	Achim	7
Aminadab	8	Joatham	8	Eliud	8
Naasson	9	Achaz	9	Eleazar	9
Salmon	10	Ezekias	10	Matthan	10
Booz	11	Manasses	11	Jacob	11
Obed	12	Amon	12	Joseph	12
Jesse	13	Josias	13	Yeshua	13
David	14	Jechonias	14		14*

2nd Column with missing kings and details

	Solomon	1	
	Roboam	2	
	Abia	3	
	Asa	4	
	Josaphat	5	
	Joram	6	
3 missing names — 3	Ahaziah		(6+7 = 13)
	Joash		
	Amaziah		
	Ozias	7	
	Joatham	8	
	Achaz	9	70
	Ezekias	10	
	Manasses	11	
	Amon	12	
	Josias	13	
1 missing name — 1	Jehoiakim		Daniel's captivity begins between 13/14
	Jechonias	14	

* implied not stated

Before we fully turn our attention to the lineage of Yeshua, biblical time, and the Messiah factors, there is one more treasure to be found related to the word shabuwa. This biblical treasure points us back to one of the most important covenants in the Bible. Let's take one more brief look.

The Sevenfold Oath

As mentioned before, the word shabuwa comes from the Hebrew root *shaba*. Shaba means to swear or take an oath. In the biblical record, the first *shaba* or oath that YHWH swears with anyone is recorded in Genesis 22:13–18. This is that famous passage we talked about in Part I of this book, where YHWH promises that in Abraham's seed all nations of the earth will be blessed. This, as we learn from the apostle Paul, was a direct reference to the promised Messiah. Now, how awesome is this? In beautiful biblical congruency, the very root word from which the *sevens* of the 70 sevens prophecy originates is used in reference to the promise YHWH made with Abraham concerning the coming of the Messiah.

> [13] And Abraham lifted up his eyes, and looked, and behold behind him a ram caught in a thicket by his horns: and Abraham went and took the ram, and offered him up for a burnt offering in the stead of his son. [14] And Abraham called the name of that place Jehovahjireh: as it is said to this day, In the mount of YHWH it shall be seen. And the angel of YHWH called

unto Abraham out of heaven the second time, And said, *By myself have I sworn [shaba], saith YHWH,* for because thou hast done this thing, and hast not withheld thy son, thine only son: that in blessing I will bless thee, and in multiplying I will multiply thy seed as the stars of the heaven, and as the sand which is upon the sea shore; and thy seed shall possess the gate of his enemies; *and in thy seed shall all the nations of the earth be blessed;* because thou hast obeyed my voice. (Genesis 22:13–18, emphasis mine)

Now to Abraham and his seed were the promises made. *He saith not, And to seeds, as of many; but as of one, And to thy seed, which is Christ.* (Galatians 3:16, emphasis mine)

On that thrilling note, let's now turn our attention to a biblical reckoning of time, the lineage of Yeshua, and the Messiah factors. Our goal in the coming chapters is to find the biblical measure of time used in the prophecy of 70 sevens. To accomplish this, we must revisit some of fascinating information we covered in Book I, *The 13th Enumeration: Key to the Bible's Messianic Symbolism.*

Chapter 2:

Biblical Time and the Messiah Factors

"And God said, Let there be lights in the firmament of the heaven to divide the day from the night; and let them be for signs, and for seasons, and for days, and years."
Genesis 1:14

Living in a world that no longer keeps time according to a biblical standard, we sometimes inadvertently assume our own concept of timekeeping when interpreting passages of Scripture. In this chapter, I would like to look at biblical time and its messianic significance in the context it was given. Our goal here is to understand biblical time so that we might use it to accurately measure the 70 sevens of Daniel 9—and thus accurately identify the promised Messiah.

Much of the information in the next few chapters will be familiar to readers of Book I, but I think it will benefit all of us to refresh our understanding of this complex but fascinating subject.

A Cosmic Rolex

If you pulled back the cover on your expensive wristwatch, you would find gears of different sizes that allow your watch to keep track of seconds, minutes, days, weeks, months, and years. Each gear is a specific size that allows it to precisely measure time.

Our Creator's watch works the same way, only His gears are the sun, moon, earth, and stars. This cosmic Rolex, if you will, measures time according to a standard He set in motion at creation (Genesis 1:14). Our earth, in its orbit around the sun, is the gear that gives us our year of 365.24 days. The moon is the gear that gives us a month of 29.53 days. The rotation of the earth is the gear that gives us our day of 24 hours. And finally, the interaction of these gears is what drives the biblical calendar.

The biblical calendar, however, does not operate on quite the same basis as our modern model of timekeeping. The rising and setting of the sun measures our modern day. It takes 365.24 of these days to make one solar year, and it's by these days that our Western solar calendar functions. The biblical month, on the other hand, is based upon the 29.53-day cycle of the moon. Twelve lunar cycles (months) of 29.53 days equals 354.36 days. This makes the biblical lunar year about eleven days shorter than each solar cycle.

But it would be a mistake to believe the only "biblical" year is the lunar one. The reason this difference is important to our discussion is that the biblical calendar incorporates *both*—it uses both the solar and the lunar year to measure time.

The Bible institutes a solar year in Genesis 1 and elsewhere, where it regulates our day-to-day "labor" by the setting and rising of the sun—a pattern of six days of labor followed by a day of rest, instituted by YHWH at creation and measured by the sun. Another way to see this pattern is to picture it as mankind's struggle under the curse of sin for the past six thousand years and of a yet-future promise of rest from that curse during the millennial reign of Christ. Even today, this pattern of 6 and 7 is acknowledged by our modern society.

The lunar aspect of the calendar, on the other hand, is used to calculate the biblical holy days or sacred assemblies (*miqras*). These feasts, also called *mow'ed* or divine appointments, were first given to Israel after the exodus from Egypt and are pictures of mankind's deliverance from the curse of sin and our reconciliation to our Creator.

These biblical holy days are pictured in the New Testament as "shadows" of things to come. There are seven of these divine appointments in the Bible, and they are frequently divided into two groups. The first group is celebrated in the spring and the second group in the fall.

A whole book could be written on the prophetic significance of the holy days—and many books have been!—but for the present, we will only briefly look at the spring feasts and their fulfillment in Yeshua. Keep in mind that Yeshua fulfilled these spring feasts according to the Biblical calendar which uses a 365.24 day solar cycle and a 29.53 day lunar cycle.

Spring Feasts
1. Passover
2. Unleavened Bread
3. Firstfruits
4. Pentecost (Shavuot)

Fall Feasts
5. Feast of Trumpets (Rosh Hashanah)
6. Day of Atonement (Yom Kippur)
7. Feast of Tabernacles (Sukkoth)

What is so awesome about these biblical holy days is that the New Testament makes it clear that the events surrounding Yeshua's death and resurrection were a fulfillment of the first four as listed below:

1 *and* **2: Passover and the Feast of Unleavened Bread:** The gospel accounts show that Yeshua was the Passover lamb which "taketh away the sins of the world."

> The next day John seeth Jesus coming unto him, and saith, Behold the Lamb of God, which taketh away the sin of the world. (John 1:29)

> Purge out therefore the old leaven, that ye may be a new lump, as ye are unleavened. For even Christ our passover is sacrificed for us: Therefore let us keep the feast, not with old leaven, neither with the leaven of malice and wickedness; but with the unleavened bread of sincerity and truth. (1 Corinthians 5:7–8)

3: Firstfruits: The apostle Paul explains that Yeshua became the firstfruits of the resurrection:

> But now is Christ risen from the dead, and become the firstfruits of them that slept. For since by man came death, by man came also the resurrection of the dead. For as in Adam all die, even so in Christ shall all be made alive. But every man in

his own order: Christ the firstfruits; afterward they that are Christ's at his coming. (1 Corinthians 15:20–23)

4: Pentecost: Later, the book of Acts explains that Yeshua commanded the apostles to wait for the Holy Spirit. The Spirit's coming took place on the day of Pentecost, just ten days after Yeshua ascended into heaven. For those willing to dig a little deeper, the parallels between the exodus and the giving of the law at Sinai and the Holy Spirit sent to the early church after Yeshua's resurrection are full of wonderful symbolism and insights.

> And when the day of Pentecost was fully come, they were all with one accord in one place. And suddenly there came a sound from heaven as of a rushing mighty wind, and it filled all the house where they were sitting. And there appeared unto them cloven tongues like as of fire, and it sat upon each of them. And they were all filled with the Holy Ghost, and began to speak with other tongues, as the Spirit gave them utterance. (Acts 2:1–4)

> Forasmuch as ye are manifestly declared to be the epistle of Christ ministered by us, written not with ink, but with the Spirit of the living God; not in tables of stone, but in fleshy tables of the heart. (2 Corinthians 3:3)

It is clear from the above accounts that the New Testament writers saw Yeshua as the fulfillment of the Bible's spring holy days.

Just like the prophecy of Daniel 9, the essence of the typology found in the biblical holy days speaks of a coming Redeemer who will pay the price of mankind's sins. It is the lunar cycles that have carried this prophecy from the past to the present.

Thanks to the Jewish people and their YHWH-given tenacity, for thousands of years the hope of the promised Redeemer has been kept alive in the biblical holy days. Each day after our labor under the sun, mankind can look up into the night sky and be reminded of the promise of reconciliation offered by Yeshua. Like a giant billboard, YHWH has used the lunar cycle to remind us of His past, present, and future plan of reconciliation for all mankind.

The Lunar Cycle and the Messiah Factors

We know from existing eclipse records dating back nearly three thousand years that the lunar cycle of 29.53 days has been relatively constant. For those interested in pursuing this line of investigation, I recommend the book *Historical Eclipses and the Earth's Rotation* by Richard Stephenson. You'll be hard-pressed to find a more exhaustive rendering of the historical eclipse record than what is given in this book.

For thousands of years, this lunar cycle of 29.53 days has waxed and waned in a manner that forever identifies it with only one person in biblical history. It shouldn't surprise us to find that from the moment YHWH set in motion the lunar cycle of 29.53 days, He hid the symbolism of 13 and 14 in its very structure! You see, from the first visible glimmer of the lunar cycle, the moon's light waxes for 13 or 14 days. Then, after a short pause, its light wanes for another 13 or 14 days.

Yes, even in the very cycles of the moon, YHWH has hidden the Messiah factors. Think about the implications! The very cycles of the moon do indeed declare the glory of God.

Take a look again at the lineage of Yeshua in the following chart. Appropriately, it is arranged by the apostle Matthew to emphasize the numbers 13 and 14 in relation to Yeshua, along with several other pieces of information. Keep this in mind, because Matthew 1 is indeed the key to understanding the prophecy of 70 weeks, and more particularly, it is the key that unlocks the prophetic word puzzle of Daniel 9:25a.

Lineage of Yeshua (Jesus)
As Summarized in Matthew 1

14 Generations From Abraham to David		14 Generations From David to the captivity		14 Generations From the captivity to Yeshua/Jesus	

As Given in Matthew 1

Abraham	1	Solomon	1	Salathiel	1
Isaac	2	Reaboam	2	Zorobabel	2
Jacob	3	Abia	3	Abiud	3
Judas	4	Asa	4	Eliakim	4
Phares	5	Josaphat	5	Azor	5
Esrom	6	Joram	6	Sadoc	6
Aram	7	Ozias	7	Achim	7
Aminadab	8	Joatham	8	Eliud	8
Naasson	9	Achaz	9	Eleazar	9
Salmon	10	Ezekias	10	Matthan	10
Booz	11	Manasses	11	Jacob	11
Obed	12	Amon	12	Joseph	12
Jesse	13	Josias	13	Yeshua	13
David	14	Jechonias	14		14*

2nd Column with missing kings and details

	Solomon	1	
	Roboam	2	
	Abia	3	
	Asa	4	
	Josaphat	5	
	Joram	6	
3 missing names — 3	Ahaziah		(6+7 = 13)
	Joash		
	Amaziah		
	Ozias	7	
	Joatham	8	
	Achaz	9	} 70
	Ezekias	10	
	Manasses	11	
	Amon	12	
	Josias	13	
1 missing name — 1	Jehoiakim		Daniel's captivity begins between 13/14
	Jechonias	14	

* implied not stated

"The heavens declare the glory of God; and the firmament sheweth his handywork. Day unto day uttereth speech, and night unto night sheweth knowledge. There is no speech nor language, where their voice is not heard. Their line is gone out through all the earth, and their words to the end of the world. In them hath he set a tabernacle for the sun, which is as a bridegroom coming out of his chamber, and rejoiceth as a strong man to run a race. His going forth is from the end of the heaven, and his circuit unto the ends of it: and there is nothing hid from the heat thereof."

Psalm 19:1–6

Chapter 3:

The Elusive 13th Month

"And it shall come to pass, that from one new moon to another, and from one sabbath to another, shall all flesh come to worship before me, saith YHWH."
Isaiah 66:23

As we've seen, the biblical calendar has two main gears. The first gear, the sun, drives mankind's day-to-day activities within a solar cycle of 365.24 days. These days are further arranged into a cycle of six days of labor and a seventh of rest, as first exemplified by YHWH at creation.

The Primary Gear

After the flood, YHWH promised Noah that as long as the "earth remaineth," there would be day and night as well as four seasons: seedtime, harvest, summer, and winter (Genesis 8:21–22). By ordering a weekly cycle of 6/7 days within a solar year of 365.24 days, YHWH forever stamped the four seasons with the number 13. You see, not only do 6 + 7 equal 13, but our solar year has 4 x 13 weeks (52), so each season is 13 weeks long.

This brings to mind the New Testament story about Yeshua's disciples plucking ears of corn on the Sabbath day and the Pharisees complaining that they were doing that "which is not lawful." Knowing that YHWH designed the biblical calendar to exemplify the Messiah, Yeshua's response to the Pharisees is enlightening:

> But he said unto them, Have ye not read what David did, when he was an hungred, and they that were with him; how he entered into the house of God, and did eat the shewbread, which was not lawful for him to eat, neither for them which were with him, but only for the priests? Or have ye not read in the law, how that on the sabbath days the priests in the temple profane the sabbath, and are blameless? But I say unto you, That in this place is one greater than the temple. But if ye had known what this meaneth, I will have mercy, and not sacrifice, ye would not have condemned the guiltless. *For the Son of man is Lord even of the sabbath day.* (Matthew 12:3–8, emphasis mine)

A Sabbath cycle is 6 days of labor in a cycle of 7. The labor of man (6) and the rest (7) of YHWH are completed by the "Son of man," Yeshua, the 13th Enumeration.

The Secondary Gear—And a Problem

As we learned in the previous chapter, the lunar cycle of 29.53 days is the gear that controls the other half of the biblical calendar. This side of the calendar reminds mankind of YHWH's promised reconciliation for all of us through the Messiah, the Lord of the Sabbath.

But there is a problem. Twelve lunar months of 29.53 days only equal 354.36 days in a year. That means the lunar year is about eleven days shorter than the solar year of 365.24. This difference of eleven days creates a challenge in reconciling the two sides of the biblical calendar. If left unreconciled, those missing days would cause the lunar or religious side of the biblical calendar to move out of synchronization with the solar year.

That YHWH intended the solar and lunar year to be synchronized with each other is evidenced by the fact that after the exodus, YHWH commanded Israel to start their first month relative to the agricultural cycle of *abib*. (Exodus 13, 23, 34; Deuteronomy 16). *Abib* in the context of the exodus describes the state of ripeness of barley. By instructing Israel to start their first month in abib, YHWH ensured that the lunar cycle would always be fixed relative to the agricultural cycle, which was governed by the sun.

Irreconcilable Differences?

That's all fine and good in theory, but how are these two parts of the biblical calendar reconciled in actuality? How is the practical side of the calendar—the side that represents mankind's struggle under the curse of sin—reconciled with the side of the calendar that represents the hope of mankind's reconciliation to their Creator?

By now you've probably guessed the answer. The two sides of the biblical calendar are reconciled by a 13th month. Every three years or so, the biblical calendar requires that a 13th month be added in order to reconcile the solar and lunar cycles. This, in calendric terms, is called an intercalation.

Historically, it is worth noting that some cultures did not intercalate their calendars like the Jewish people were implicitly instructed to do in the book of Exodus. An ancient example is found in the calendric systems of the Egyptians; a modern example is the Islamic calendar. Both of these calendar systems have months that wander throughout the solar year because they are not reconciled by a 13th month.

Ezekiel's 13th Month

Although Exodus requires a de facto intercalation (Exodus 13:4, 23:15, 34:18; Deuteronomy 16:1), an actual biblical example of a 13th month requires a little effort to find. The only place I'm aware of that gives chronological evidence for an intercalated lunar/solar cycle is found in the book of Ezekiel. Once again, this will be very familiar to readers of the first book in this series, but I believe this fascinating information is worth revisiting.

In the first few chapters, YHWH uses the prophet Ezekiel to give Israel and Judah an object lesson. YHWH instructs Ezekiel to lie on his side for 390 (13 x 30) days for the sins of Israel. He goes on to instruct him to lie on his other side for forty days for the sins of Judah. These unusual instructions provide us with a rare opportunity to define the lunar/solar calendar and its intercalations as they relate to the chronology of the Bible.

> Now it came to pass in the thirtieth year, in the fourth month, in the fifth day of the month, as I was among the captives by the river of Chebar, that the heavens were opened, and I saw

visions of God. In the fifth day of the month, which was the fifth year of king Jehoiachin's captivity . . . (Ezekiel 1:1–2)

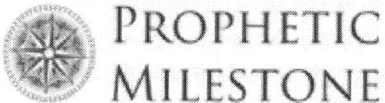

Prophetic Milestones: The Thirtieth year of Ezekiel

Keep the thirtieth year mentioned in the passage above in mind for future reference. In Book III of this series, *The Jubilee Code: Prophetic Milestones in the Bible*, this verse becomes an important focal point in the chronology of the Old Testament as it relates to the Jubilee and Sabbath cycles and YHWH's redemptive plan for mankind.

The Fifth Year of Jehoiachin

Ezekiel was commanded to lie on either side for a total of 430 days.

> For I have laid upon thee the years of their iniquity, according to the number of the days, three hundred and ninety days: so shalt thou bear the iniquity of the house of Israel. And when thou hast accomplished them, lie again on thy right side, and thou shalt bear the iniquity of the house of Judah forty days: I have appointed thee each day for a year. (Ezekiel 4:5–6)

In the sixth month of the following year, after completing his object lesson, Ezekiel was sitting in his house with some of the elders of Judah. From this gathering, YHWH physically took Ezekiel and showed him the departure of the shekinah glory of YHWH from Jerusalem (Ezekiel 8–10).

There are three possible ways to calculate the amount of time between the fourth month of Jehoiachin's fifth year and the sixth month of his sixth year, and only one of these provides enough time to accommodate the 430 days Ezekiel was required to lie on his side before we find him sitting in his own house among the elders of Judah.

They are listed in the chart below:

Ezekiel's 430 days

390 days on his left side + 40 days on his right side (Eze. 1-4)

	30 day months	29.53 day lunar months	29.53 day lunar + intercalary 13th month
Start 5th day of 4th month	4th month - 5th yr.	4th month - 5th yr.	4th month - 5th yr.
	5th month - 5th yr.	5th month - 5th yr.	5th month - 5th yr.
	6th month - 5th yr.	6th month - 5th yr.	6th month - 5th yr.
	7th month - 5th yr.	7th month - 5th yr.	7th month - 5th yr.
	8th month - 5th yr.	8th month - 5th yr.	8th month - 5th yr.
	9th month - 5th yr.	9th month - 5th yr.	9th month - 5th yr.
	10th month - 5th yr.	10th month - 5th yr.	10th month - 5th yr.
	11th month - 5th yr.	11th month - 5th yr.	11th month - 5th yr.
	12th month - 5th yr.	12th month - 5th yr.	12th month - 5th yr.
	1st month - 6th yr.	1st month - 6th yr.	13th month - 5th yr.
	2nd month - 6th yr.	2nd month - 6th yr.	1st month - 6th yr.
	3rd month - 6th yr.	3rd month - 6th yr.	2nd month - 6th yr.
	4th month - 6th yr.	4th month - 6th yr.	3rd month - 6th yr.
	5th month - 6th yr.	5th month - 6th yr.	4th month - 6th yr.
End 5th day of 6th month	6th month - 6th yr.	6th month - 6th yr.	5th month - 6th yr.
			6th month - 6th yr.
Total months	14	14	15
Total days	420	413.42	442.95

And it came to pass in the sixth year, in the sixth month, in the fifth day of the month, as I sat in mine house, and the elders of Judah sat before me, that the hand of the Lord YHWH fell there upon me. Then I beheld, and lo a likeness as the appearance of fire: from the appearance of his loins even downward, fire; and from his loins even upward, as the appearance of brightness, as the colour of amber. And he put forth the form of an hand, and took me by a lock of mine head; and the spirit lifted me up between the earth and the heaven, and brought me in the visions of God to Jerusalem, to the door of the inner gate that looketh toward the north; where was the seat of the image of jealousy, which provoketh to jealousy. (Ezekiel 8:1–3)

Of the three options in this chart, only the third allows for the necessary time given the chronological evidence provided in the text. In order for Ezekiel to have lain on his side for 430 days and still be sitting in his house by the sixth month, the fifth year of Jehoiachin's captivity must have had an intercalary or 13th month. (Please note that if the seven days of Ezekiel 3:15 are taken into account, seven additional days must be subtracted from the above totals, which makes it even more certain that a 13th month was used).

Incidentally, this passage is of great value to the chronologist who is interested in synchronizing the lunar/solar cycle in terms of the macrochronological record. As far as I know, this is the only place in the Scripture that provides specific chronological evidence of an intercalary month. Contextually, this shows that during the captivity period, the Jewish people understood time in the sense of an intercalated lunar/solar calendar—a calendar reconciled by a 13th month.

Reconciled by the 13th Enumeration

It's worth mentioning again that in a symbolic sense, the rising and setting of the sun regulates man's labor and rest throughout the solar year, symbolism which can be extrapolated out to man's labor under the curse of sin and the coming rest of God. The lunar cycle, on the other hand, regulates the Bible's religious calendar and its miqras (sacred assemblies) and mow'ed (appointed times). These two parts of the calendar, since at least the Second Temple era, have been synchronized by a 13th month. The very essence of biblical time is meant to focus our attention on Yeshua, the 13th Enumeration, whose purpose to reconcile mankind to YHWH has been evidenced by the heavenly luminaries since the very moment our Creator set them in motion.

In the next chapter we will look at biblical time in an unusual context. By the time we are done, I'm pretty sure you'll have a new appreciation for how our ancestors understood the concept of time.

Chapter 4:

Of Circles, Cubits, and Context

"His going forth is from the end of the heaven, and his circuit unto the ends of it: and there is nothing hid from the heat thereof."
Psalm 19:6

Context is an indispensable part of correctly understanding the Bible. When investigating the messianic symbolism and prophecies of the Bible, the context of *time* is especially relevant, because time is the thread that connects the past to the present and the present to the future. Our Creator, YHWH, has a plan to reconcile mankind through Yeshua, and time is one of the means by which He provides evidence of this purpose in the Bible.

A few passages of Scripture are sufficient to explain:

> To every thing there is a season, and a time to every purpose under the heaven. (Ecclesiastes 3:1)

> But when the fulness of the time was come, God sent forth his Son, made of a woman, made under the law . . . (Galatians 4:4)

> Remember the former things of old: for I am God, and there is none else; I am God, and there is none like me, declaring the end from the beginning, and from ancient times the things that

are not yet done, saying, My counsel shall stand, and I will do all my pleasure. (Isaiah 46:9–10)

Behold, the days come, saith YHWH, that I will perform that good thing which I have promised unto the house of Israel and to the house of Judah. In those days, and at that time, will I cause the Branch of righteousness to grow up unto David; and he shall execute judgment and righteousness in the land. In those days shall Judah be saved, and Jerusalem shall dwell safely: and this is the name wherewith she shall be called, YHWH our righteousness. (Jeremiah 33:14–16)

Prophecy and the Blueprint of Eschatology

Through the use of predictive prophecy, the Bible makes it abundantly clear that history is playing out according to YHWH's plan. As we try understand Daniel 9, it is imperative that we keep a biblical concept of time firmly fixed in our minds.

Today, some well-meaning Bible scholars are using the wrong measure of a "year" when trying to follow the biblical blueprint of time, especially when it comes to "last things"—eschatology. Though sincerely offered and apparently functional, their measures of time have given them an erroneous perspective on YHWH's prophetic blueprint for Daniel 9. This error in fact has led scholars to make assumptions about the prophecy of 70 sevens that have profound theological implications. The truth of the matter is that Daniel 9 and the prophecy of 70 sevens has had a great influence on how we see Messiah's purpose at His first coming and at His second. The prophecy has also influenced how we see the culmination of this age regarding such subjects as the rapture, the tribulation, the Antichrist, and numerous other intertwined prophetic events. So with this sobering weight of interpretational influence reminding us of the importance of biblical time, let's take another look at the evidence to ensure that we are building our eschatological house upon a solid foundation.

As It Stands Today

Today, there are basically three ways in which scholars calculate a biblical year:

1. As a solar year of 365.24 days
2. As a lunar "prophetic" year of 360 days (more about this strange innovation below)
3. As a lunar/solar year of 12 or 13 cycles of 29.53 days each (354.36 or 383.89 days respectively)

As we have briefly seen, from the time of the Second Temple era to the present, the Bible's lunar/solar calendar has been based upon the interaction of the solar year of 365.24 days with the lunar month of 29.53 days. Since the Bible has never given any indication that a solar year of 365.24 days is the sole factor in determining the biblical calendar, we can reasonably conclude that to calculate prophetic events using such a measure of time is unreasonable.

But what about a 360-day lunar or "prophetic" year? Is there any reasonable grounds to use such a calendar alongside the biblically mandated lunar/solar calendar of today? Keep in mind that Yeshua already fulfilled half the Biblical holy days using a intercalated lunar/solar year, not a so called 360 day "prophetic" year.

Today, a majority of scholars claim that the Bible's prophecies should be calculated using such a "prophetic" year of 360 days (twelve 30-day months), believing that at some point in the past, the solar year was exactly 360 days long and the monthly lunar cycle was exactly 30 days in length. (They use the events of Joshua's extended day and Hezekiah's backward-moving sundial, in part, to explain why things changed.) They further contend that during the events described in the book of Revelation, the lunar/solar cycle will once again revert to such an arrangement. One of the first to propose such a "prophetic year" was our old friend Sir Robert Anderson of Scotland Yard, whose book *The Coming Prince* set the standard for modern-day biblical interpretation of the prophecy of Daniel 9, including the chronological claims we have already examined in these pages.

Personally, I think it is unreasonable to claim that such a "prophetic" year is relevant when we have biblical evidence that from the time of the exodus onward, the Bible's calendar has been lunar/solar with an intercalated 13th month. Further we already have proof that Yeshua fulfilled the spring feast schedule using the Biblically mandated lunar/solar calendar. Are we to believe the second half of the Biblical feasts are to be calculated using a different measure of time? To superimpose a 360-day calendar over the lunar/solar calendar of the post-exodus era is a tenuous move at best.

But let's look for such a year. If a lunar "prophetic year" of twelve 30-day months actually existed in the pre-flood age, as has already been suggested, the solar year must have been of equal length;

otherwise the lunar calendar would still have required an intercalation in order to keep it synchronized with the solar year of 365.24 days. Such an intercalation would, by necessity, require the five missing days to be added back into the lunar calendar for any prophetic calculations to be accurate. This intercalation, surprisingly, is something modern scholarship on Daniel 9 does not take into account.

Considering the importance of a biblical year to our understanding of Daniel 9 and the events leading up to the return of Yeshua, I think it is well worth our effort to define as best we can the exact length of a biblical solar year in antiquity.

Of Circles and Context

Would it mean anything to you if I told you that the first circle below is 970.71 centimeters in circumference? Probably not, right?

But what if I told you the circumference of that same circle was originally intended to be expressed in inches, and said circumference was 365.24 inches? Both circles are the same size, but the first circle as expressed in centimeters means little to most of us. The second circle, on the other hand, as expressed in inches, makes us associate its circumference with a solar year. Such an association makes us realize that the circumferential length of the circle was likely intentional. That is context!

The Cubit

Let's take the illustration a step further. In ancient Egypt, the year was sometimes represented as a circle 365.25 inches in circumference. This "year circle" was also called a "quarter" because it was equal to one-fourth of an Egyptian area measurement called an aroura. If expressed as a square, an aroura would be 2060.7 x 2060.7 inches. One one-hundredth of such a square aroura is the origin of the 20.6-inch Egyptian cubit measurement.

In the fifth century, an Egyptian priest named Horapollo made the following statement in his book *Hieroglyphica,* Book I, Part V:

> To represent the current year, they (the Egyptians) depicted the fourth part of an aroura: now the aroura is a measure of land of an hundred cubits. And when they would express a year they say a quarter.

Herodotus, in his *Histories,* Book II, 168 made a similar observation:

> ... now the yoke [aroura] of land measures a hundred Egyptian cubits every way, and the Egyptian cubit is, as it happens, equal to that of Samos.

This little bit of history proves the ancient Egyptians were using a relatively accurate representation of pi to express a relationship between a solar year of 365.25 days and one of their most basic units of measure, a cubit. It is worth noting that another Egyptian cubit, the rod cubit, was also based upon a similar relationship. The rod or circumferential cubit of 18.2 inches was half the circumference of a circle of 36.525 inches. Kind of makes you wonder about the origins of the Metric system doesn't it? Maybe the French "enlightenment" was so enlightened after all.

Intriguing, isn't it? When I stumbled upon this in a book about Egyptian history and the pyramids a couple of decades ago, it made me realize how little we understand about the past and how much has been forgotten.

A full rendering of the subject is beyond the scope of this book, but for those who would like to dig a little deeper into the subject, you can read an article I wrote on the subject at my blog:

http://www.the13thenumeration.com/Blog13/2012/09/09/the-ancient-origins-of-the-cubit/

The Cubit and the Solar Year

Okay, so that's a neat bit of history, you might be thinking, but what does it have to do with true biblical time? Well, if scholars like Sir Robert Anderson are correct and the Bible had a 360-day lunar year at some point in the past, then we must be able to prove that the solar year was also 360 days long. Remember, the biblical calendar has both a solar and lunar side to it. They work in synchronization. If they are not equal, then they require an intercalation—but such an intercalation is not taken into account by scholars such as Sir Robert Anderson and those who have followed in his footsteps.

The history of the cubit is just one way to provide tangible evidence that the solar year of 365.24 days has been relatively constant since the cubit was first developed from pi and its relationship to the solar year of 365.25 days. At some point in the past there may have been a lunar year of twelve 30-day months, but there is no evidence that the solar year has ever been 360 days long.

As we've already shown, the biblical calendar after the exodus was designed specifically to show that Yeshua, the 13th Enumeration of Matthew's list, was the Messiah promised in the Scripture. A prophetic lunar year of 360 days undermines this biblical symbolism severely much the same way the metric system obfuscates the historical context of the inch, pi, and the cubit.

Stonehenge and the Year Circle

For the skeptics out there, the year circle of 365.24 is also found in the measurements of Stonehenge and the Great Pyramid. The former structure dates to somewhere between 3000–2000 BC and the latter to the Fourth Dynasty of Egypt, approximately 2560 BC.

In the image below, I have added a blue circle to a drawing of Stonehenge. This blue circle is a year circle, or a quarter of an aroura, based upon the measurements of Sir Flinders Petrie (W.M. Flinders Petrie, *Stonehenge: Plans, Description, and Theories.* London: Edward Stanford, 1880).

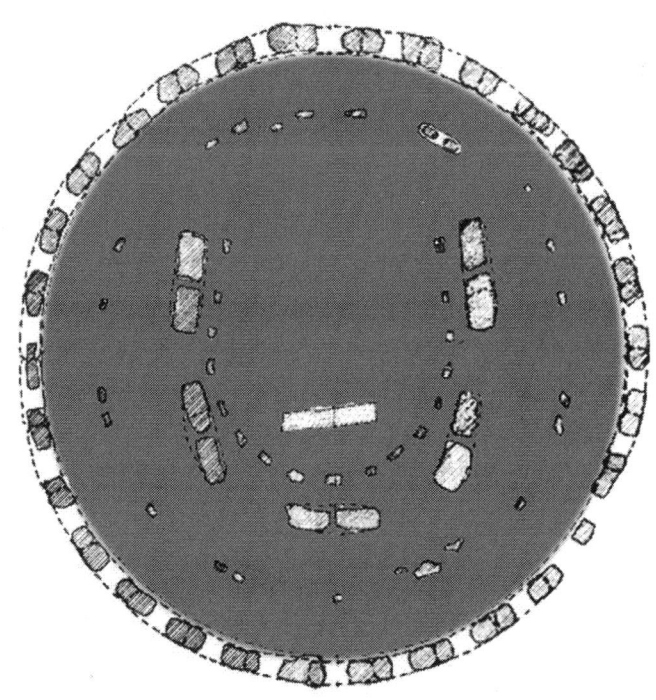

The bottom line is that we have reasonable historical records, as well as actual, measureable megalithic structures, to show that the solar year of 365.24 days has remained relatively constant for the last 4500 years. This means that, no matter what type of lunar year you believe was kept during the pre-exodus biblical era, it had to be intercalated with a 365.24-day solar year. Any "year" calculations that do not take such an intercalation into consideration are erroneous.

As an aside, one can't help but wonder how early "Bronze Age" people managed to construct structures with a fully developed understanding of pi and the solar year. It makes me think of the two-thousand-year-old quote by the famous Jewish historian Josephus:

> Now this Seth . . . did he leave children behind him who imitated his virtues . . . *They also were the inventors of that peculiar sort of wisdom which is concerned with the heavenly bodies, and their order.* And that their inventions might not be lost before they were sufficiently known, upon Adam's prediction that the world was to be destroyed at one time by the force of fire, and at another time by the violence and quantity of water, they made two pillars, the one of brick, the other of stone: they inscribed their discoveries on them both, that in case the pillar of brick should be destroyed by the flood, the pillar of stone might remain, and exhibit those discoveries to mankind; and also inform them that there was another pillar of brick erected by them. Now this remains in the land of Siriad

[Egypt] to this day. *(Antiquities of the Jews* 1:68–71, emphasis mine)

So much for those who would have us believe that ancient man was a Neanderthal-like cave dweller!

In summary, then, we have 4500 years of history to show that the solar year is still relatively constant. If a lunar calendar of 360 days was used during the pre-deluge age, it was not of equal length to the solar year. Therefore, as history demonstrates, it was either intercalated with the 365.24-day year or it was left to wander through the seasons like the Islamic calendar today.

With this in mind, it would be good to once more affirm the biblical definition of time from Genesis:

> And God said, Let there be lights in the firmament of the heaven to divide the day from the night; and let them be for signs, and for seasons, and for days, and years: and let them be for lights in the firmament of the heaven to give light upon the earth: and it was so. And God made two great lights; the greater light to rule the day, and the lesser light to rule the night: he made the stars also. And God set them in the firmament of the heaven to give light upon the earth, and to rule over the day and over the night, and to divide the light from the darkness: and God saw that it was good. (Genesis 1:14–18)

Folks, the Bible is clear that from the time of creation, the "greater light," the sun, has ruled the day and the "lesser light," the moon, has ruled the night. These two gears in YHWH's Rolex are working together to drive the biblical calendar, just as they always have. In a biblical sense, as it relates to eschatology, there is no such thing as a 360-day "prophetic" lunar year, much less one that is not intercalated with the greater light of the solar cycle. Any attempt to use such a measure of time in regard to the Bible's prophetic record can only end in serious errors that will undermine the intended design of YHWH's prophetic blueprint of time.

Chapter 5:

70 Sevens and the Messiah Factors

"So teach us to number our days, that we may apply our hearts unto wisdom. Return, O YHWH, how long? and let it repent thee concerning thy servants. O satisfy us early with thy mercy; that we may rejoice and be glad all our days."

Psalm 90:12–14

Now that we have a better understanding of how the Bible reckons time, let's apply that knowledge to understanding the prophecy of Daniel 9. Biblical time in the strictest sense is a lunar/solar calendar that varies between 12 and 13 months. A biblical "year," then, is not 365.24 solar days or 360 so-called "prophetic" lunar days, but rather a certain number of lunar cycles of 29.53 days each. Normally there are 12 lunar cycles in a biblical year, but every three years or so an intercalary or 13th lunar cycle is added.

The bottom line is that the biblical year is *not* a specific number of days, but rather a varying number of lunar cycles.

Putting the Pieces Together

Here are the pieces of our prophetic puzzle:

- We have a 70 sevens prophecy which speaks of a coming Messiah, the timing element of which is not given.

- We have a biblical calendar which varies between 12 and 13 lunar cycles of 29.53 days each.
- From the very lunar cycles in the heavens, the lineage of Yeshua in the first chapter of the New Testament, and throughout the Old Testament's sacrificial system, we have the numbers 13 and 14 woven into the very heart of the Bible's messianic symbolism.

In Book I, I made the case that the numbers 13 and 14 in the Bible are unique markers that identify only one hero in biblical history as the Messiah promised in the Scripture. That messianic hero is Yeshua of Nazareth. Now, let's put that symbolism to the test with the prophecy of Daniel 9.

For nearly two thousand years now, Matthew 1 has represented Yeshua as the 13th and by inference the 14th generation. For at least three thousand years, the Bible's own religious calendar, a calendar which beautifully symbolizes the redemptive plan of YHWH, has been based upon the two cycles of waxing and waning light of 13 or 14 days each. What if, when YHWH set His redemptive plan for mankind in motion, He tuned His cosmic Rolex so that at a very specific juncture in history the prophecy of 70 sevens could be set in motion, a juncture which, when fully understood, would illustrate His divine love for His creation? Does that sound farfetched to you? It shouldn't. Let me show you why.

The Messiah Factors and 70 Sevens

First, let's take the entire prophecy of 70 sevens and test our Messiah factors as the measurement of time for this prophecy—the blueprint that will give us the correct measurement. Here are the numbers.

Biblical "time" & the Messiah Factors

Lunar month	29.53 days
Solar year	365.24 days

13 lunar cycle "year"	383.89 days	(13 x 29.53)
14 lunar cycle "year"	413.42 days	(14 x 29.53)

70 Sevens x 13 cycles	515.02 solar years	(490 x 13 x 29.53 / 365.24)
70 Sevens x 14 cycles	554.63 solar years	(490 x 14 x 29.53 / 365.24)

Our starting point is the dabar or word of YHWH to "return and build Jerusalem" that was given in the year 520 BC.

Using 520 BC as the starting point, a 13-lunar-cycle year times 70 sevens brings us to an initial end date of 5 BC. A 14-lunar-cycle year times 70 sevens gives us a terminal date of 35–36 AD. What does that mean in terms of real history? According to many chronologists, Yeshua (Jesus) was conceived and born in 5/4 BC. It is believed that the apostle Paul was called to be the apostle to the Gentiles sometime between the years 31–36 AD. His calling by Yeshua on the road to Damascus is the Bible's last recorded calling of an apostle. Appropriately, this would have made Paul the 13th apostle and the last eyewitness called by Yeshua. Here is a scriptural summary of the two events:

> *But when the fulness of the time was come,* God sent forth his Son, made of a woman, made under the law, to redeem them that were under the law, that we might receive the adoption of sons. (Galatians 4:4–5, emphasis mine)
>
> For I delivered unto you first of all that which I also received, how that Christ died for our sins according to the scriptures; and that he was buried, and that he rose again the third day according to the scriptures . . . *and last of all he was seen of me also, as of one born out of due time.* For I am the least of the apostles, that am not meet to be called an apostle, because I persecuted the church of God. (1 Corinthians 15:3–9, emphasis mine)

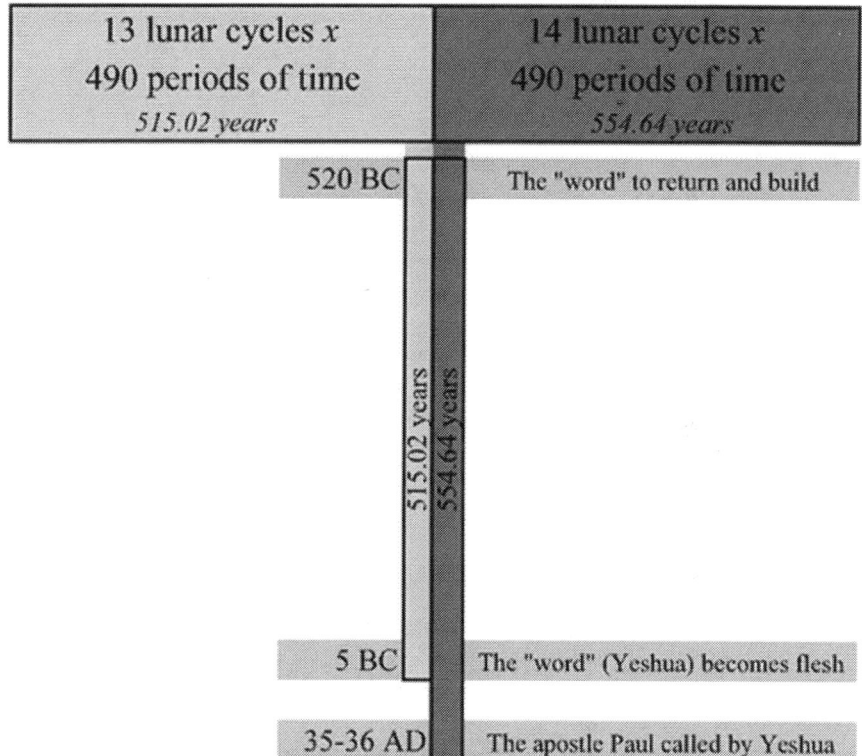

In general terms, then, our use of the Messiah factors as a biblical measurement of time for the prophecy of 70 sevens encapsulates a period of time that starts with the conception or birth of Yeshua (Jesus) and ends with the call of the apostle Paul, YHWH's chosen spokesperson to bring the gospel message to the Gentiles. Okay, so it appears that we've got the right era in biblical history—but what about the three time units or epochs the prophecy is broken down into? How do the Messiah factors handle the 7 sevens (plural masculine), the 62 sevens, and the 1 seven of Daniel 9? Let's take a look.

Chapter 6:

7 Shabuwa Until the Messiah

"Know therefore and understand, that from the going forth of the commandment to restore and to build Jerusalem unto the Messiah the Prince shall be seven weeks."
Daniel 9:25

Do you remember my little chart from the beginning of this book which showed the prophecy of 70 weeks broken down into its three basic periods or epochs of time? Take a look at it again with a perspective freshened by the knowledge gained in the preceding chapters.

Overview of 70 Sevens

- Commandment to Restore and Build
- 7 Sevens until the Messiah (49)
- 62 Sevens the Plaza & Wall Rebuilt (434)
- Messiah Cut off After 62 Sevens
- 1 Seven the Covenant Confirmed (7)

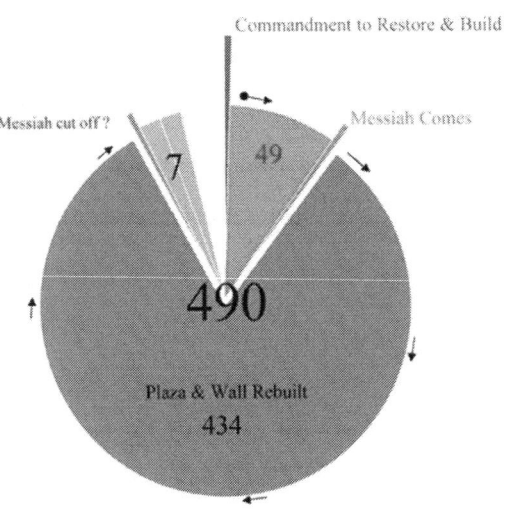

Does it still seem strange to you that Daniel 9 predicts that the Messiah will come 7 sevens (49 units) after the "word to restore and build Jerusalem," yet He will still be alive to be "cut off" sometime after 62 sevens (434 units) later in history?

> Know therefore and understand, that from the going forth of the commandment to restore and to build Jerusalem unto the Messiah the Prince shall be *seven weeks*, and threescore and two weeks: the street shall be built again, and the wall, even in troublous times. (Daniel 9:25, emphasis mine)

Prophetic Milestone: The Coming of the Messiah

Here is where the hair-raising brilliance of Daniel 9 really shines. YHWH, by giving the prophecy as 7 sevens, 62 sevens, and 1 seven, set the prophecy out as a total unit of 70 sevens or 490 units. But in so doing, He also gave a chronological order to the prophecy. The 7 sevens come first, the 62 sevens next, and the final seven last.

Yet, as we learned in chapter 1, shabuwa or sevens in the case of Daniel 9:25a is written in a very peculiar way, using the masculine plural form of the word. As written back when the prophecy was given to Daniel, there were no vowel pointings. This means that Daniel 9:25a actually reads *70 seven.* Only by reading the context of the entire passage of Daniel 9:24–27 can one see the plural masculine form of the Hebrew word shabuwa and its implied meaning of 7 sevens. So in reality Daniel 9:25a is a brilliant play on words. The only way the "Messiah the Prince" of Daniel 9:25 could refer to the same Messiah who is "cut off" in Daniel 9:26 is if the text somehow indicated that the 7 shabuwa, *that first epoch* of Daniel 9:25a, were of a unit of time with a larger magnitude than the other epochs. That is exactly what we find here with the plural masculine form of shabuwa.

Shabuwa
A Relative Comparison

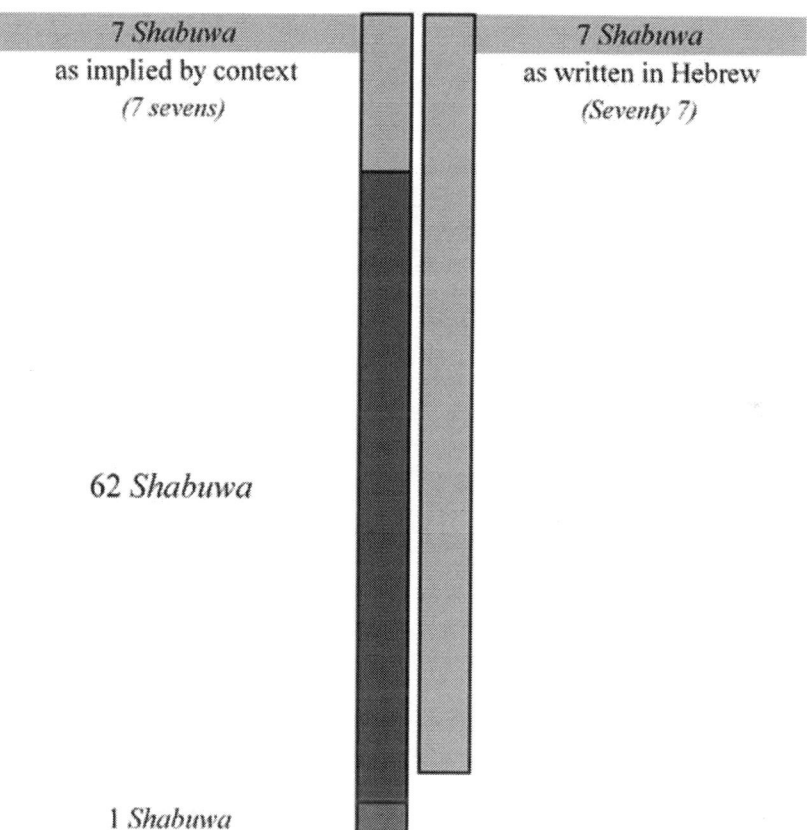

7 *Shabuwa*
as implied by context
(7 sevens)

7 *Shabuwa*
as written in Hebrew
(Seventy 7)

62 *Shabuwa*

1 *Shabuwa*

The First Coming of the Messiah

Here is how YHWH's genius designed this to work.

> Know therefore and understand, that from the going forth of the *word* to *return* and to build Jerusalem unto the Messiah the Prince shall be *70 seven*. (Daniel 9:25, emphasis and paraphrase mine)

In consideration of the symbolism associated with Yeshua as the 13th Enumeration, let's figure this first section of Daniel 9 using a 13-lunar-cycle year.

Instead of the implied 7 sevens of Daniel 9:25a, let's use what was actually written back when the prophecy was given to Daniel and make this epoch a period of "70 seven." Thus, we have 490 periods of time between the word of YHWH to return and build Jerusalem until the coming of the Messiah.

7 Shabuwa to the Messiah

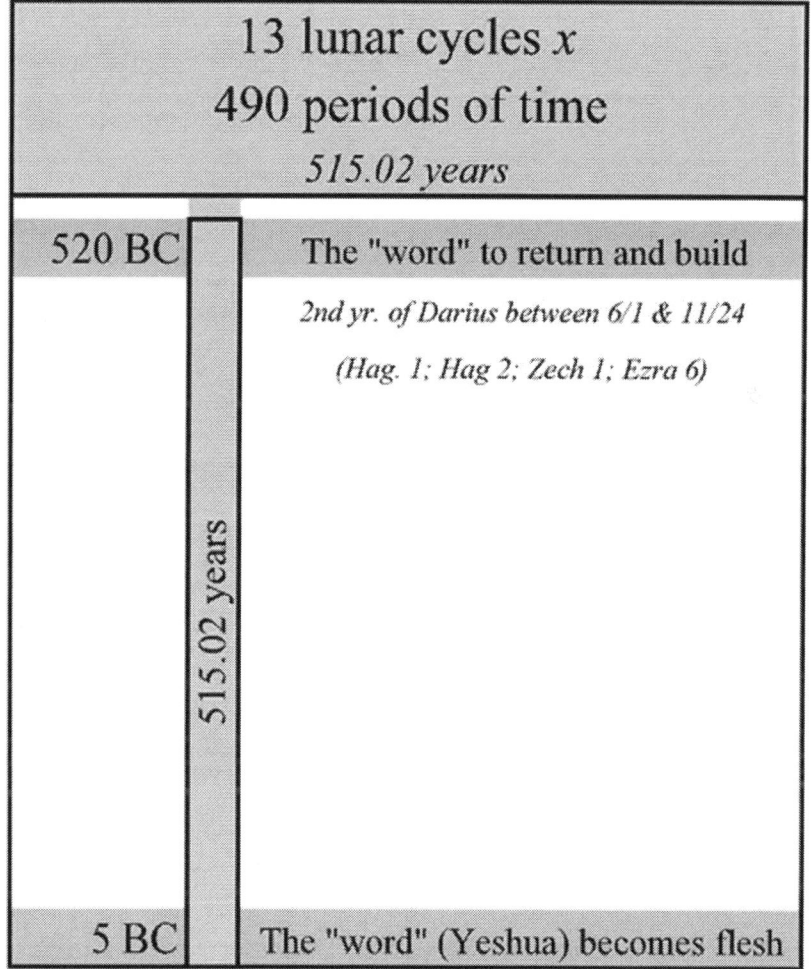

Think about the implications of this. Many respected New Testament chronologists place the birth of Yeshua in the fall of 4 BC around the Feast of Tabernacles. His conception, that point when Yeshua became human flesh (when his human "foundation was laid") would have occurred nine months earlier in the winter of 5 BC. The divine command witnessed by Haggai, Zechariah, and Ezra gives us a window for the beginning of the countdown between the first day of the sixth month and the twenty-fourth day of the eleventh month. I don't know that it is even necessary to show a more exact date, but if we're to use the date of Haggai 2 where we are told to consider or count from the twenty-fourth day of the ninth month of the second year of Darius (when the temple foundation was laid), our 515.02 years take us to the Feast of Dedication (Hanukah) in the year 5 BC, just nine months before the birth of Yeshua. Another way to look at this is that Daniel 9:25a, as written, shows it was 70 seven (*shib'iym sheba*) from the word of YHWH until that "word" became flesh in Yeshua.

> And the Word was made flesh, and dwelt among us, (and we beheld his glory, the glory as of the only begotten of the Father,) full of grace and truth. (John 1:14)

Hidden in Plain Sight

No longer do we have to ignore Daniel 9:25a and the prediction that the Messiah will come after 7 shabuwa. Hidden in plain sight, in one of the cleverest ciphers ever conceived, is mathematical proof that Yeshua was the Messiah promised in the Scriptures. We find this proof in a brilliant wordplay, the roots of which can be traced all the way back to the first recorded biblical oath (*shaba*) YHWH made with a man—that oath of sevens made with Abraham, which promised that someday in Abraham's seed all nations of the earth would be blessed. The 7 shabuwa of Daniel 9 then gives us the precise date for when the first part of that divine plan would take effect. Praise be to YHWH!

Now to Abraham and his seed were the promises made. He saith not, *And to seeds, as of many; but as of one, And to thy seed, which is Christ.* And this I say, that the covenant, that was confirmed before of God in Christ, the law, which was four hundred and thirty years after, cannot disannul, that it should make the promise of none effect. (Galatians 3:16–17, emphasis mine)

A Once and Future King

Those who were rocked by this information, stay tuned. There is more than one Messiah factor. In the next chapter we will look at the Messiah factor 14, a number often associated with the Messiah, sacrifice, and a once and future king.

Chapter 7:

The Messiah Cut Off

"Surely he hath borne our griefs, and carried our sorrows: yet we did esteem him stricken, smitten of God, and afflicted. But he was wounded for our transgressions, he was bruised for our iniquities: the chastisement of our peace was upon him; and with his stripes we are healed."

Isaiah 53:4–5

In Book I of the Prophecies and Patterns series, we looked at the symbolism of 14 as it relates to the Messiah and the sacrificial system. We noted that Matthew 1 not only draws our attention to Yeshua as the 13th generation but also symbolizes Yeshua as the 14th generation, the risen Savior and King. Let's recap some of the Messianic symbolism of the number 14 before we look at how this Messiah factor might relate to the timing of Daniel 9 and the prophecy of 70 sevens.

Of Sacrifices and Kings

- On the 14th day of the month Nisan at even, the Passover lamb is sacrificed. John the Baptist described Yeshua as "the lamb of God which taketh away the sins of the world."
- Fourteen lambs are killed for each of the first seven days of the burnt offering sacrifices during the Feast of Tabernacles.

- According to Numbers 28 and Exodus 12, the first day of the Feast of Unleavened Bread requires 13 sacrifices to be made but 14 consumed. (More on this in chapter 10 of Book I, *The 13th Enumeration: Key to the Bible's Messianic Symbolism*.)

Worth considering are the words of the apostle Paul concerning Jesus and His ancestor David:

> ... concerning his Son Jesus Christ our Lord, which was made of the seed of David according to the flesh [13]; and declared to be the Son of God with power, according to the spirit of holiness, by the resurrection from the dead [14]. (Romans 1:3–4, insertions mine)

Notice that the passage above describes two aspects of the Messiah's existence. The first is when He was made "of the seed of David according to the flesh." This, as we saw in the previous chapter, was fulfilled at Yeshua's conception/birth, which we dated from the start of Daniel's countdown using a Messiah factor of 13. The second part of this passage tells us of His death and resurrection as symbolized in the biblical record by the Messiah factor of 14.

Did you know that in ancient Hebrew, letters were used to represent numbers? It is fascinating to learn, then, that the Hebrew name *David* has a numerical value of 14. Further solidifying this symbolism is that David is listed as the 14th generation in Matthew 1:

David

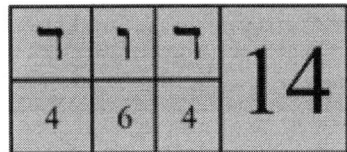

As you can see below, the symbolism is stunning! Just as King David is represented as the 14th generation in the first column of Matthew 1, Yeshua the 13th Enumeration, the risen Messiah, becomes the 14th generation in the third column. How beautiful, then, to acknowledge the words of Luke:

> And, behold, thou shalt conceive in thy womb, and bring forth a son, and shalt call his name JESUS [Yeshua]. He shall be great, and shall be called the Son of the Highest: *and the Lord God shall give unto him the throne of his father David.* (Luke 1:31–32, emphasis mine)

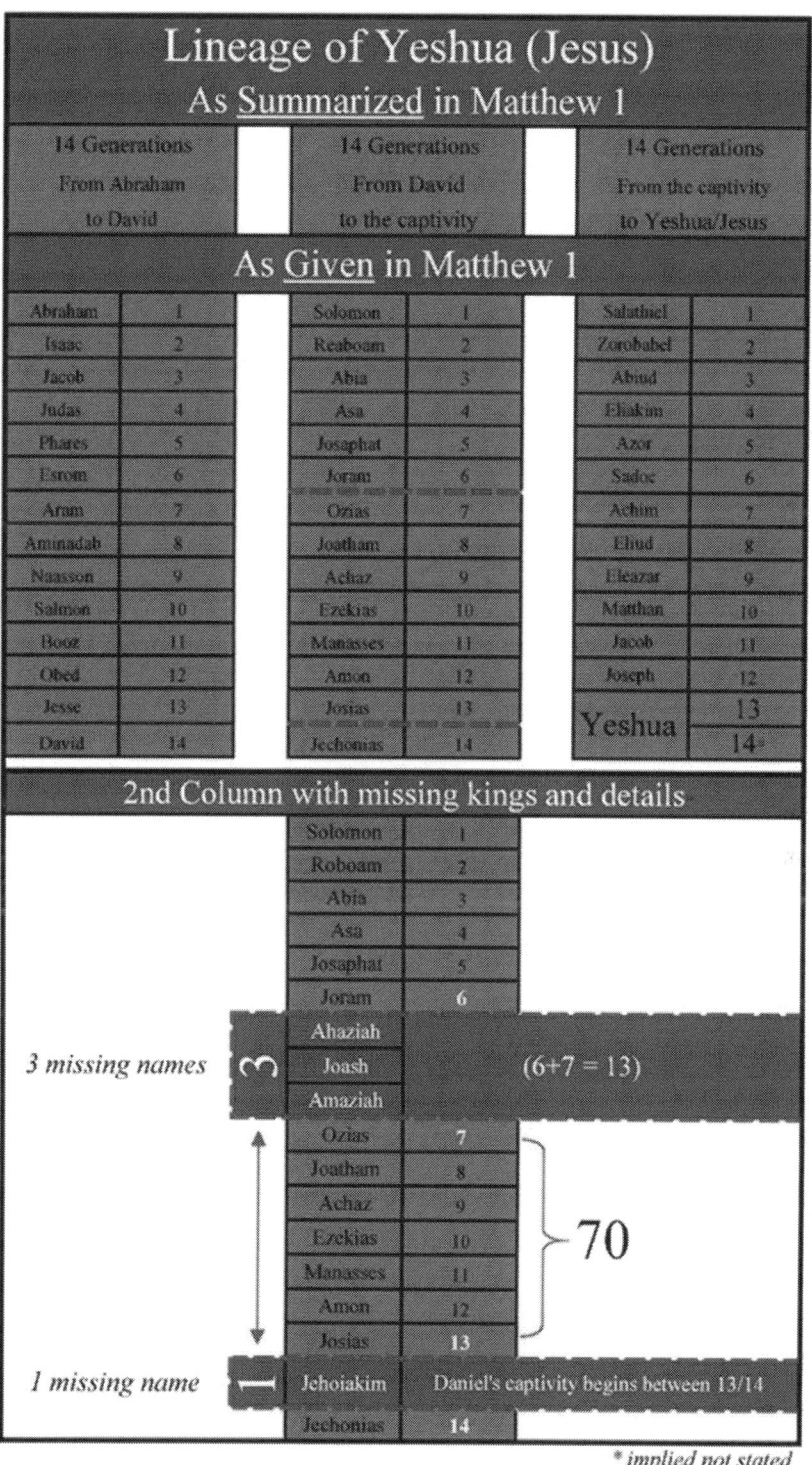

Daniel 9 and the 62 Sevens

As we learned in the previous chapter, Daniel 9 is a chronological prophecy, but with added depth few have realized. Let's now turn our attention to the second epoch in the prophecy of 70 sevens and see how the 62 sevens, calculated with a Messiah factor of 14 (appropriate given the connotation of sacrifice and kingship), might fit into YHWH's prophetic blueprint for the Messiah.

> Know therefore and understand, that from the going forth of the commandment to restore and to build Jerusalem unto the Messiah the Prince shall be seven weeks, and threescore and two weeks: the street shall be built again, and the wall, even in troublous times. And after threescore and two weeks shall Messiah be cut off, but not for himself. (Daniel 9:25–26a)

Overview of 70 Sevens

- Commandment to Restore and Build
- 7 Sevens until the Messiah (49)
- 62 Sevens the Plaza & Wall Rebuilt (434)
- Messiah Cut off After 62 Sevens
- 1 Seven the Covenant Confirmed (7)

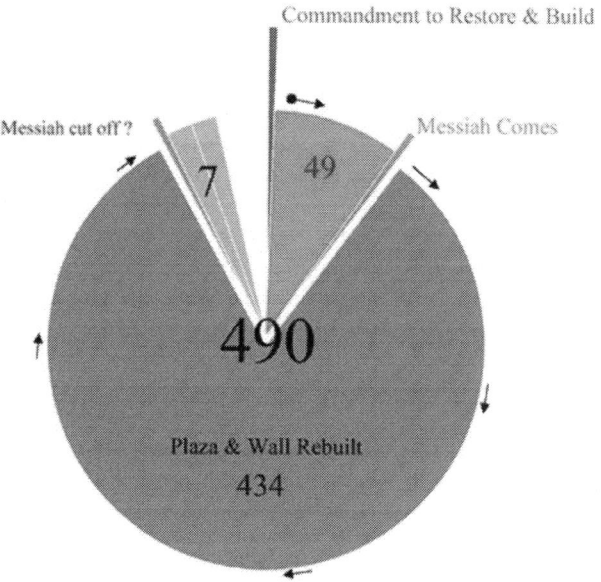

Once again take a look at the chart above. We've already looked at the first 7 shabuwa (49) of the 70 shabuwa (490) and saw how they provided a means for us to determine the timing of Yeshua's conception and birth in 4/5 BC.

Since the prophecy is chronological, let's now take the next piece of our chronological pie and add it to the first piece. Seven shabuwa (49) plus 62 shabuwa (434) equals 69 shabuwa, or 483 periods of prophetic time, after which Daniel 9:26 states the Messiah will be "cut off."

> And after threescore and two weeks shall Messiah be cut off, but not for himself. (Daniel 9:26a)

Instead of using our Messiah factor of 13 this time, let's look at 14, the number the Bible associates with sacrifice, resurrection, and a king. Once again, our starting point is the twenty-fourth day of the ninth month of 520 BC. A 14-lunar-cycle year times the 62 + 7 shabuwa (483 periods of time) equals 546.71 solar years. Counting down, 546.71 years from YHWH's divine word for the Israelites to "return and build" brings us to the fall of 28 AD. The chart below gives the math.

Biblical "time" & 62 *Shabuwa*

Lunar month	29.53 days	
Solar year	365.24 days	

13 lunar cycle "year"	383.89 days	(13 x 29.53)
14 lunar cycle "year"	413.42 days	(14 x 29.53)

62 + 7 *Shabuwa*	483 periods of time	((62 x 7) + (7 x 7) = 483)
69 *Shabuwa* x 14 cycles	546.71 solar years	(483 x 14 x 29.53 / 365.24)

The Messiah's Ministry

Okay, so the 62 + 7 shabuwa end in the fall of 28 AD in the seventh month of the biblical calendar. Before trying to determine whether this date has any relevance to the New Testament chronology of Yeshua, let's back up a moment and look at the chronology from another angle. In the previous chapter we used Daniel 9:25 and the 7 shabuwa to calculate the conception of Yeshua in the winter of 5 BC and his subsequent birth nine months later in September/October of 4 BC. Using this date as a basis, Yeshua would have turned thirty years old in the fall of 27 AD. Here is a New Testament account that helps confirm this and provides us another way to date the start of Yeshua's ministry.

> Now in the fifteenth year of the reign of Tiberius Caesar, Pontius Pilate being governor of Judaea, and Herod being tetrarch of Galilee, and his brother Philip tetrarch of Ituraea and of the region of Trachonitis, and Lysanias the tetrarch of Abilene, Annas and Caiaphas being the high priests, the word of God came unto John the son of Zacharias in the wilderness . . .
>
> Now when all the people were baptized, it came to pass, that Jesus also being baptized, and praying, the heaven was opened, and the Holy Ghost descended in a bodily shape like a dove upon him, and a voice came from heaven, which said, Thou art my beloved Son; in thee I am well pleased. And *Jesus himself began to be about thirty years of age,* being (as was supposed) the son of Joseph, which was the son of Heli. (Luke 3:1–23, emphasis mine)

The Fifteenth Year of Tiberius

The passage above indicates that Yeshua was about thirty years old in the fifteenth year of Tiberius Caesar when he was baptized by John. After his baptism by John, Yeshua goes into the wilderness for forty days to be tempted by Satan. He then returns from the wilderness, and his official ministry begins in Capernaum (Matthew 4:17), where he starts to gather his disciples. In keeping with the Old Testament example of priestly service beginning in one's thirtieth year (Numbers 4), I think it likely that at some point between his baptism and his journey to Capernaum, Yeshua turned thirty years old. In any case, the fifteenth year of Tiberius provides another way to synchronize the start of Yeshua's ministry.

Historically speaking, there are two ways to date the reign of Tiberius. One method reckons the fifteenth year of Tiberius from his sole rule beginning August 19 of 14 AD. The other, a provincial method, reckons the fifteenth year of Tiberius from his joint rule with Augustus beginning January 16 of 13 AD. As we will see in a moment, we have historical accounts that use both methods.

Adding an additional layer of complexity is the fact that our modern "AD" dating was not used until several centuries after the crucifixion. The early church fathers and others dated the ministry and crucifixion of Jesus according to the Roman year AUC (*Anno Urbis Conditae*). The AUC year begins on April 21, not on January 1 as does our modern year. This fact is often overlooked when considering the dates of the early church fathers and others. Keeping this in mind is very important as we investigate further. As in many cases where historical accounts seem to differ, both sides can actually be in agreement depending on the contextual perspective.

With these facts in mind, we now have two possible dating schemes with which to date the start of Yeshua's ministry. The provincial method, based on Tiberius's joint rule with Augustus, would place the call of John the Baptist in the spring of 27 AD or the year 780 AUC. The other method, based on the sole rule of Tiberius after the death of Augustus, would place the call of John the Baptist in the spring of 29 AD or 782 AUC. The start of Yeshua's ministry began approximately six months later, either in the fall of 27 AD in the former case or the fall of 29 AD in the latter. Of the two possible dating schemes above, the earlier date most congruently fits the available evidence from the perspective of Luke 3 and the other Gospels. In support of the provincial method, it might also be added that it was used in the Bible to date the reign of Cyrus and others.

Adding further support to the two methods of reckoning is, ironically, what appears to be a contradiction between Julius Africanus and Hippolytus concerning the crucifixion.

Julius Africanus stated that the crucifixion occurred in the sixteenth year of Tiberius (Julius Africanus, *Chronography,* XV.1,2; XVIII.1–3). Hippolytus, on the other hand stated that the crucifixion occurred in the eighteenth year of Tiberius (Hippolytus, *Commentary on Daniel,* Book 4, 23.3, as translated by T.C. Schmidt). The most reasonable explanation of this apparent discrepancy is that Julius Africanus based his reckoning from the sole rule of Tiberius, while Hippolytus reckoned from Tiberius's joint rule with Augustus, thus both placing the crucifixion in 782 AUC or early April of 30 AD.

(Note: 783 A.U.C. did not begin until April 21 of 30 AD. Passover that year began April 6 or 7. So Yeshua's death and resurrection took place in 782 AUC, just two weeks before the new Roman year of 783.)

Two or Three Years

Traditionally, scholars have calculated the length of Yeshua's ministry as three and a half years. But as with many of the chronological subjects we have looked at, this belief is based upon a weak presuppositional bias, not reasonable biblical evidence. In fact, the gospel of John is the only gospel account that provides a relatively congruent chronological timeline of the events related to Yeshua's ministry. John only mentions three Passover celebrations during the entire period, making for a ministry that lasted only two and a half years. Adding another year to John's account goes beyond the most natural reading of the text. So for the purposes of this book, I will be using 2.5 years for Yeshua's ministry.

If Yeshua's crucifixion took place on the third Passover of His ministry, as John suggests, this would mean it was the year 30 AD. The following chart gives the pertinent details:

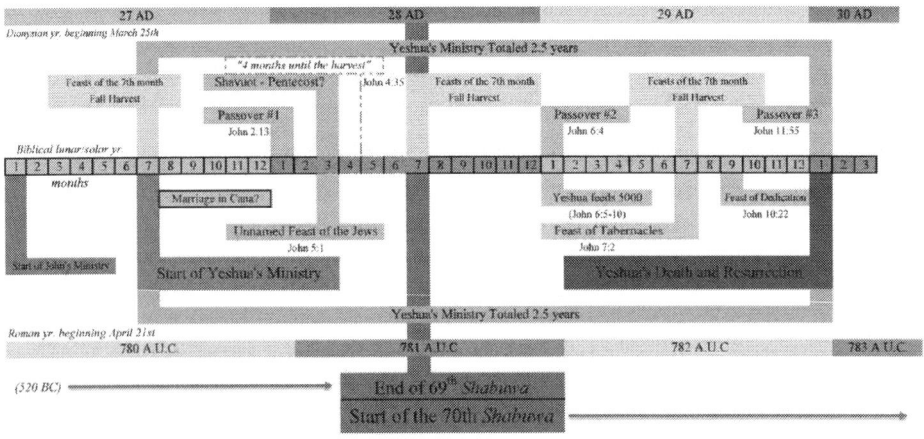

The End of 62 Shabuwa

With the above chronology in place, we have a context for understanding what was taking place in the late summer and early fall of 28 AD when the 7 + 62 shabuwa ended. If the chronology we've described in the preceding pages is correct, then the summer of 28 AD marked the end of Yeshua's first year of ministry, a ministry which began with his baptism. During the following year, the transfiguration—one of the most intriguing and least understood events of Yeshua's ministry—took place. In the following chapters we will look at the transfiguration, Yeshua's death and resurrection, and the possible implications these have for the final shabuwa of the 70 sevens prophecy.

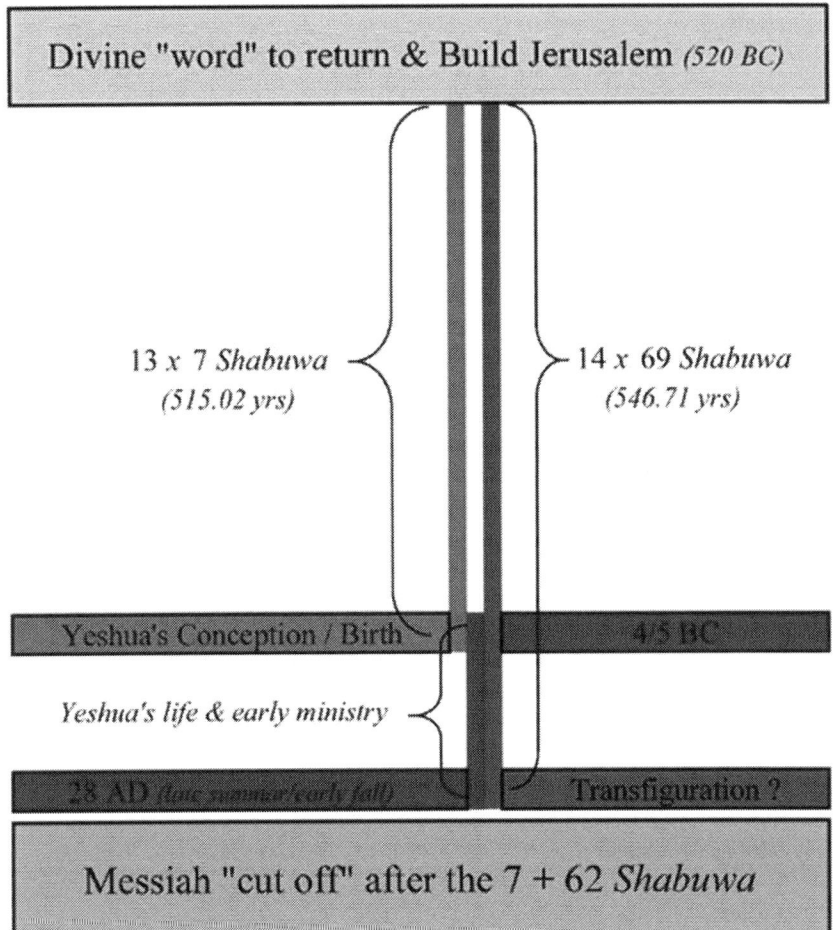

Chapter 8:

The Final Shabuwa

"And he shall confirm the covenant with many for one week: and in the midst of the week he shall cause the sacrifice and the oblation to cease, and for the overspreading of abominations he shall make it desolate, even until the consummation, and that determined shall be poured upon the desolate."

Daniel 9:27

Of all the controversy surrounding the 70 sevens prophecy, the most divisive by far is the timing of its final epoch. The antagonists in this controversy fall into two main camps: one which sees the fulfillment of the 70th shabuwa in the first century AD and the other which sees a yet-future fulfillment just before the second coming of Christ. Briefly, I will summarize the two positions so that those unfamiliar with the discussion will have at least some understanding of the issues involved as we dig into the biblical context of the 70th shabuwa.

The Historicist Camp

Generally speaking (there are exceptions), historicists believe that the 70th shabuwa of Daniel 9 was fulfilled in the first century with the destruction of Jerusalem in 70 AD. Typically, they hold to a dominion theology that sees many if not all the prophecies of the Bible as fulfilled by Yeshua and the early church in the first century. According to this position, Daniel 9 was fulfilled in Yeshua, and we are now living in the kingdom age. This position also sees the unfulfilled Old Testament prophecies related to the Jewish people and the nation of Israel as fulfilled in the church. These beliefs are sometimes called supercessionism or replacement or divestment theology. Many in this camp demand a literal reading of Daniel 9 as it applies to Yeshua, yet spiritualize many of the prophecies that speak to a future restoration of the Jewish people and the nation of Israel.

The Futurist Camp

Generally speaking (and there are exceptions here as well), futurists believe that the 70th shabuwa of Daniel 9 is yet to be fulfilled in a future 7-year period of apocalyptic upheaval known as the Great Tribulation. The final shabuwa of Daniel 9 (understood as a period of 7 years) is a main pillar in this eschatological worldview. Futurists believe that the Old Testament covenants and promises made by YHWH to Abraham and his seed will be literally fulfilled and that these events will culminate with the second coming of Yeshua and His literal rule from Jerusalem for a thousand years. Many futurists demand a literal, straightforward interpretation of the prophetic record when it comes to Yeshua's second coming and the Jewish people, but when it comes to Daniel 9 and the 70th shabuwa, they employ a more relaxed interpretive method by deferring the 70th shabuwa to a yet-future date without any textual reason to do so.

Taking the Bible's Prophecies Literally

Let me state unequivocally that I believe in a literal return of Yeshua and a literal reign from Jerusalem for one thousand years—what is popularly known as the Millennium. I also believe in the literal regathering of the Jewish people to their ancestral homeland and a literal future fulfillment of the Bible's unfulfilled prophecies concerning them. Simply put, I believe that YHWH keeps His word. To my way of looking at the biblical record, if I cannot trust all of YHWH's covenants and promises made with Abraham and his descendants, then I have no foundation upon which to base my own faith.

Having said that, I believe it is my brethren in the futurist camp who, in a well-meaning but overzealous attempt to buttress their futurist position, have done the greatest damage to the prophecy of 70 shabuwa. As you will see in the coming pages, the prophecy of 70 sevens is a testimony to the Jewish people and indeed all mankind that Yeshua is the promised Old Testament Messiah and that His death and resurrection as our substitutionary sacrifice are the means by which we are reconciled to our Creator. Sadly, many futurists point an accusatory finger at their brethren in the historicist camp, accusing them of undermining the impact of prophecy, yet when it comes to the greatest messianic prophecy in the Bible, we are the ones guilty of divesting it of its messianic glory and replacing it with a focus on the "Man of Sin."

As we explore the 70th shabuwa in more detail in the coming pages, ask yourself if it really makes reasonable interpretive sense for the messianic message of Daniel 9 to end with the death of Messiah in

Daniel 9:26 and not a single hint of His redemptive purpose in the final two verses, with the focus instead moving to the Antichrist. If that doesn't make sense to you, then I ask you to consider the final shabuwa with me from another perspective, a perspective freshened with the expectancy of the Messiah's return, but one which does not leave us hanging without at least a thread of redemptive hope found in the death and resurrection of Yeshua. Let's see if we can discern exactly what YHWH had in mind when He described the events of the 70th shabuwa.

> And after threescore and two weeks shall Messiah be cut off, but not for himself:
> > *and the people of the prince that shall come shall destroy the city and the sanctuary; and the end thereof shall be with a flood, and unto the end of the war desolations are determined.*
>
> And he shall confirm the covenant with many for one week: and in the midst of the week he shall cause the sacrifice and the oblation to cease, and for the overspreading of abominations he shall make it desolate, even until the consummation, and that determined shall be poured upon the desolate. (Daniel 9:26–27 emphasis mine)

Our Cast of Characters

As we saw above, we have two prophetic camps as it relates to the final verses of Daniel. One side sees Daniel 9:26–27 fulfilled with the death and resurrection of the Messiah and the subsequent events of

70 AD. The other side see Daniel 9:26–27 unfulfilled, and its final epoch shifted away from the Messiah to a coming Anti-Messiah. So who do you see in Daniel 9:26–27? Do you see a risen Messiah or a reigning Anti-Messiah?

To try to simplify the people and events described in these final two verses, I've broken them out into two categories.

People Described:
- The Messiah
- The people who destroy the city
- The prince (of the people)
- He (who confirms a covenant)
- He (who causes the sacrifice and oblation to cease)
- He (who makes it desolate—until the consummation)

Events Described:
- After 62 shabuwa the Messiah is cut off.
- Jerusalem and the temple are destroyed (by the people of the prince).
- He (unspecified) confirms a covenant with the "many" for one shabuwa.
- He (unspecified) causes the sacrifice and oblation to cease in the midst of the shabuwa.
- On the "wings" of abomination he (unspecified) makes it desolate until the consummation and those events which are to be poured upon the desolate/desolator.

That is quite a bit of intriguing information, isn't it? Well, let's do our best to unpack it. In the next chapter we will start by looking at several key Hebrew words that have great bearing on the text. One of the fascinating (and often overlooked) aspects of Daniel 9:26–27 is that it seems to point us back to Noah's flood, one of the greatest human tragedies recorded in the Bible—and this connection will provide us with a much deeper understanding of Daniel's prophecy. By the time we're done, I think you will have a new appreciation for Daniel 9 and YHWH's plan to reconcile all mankind through Yeshua, the promised Messiah.

Chapter 9:

Daniel 9, the Flood, and YHWH's Redemptive Purpose

"And after threescore and two weeks shall Messiah be cut off, but not for himself."
Daniel 9:26a

In a previous chapter we learned that by a biblical reckoning of time, the 69th shabuwa ended in the fall of 28 AD, sometime around the end of Yeshua's first year of ministry. Daniel 9:26 tells us that after this 69th shabuwa, the Messiah is "cut off." The phrase "cut off" comes from the Hebrew *karath*. Karath is a primitive Hebrew root word which means to cut, cut off, eliminate, or cut a covenant. As many Hebrew scholars have noted over the years, the first occurrence of a Hebrew word in the Bible often provides additional underlying context that is valuable when trying to understand its meaning. Karath is not an exception to this rule. Here, take a look:

> And God spake unto Noah, and to his sons with him, saying, And I, behold, I establish my covenant with you, and with your seed after you; And with every living creature that is with you, of the fowl, of the cattle, and of every beast of the earth with you; from all that go out of the ark, to every beast of the earth. And I will establish my covenant with you; neither shall all flesh be *cut off* [karath] any more by the waters of a flood;

neither shall there any more be a flood to destroy the earth.
(Genesis 9:8–11, emphasis mine)

We find the first occurrence of *karath* (cut off) in the context of YHWH's covenantal promise with Noah and his seed that never again would He karath (cut off) all mankind with a flood of water. The Bible tells us that this great destruction of mankind, this cutting off, was due to the sinfulness of mankind, and only Noah and his family were saved.

Now consider this cutting off in light of the prophecy of 70 shabuwa. In contrast to mankind being cut off because of their sins as Genesis 9 describes, the Messiah of Daniel 9 is "cut off," "not for himself" but for the sins of others. He died so that all who trust in Him might live. He died so that the six goals of Daniel 9:24 might be accomplished.

Hundreds of years before the 69th shabuwa ended in 28 AD, the prophet Isaiah described the "cutting off" of the Messiah this way:

> He is despised and rejected of men; a man of sorrows, and acquainted with grief: and we hid as it were our faces from him; he was despised, and we esteemed him not. Surely he hath borne our griefs, and carried our sorrows: yet we did esteem him stricken, smitten of God, and afflicted. But he was wounded for our transgressions, he was bruised for our iniquities: the chastisement of our peace was upon him; and with his stripes we are healed. All we like sheep have gone

astray; we have turned every one to his own way; and YHWH hath laid on him the iniquity of us all.

He was oppressed, and he was afflicted, yet he opened not his mouth: he is brought as a lamb to the slaughter, and as a sheep before her shearers is dumb, so he openeth not his mouth. He was taken from prison and from judgment: and who shall declare his generation? For he was cut off out of the land of the living: for the transgression of my people was he stricken. And he made his grave with the wicked, and with the rich in his death; because he had done no violence, neither was any deceit in his mouth. Yet it pleased YHWH to bruise him; he hath put him to grief: when thou shalt make his soul an offering for sin, he shall see his seed, he shall prolong his days, and the pleasure of YHWH shall prosper in his hand.

He shall see of the travail of his soul, and shall be satisfied: by his knowledge shall my righteous servant justify many; for he shall bear their iniquities. Therefore will I divide him a portion with the great, and he shall divide the spoil with the strong; because he hath poured out his soul unto death: and he was numbered with the transgressors; and he bare the sin of many, and made intercession for the transgressors. (Isaiah 53:3–13)

Fascinating, isn't it? Karath is first associated with the righteous judgment of mankind's sins by an angry God in the days of Noah. But in Daniel 9, karath tells of a loving God who became flesh so that he might reconcile mankind as described in Daniel 9:24 and Isaiah 53. Yeshua was karath so we would not have to be.

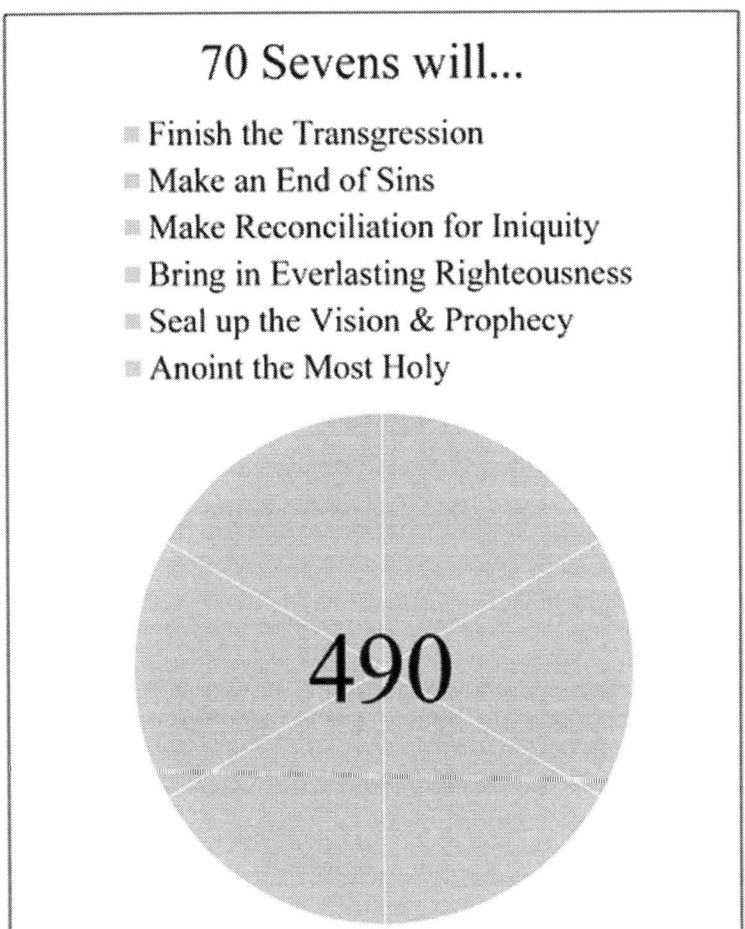

Cutting the Covenant

But there is more to karath than just cutting off as described in the flood account and Daniel 9. Karath is also used in the Bible to described the cutting of a covenant. For those unfamiliar with the terminology, it's kind of like me saying, "Let's cut a deal." In the Ancient Near East when two sides got together to make a covenant, they would say the two sides "cut" or karath a covenant. In the Bible, this cutting of a covenant between God and man is first mentioned when YHWH promised the childless Abraham that he would have an heir and that he and his seed would inherit the promised land. As part of YHWH's confirmation of the covenant, he caused Abraham to divide a sacrifice, and YHWH's fire passed between the pieces. From this point forward in biblical history, we have the Hebrew expression of making or cutting a covenant.

> And he said, Lord YHWH, whereby shall I know that I shall inherit it? And he said unto him, Take me an heifer of three years old, and a she goat of three years old, and a ram of three years old, and a turtledove, and a young pigeon. And he took unto him all these, and divided them in the midst, and laid each piece one against another . . .
>
> And it came to pass, that, when the sun went down, and it was dark, behold a smoking furnace, and a burning lamp that passed between those pieces. *In the same day YHWH made* [cut/karath] *a covenant with Abram,* saying, Unto thy seed have I given this land, from the river of Egypt unto the great river, the river Euphrates. (Genesis 15:8–18, emphasis mine)

Let's now consider "*karath*" in Daniel 9 with this underlying context in mind. To the Hebrew reader, the word brings to mind the biblical flood and mankind's destruction as a result of YHWH's righteous judgment. It also brings to mind YHWH's promise to Abraham that his seed would inherit the promised land from the Nile to the Euphrates. In wonderful biblical prophetic symbolism, we find both of these underlying threads converging in Yeshua. YHWH, in keeping with His covenant to Noah and his seed that He would never again cut off all mankind with a flood of water, instead cuts a covenant with faithful Abraham, one of Noah's descendants—a covenant which centuries later results in mankind's ultimate deliverance from death through Abraham's seed, a "seed" we know as Yeshua, the salvation of YHWH.

The Rule of Antecedent

But there is an even deeper connection between Daniel 9 and the events of the flood, and it is related to two more Hebrew words found in Daniel 9:27, words that also have their origins in the flood story. First, though, we have to deal with Daniel 9:26b and the rule of antecedent.

> And after threescore and two weeks shall Messiah be cut off, but not for himself:
> > *and the people of the prince that shall come shall destroy the city and the sanctuary; and the end thereof shall be with a flood, and unto the end of the war desolations are determined.*
>
> And he shall confirm the covenant with many for one week: and in the midst of the week he shall cause the sacrifice and the oblation to cease, and for the overspreading of abominations he shall make it desolate, even until the consummation, and that

determined shall be poured upon the desolate. (Daniel 9:26–27, 26b emphasized)

After the Messiah is "cut off," the text jumps to a description of the destruction of Jerusalem by "the people" of the "prince that shall come." Many respected scholars in the futurist camp believe this prince is the yet-future Antichrist and that it is to this individual that the balance of Daniel 9 refers when it mentions "he."

Respected scholars in the historicist camp, by contrast, believe this prince was the Roman general Titus and that Daniel 9:26b is a description of Jerusalem's destruction in 70 AD by Titus's armies. The "he" of verse 27, they believe, is the Messiah, and Daniel 9:26b is merely a parenthetical insertion.

Does this interpretation make sense? It is important to note here that up to this point, 98.6 percent of the prophecy has been about the Messiah. It's clear that there's been a shift here, but is this new information in Daniel 9:26b an overall change of focus from the Messiah to the Antichrist, as futurists maintain, or is it just a parenthetical insertion that gives additional details related to the city of Jerusalem? In my opinion, the historicists are on solid ground here: changing the focus of the prophecy from the Messiah to an unnamed prince of an unnamed army—making that prince the central figure in all that follows—is a shaky interpretation. It seems to me that if YHWH had wanted us to change the focus of the prophecy from the Messiah to "the prince" of Daniel 9:26b, He would have made "the prince" the primary focus of the verse and not the "the people" of the prince. To my mind, it is a dangerous precedent to turn our focus away from the Messiah and toward the Anti-Messiah without a clear contextual reason. Daniel 9:26b definitely does not meet that criterion.

"But the rule of antecedent!" you protest. Doesn't the rule of antecedent require the "he" of Daniel 9:27 to refer back to the closest noun, i.e. "the prince" of Daniel 9:26b? This would be a reasonable determination if we had contextual grounds to believe the text intended to leave us hanging regarding the Messiah, but frankly that is an unreasonable assumption. Firstly, the prince of Daniel 9:26b is not even the subject of the verse; it is the "people" who are in focus here. Can we really justify making an unnamed people and their prince the sole focus of the rest of the prophecy to the neglect of the Messiah? I don't think so. Further supporting this position is the fact that in the Hebrew Scriptures, the rule of antecedent isn't a hard and fast rule. Daniel 8:25 provides us with a good example of why the overall contextual theme of a passage is more important than the rule of antecedent:

> And through his policy also he shall cause craft to prosper in his hand; and he shall magnify himself in his heart, and by peace shall destroy many:
> *he shall also stand up against the Prince of princes;* but *he* shall be broken without hand. (Daniel 8:25, emphasis mine)

If we interpreted Daniel 8:25 in the same way Daniel 9:26–27 is commonly interpreted, we would have the "he" referring back to the Prince of princes. In other words, we would have the Messiah broken without hand. Clearly that is not the most reasonable or intended rendering of this passage. The focus or general thrust of this passage is about the "king of fierce countenance," and even though the Prince of princes is inserted in verse 25, there is no contextual justification for changing the focus of the final part of the passage.

Daniel 9:26–27, by the most reasonable interpretive method, must be treated the same way. A mention of "the "people of the prince" is not sufficient grounds to drop the Messiah cold in Daniel 9:26a and then leave Him there while we refocus the rest of the prophecy on the Antichrist. I admit, I don't have any theological training, but I'd like to think I have some common sense.

Just to be clear here: I am a futurist who believes in the literal second coming of Yeshua and literal fulfillment of all the Bible's unfulfilled prophecies concerning Israel and the Jewish people, but the futurist position on Daniel 9:27 just doesn't make sense on many levels. In my opinion both sides in this discussion have read too much of their theological position into their interpretation of the prophecy of 70 sevens.

But let's get back to Daniel 9 and the flood, and I'll give another reason why we should never have taken our eyes off the Messiah for the final epoch of Daniel 9.

Confirming the Covenant

For the sake of argument, let's look at Daniel 9:27 not as a departure into the future of the Antichrist, but as a continuation of the messianic focus of Daniel 9:26a. Daniel 9:26a left off with the Messiah being cut off, "but not for himself." Daniel 9:27 picks back up in the same way Daniel 9:26a ended, by using a pronoun to refer to the Messiah. It starts by stating that "he shall confirm the covenant." Take a moment once again to read the passage:

> And after threescore and two weeks shall Messiah be cut off, but not for himself:
> > *and the people of the prince that shall come shall destroy the city and the sanctuary; and the end thereof shall be with a flood, and unto the end of the war desolations are determined.*
>
> And he shall confirm the covenant with many for one week: and in the midst of the week he shall cause the sacrifice and the oblation to cease, and for the overspreading of abominations he shall make it desolate, even until the consummation, and that determined shall be poured upon the desolate. (Daniel 9:26–27)

The Hebrew words "confirm" and "covenant" in Daniel 9:27 takes us back again to the imagery of Noah's flood and the destruction of mankind. The Hebrew word translated "confirm" in this passage is *gabar,* and it means to prevail upon or have strength over. Daniel 9:27 is the only place in the Scriptures where gabar is translated this way, and frankly, "confirm" just doesn't convey the true meaning of the word. Below, take a look at the first occurrence of gabar. Intriguingly, it too takes us back to the events of the flood when mankind and their sins were karath or cut off from the face of the earth in Genesis 7.

> And the waters prevailed [gabar], and were increased greatly upon the earth; and the ark went upon the face of the waters. (Genesis 7:18)

Fascinating, isn't it, that the same waters that "prevailed" over the earth, washing away mankind's sins, also lifted the ark to safety to the saving of Noah and his family? Notice in the following passage that Peter compares Yeshua's death and resurrection (his cutting off) to the flood and mankind's deliverance from sin. (Note that it's not the baptism by water which saves us, as some have incorrectly interpreted this passage, but the baptism of Yeshua's substitutionary atonement empowered by His resurrection.)

> For Christ also hath once suffered for sins, the just for the unjust, that he might bring us to God, being put to death in the flesh, but quickened by the Spirit: by which also he went and preached unto the spirits in prison; which sometime were disobedient, when once the longsuffering of God waited in the days of Noah, while the ark was a preparing, wherein few, that is, eight souls were saved by water. The like figure whereunto even baptism doth also now save us (not the putting away of the filth of the flesh, but the answer of a good conscience toward God,) by the resurrection of Jesus Christ: who is gone into heaven, and is on the right hand of God; angels and authorities and powers being made subject unto him. (1 Peter 3:18–22)

Peter repeats this imagery in 2 Peter 3. Let's tie it all together with the Hebrew word *beriyth,* or covenant. Daniel 9:27 states that "he" (who we for the present assume is the Messiah Yeshua) prevails or strengthens the beriyth or covenant with Daniel's people, or as they are called in the text, "the many."

Remember, the New Testament is clear that Yeshua came to redeem all mankind, but there is a chronological order to YHWH's plan, and part one of that plan involved the Messiah's going to the Jewish people, His own brethren, first. This divine order of things is critically important to understand as it relates to Daniel 9 and the covenant made with the "many."

> For I am not ashamed of the gospel of Christ: for it is the power of God unto salvation to every one that believeth; to the Jew first, and also to the Greek. (Romans 1:16)

We know from the New Testament accounts that many of Yeshua's own brethren rejected Him, and that as part of the overall plan of YHWH, that rejection is but a partial blindness until the "times of the Gentiles" have been fulfilled. It's fascinating, then, to read the prophet Isaiah's words and how he explains YHWH's temporary anger toward His chosen people in the context of the Noah's flood. This is only an excerpt; to get the full depth of this promise, I recommend reading all of Isaiah 54:

> For thy Maker is thine husband; YHWH of hosts is his name; and thy Redeemer the Holy One of Israel; The God of the

whole earth shall he be called . . . For a small moment have I forsaken thee; but with great mercies will I gather thee. In a little wrath I hid my face from thee for a moment; but with everlasting kindness will I have mercy on thee, saith YHWH thy Redeemer.

> For this is as the waters of Noah unto me: for as I have sworn that the waters of Noah should no more go over the earth; so have I sworn that I would not be wroth with thee, nor rebuke thee. For the mountains shall depart, and the hills be removed; but my kindness shall not depart from thee, neither shall the *covenant of my peace* be removed, saith YHWH that hath mercy on thee. (Isaiah 54:5–10, emphasis mine)

For those of us Gentiles who have reaped the benefits of this period of time during which YHWH is calling the Gentiles to the family of God, I remind you of the words of the apostle Paul:

> For I would not, brethren, that ye should be ignorant of this mystery, lest ye should be wise in your own conceits; that blindness in part is happened to Israel, until the fulness of the Gentiles be come in. And so all Israel shall be saved: as it is written, There shall come out of Sion the Deliverer, and shall turn away ungodliness from Jacob: *for this is my covenant unto them, when I shall take away their sins.* (Romans 11:25–27)

In Part I of this book, we looked at the central covenantal theme of the Bible as it relates to Daniel 9, and I made the case that in fact this theme is the promise that mankind will someday be reconciled to our Creator through the promised seed. Indeed, it is Daniel 9 where we find this divine plan taking clear shape, when the promised Redeemer was karath for mankind's sins.

The Messiah Strengthens the Covenant

In the preceding pages of this chapter, we saw how after the "cutting off" of mankind at the flood, the same Hebrew word *karath* was often used to described the making or cutting of a covenant (beriyth). In the coming pages we will zero in on the covenant described in Daniel 9:27 to try to answer a couple of questions. Was it the Messiah, not the Antichrist, who strengthened the covenant, and if it was, then why is it strengthened for only one shabuwa (seven)?

To lay the foundation for this line of inquiry, we must journey back in time to the days of Moses and the institution of the sacrificial system and its messianic foreshadowing.

Chapter 10:

Strengthening the Covenant

"For the law made nothing perfect, but the bringing in of a better hope did; by the which we draw nigh unto God. And inasmuch as not without an oath he was made priest . . . by so much was Jesus made a surety of a better testament [covenant].*"*
Hebrews 7:19–22

Have you ever asked yourself what was the purpose of the priesthood and sacrificial law as mandated by YHWH to Moses and the children of Israel? Why was Israel required to make endless sacrifices for sin? Why, year after year, over and over again, did each sin and every trespass require a sacrifice in order for the transgressor to be considered temporarily "right" with YHWH?

The short answer is that these vivid blood rites were but reminders of mankind's fallen, sinful state and the price such sin requires of innocent blood. In the big picture, these sacrifices were shadows or rehearsals of what YHWH intended to accomplish on our behalf by becoming flesh and paying the righteous penalty for our sins. The apostle Paul explains it this way:

> Wherefore then serveth the law? It was added because of transgressions, till the seed should come to whom the promise

was made; and it was ordained by angels in the hand of a mediator. (Galatians 3:19)

But when the fulness of the time was come, God sent forth his Son, made of a woman, made under the law, to redeem them that were under the law, that we might receive the adoption of sons. (Galatians 4:4–5)

Yeshua, by dying for the sins of mankind, fulfilled the symbolism or shadow of the sacrificial law given to Israel. His blood became the surety or the strength of a better covenant, as described in Hebrews 7 above. This better covenant does not require eternal sacrifices by a fallible priesthood, but instead one sacrifice by a righteous priest that brings permanent reconciliation and everlasting righteousness in the eyes of YHWH.

The Final Sacrifice

Do you remember the famous words Yeshua spoke that Passover night before His death, a night commemorating the horrific event nearly 1500 years earlier in the land of Egypt when the angel of death killed the firstborn of every house not marked with the blood of the Passover lamb? That very night, Yeshua enjoined His disciples to remember that the wine of the Passover supper was but a symbol of a new covenant in His blood, a covenant far better than the temporary one given to Israel.

> For this is my blood of the new testament [covenant], which is shed for many for the remission of sins. (Matthew 26:28)

> The Lord Jesus the same night in which he was betrayed took bread: and when he had given thanks, he brake it, and said, Take, eat: this is my body, which is broken for you: this do in remembrance of me. After the same manner also he took the cup, when he had supped, saying, This cup is the new testament [covenant] in my blood: this do ye, as oft as ye drink it, in remembrance of me. For as often as ye eat this bread, and drink this cup, ye do shew the Lord's death till he come. (1 Corinthians 11:23–26)

You see, Yeshua's death and resurrection brought a change in the sacrificial law. His sacrifice took a covenant that was weak and incomplete and strengthened it to reach its full intended purpose. Take a moment to let the biblical record explain far better than I ever could:

> For the priesthood being changed, there is made of necessity a change also of the law. (Hebrews 7:12)

> So also Christ glorified not himself to be made an high priest; but he that said unto him, Thou art my Son, to day have I begotten thee. As he saith also in another place, Thou art a priest for ever after the order of Melchisedec. Who in the days of his flesh, when he had offered up prayers and supplications with strong crying and tears unto him that was able to save him

from death, and was heard in that he feared; though he were a Son, yet learned he obedience by the things which he suffered; and being made perfect, he became the author of eternal salvation unto all them that obey him; called of God an high priest after the order of Melchisedec. (Hebrews 5:5–10)

For David is not ascended into the heavens: but he saith himself, YHWH said unto my Lord, Sit thou on my right hand, Until I make thy foes thy footstool. Therefore let all the house of Israel know assuredly, that God hath made that same Jesus, whom ye have crucified, both Lord and Christ. (Acts 2:34–36)

YHWH said unto my Lord, Sit thou at my right hand, until I make thine enemies thy footstool. YHWH shall send the rod of thy strength out of Zion: rule thou in the midst of thine enemies . . . YHWH hath sworn, and will not repent, Thou art a priest for ever after the order of Melchizedek. (Psalm 110:1–4)

The Blood Covenant

At this point, I hope you've caught at least a glimpse of how the Bible testifies that Yeshua, the Messiah of Daniel 9:26–27, did indeed strengthen or prevail upon the covenant given to Israel, those beloved descendants of Abraham whom the text of Daniel 9 refers to as "the many." Before we move on to look at the reason this covenant was confirmed for just one *shabuwa*, I think it is important to finish this chapter by filling in a few final gaps in our understanding of why the sacrificial system was such an important symbol in YHWH's plan to reconcile all mankind through Yeshua the Messiah.

> For when Moses had spoken every precept to all the people according to the law, he took the blood of calves and of goats, with water, and scarlet wool, and hyssop, and sprinkled both the book, and all the people, Saying, *This is the blood of the testament* [beriyth – covenant (Exodus 24:8)] which God hath enjoined unto you.
>
> . . . And almost all things are by the law purged with blood; *and without shedding of blood is no remission.* It was therefore necessary that the patterns of things in the heavens should be purified with these; but the heavenly things themselves with better sacrifices than these. For Christ is not entered into the holy places made with hands, which are the figures of the true; but into heaven itself, now to appear in the presence of God for us:
>
> Nor yet that he should offer himself often, as the high priest entereth into the holy place every year with blood of others; For then must he often have suffered since the foundation of the world: but now once in the end of the world hath he appeared to put away sin by the sacrifice of himself.
>
> And as it is appointed unto men once to die, but after this the judgment: so Christ was once offered to bear the sins of many; and unto them that look for him shall he appear the second time without sin unto salvation. (Hebrews 9:19–28, emphasis mine)

Paul continues refining this theme in Hebrews 10 to show that Yeshua's death and resurrection satisfied the requirements of the law in terms of sacrificial atonement. In other words, Yeshua's blood prevailed over the inadequate Old Testament sacrificial law and once and for all brought eternal righteousness through His blood.

> For the law having a shadow of good things to come, and not the very image of the things, can never with those sacrifices which they offered year by year continually make the comers thereunto perfect. For then would they not have ceased to be offered? because that the worshippers once purged should have had no more conscience of sins. But in those sacrifices there is a remembrance again made of sins every year. For it is not possible that the blood of bulls and of goats should take away sins.
>
> Wherefore when he cometh into the world, he saith, Sacrifice and offering thou wouldest not, but a body hast thou prepared me: in burnt offerings and sacrifices for sin thou hast had no pleasure. Then said I, Lo, I come (in the volume of the book it is written of me,) to do thy will, O God. Above when he said, Sacrifice and offering and burnt offerings and offering for sin thou wouldest not, neither hadst pleasure therein; which are offered by the law; then said he, Lo, I come to do thy will, O God.
>
> *He taketh away the first, that he may establish the second.* By the which will we are sanctified through the

offering of the body of Jesus Christ *once for all*. (Hebrews 10:1–10, emphasis mine)

To round out this idea of the blood covenant and the coming Messiah, I once more remind you the famous words of Zechariah:

Rejoice greatly, O daughter of Zion; shout, O daughter of Jerusalem: behold, thy King cometh unto thee: he is just, and having salvation; lowly, and riding upon an ass, and upon a colt the foal of an ass. And I will cut off the chariot from Ephraim, and the horse from Jerusalem, and the battle bow shall be cut off: and he shall speak peace unto the heathen: and his dominion shall be from sea even to sea, and from the river even to the ends of the earth. *As for thee also, by the blood of thy covenant I have sent forth thy prisoners out of the pit* wherein is no water. (Zechariah 9:9–11, emphasis mine)

Why Only One Shabuwa?

The book of Hebrews gives us clear understanding of how Yeshua fulfilled Daniel's prophecy that the Messiah would "strengthen" or "prevail over" the covenant. The question that remains unanswered is why, if it was Yeshua who confirmed the covenant of Daniel 9:27, did He only strengthen the covenant for the final shabuwa? The answer to that question takes us to the very purpose of this prophecy, the purpose of the Jewish people in the plan of YHWH, and the story of how YHWH has worked that plan out through the ages. We'll dig into all of this in chapter 11.

"For this is my blood of the new testament [covenant]*, which is shed for many for the remission of sins."*

Matthew 26:28

Chapter 11:

The Final Shabuwa of Living Witnesses

"And for this cause he is the mediator of the new testament, that by means of death, for the redemption of the transgressions that were under the first testament, they which are called might receive the promise of eternal inheritance. For where a testament is, there must also of necessity be the death of the testator. For a testament is of force after men are dead: otherwise it is of no strength at all while the testator liveth. Whereupon neither the first testament [covenant] *was dedicated without blood."*

Hebrews 9:15–18

I've done my best to show that Yeshua's "cutting off" and resurrection were the climactic act in YHWH's covenantal plan to reconcile all mankind through Yeshua, the Messiah. Generally speaking, this plan started with YHWH's covenantal promise of the seed, which He confirmed with the biblical fathers Adam, Noah, and Abram, a covenant which promised that someday, through their seed, all nations of the earth would be blessed. Although the first stirrings are there in God's word to Adam and Noah, it is not until YHWH's covenant with Abraham, after he showed his faith in his willingness to sacrifice his only son, that we get our first real idea of what YHWH's plan of reconciliation entailed. Some centuries later, just after the exodus, the sacrificial law was added and the full hopelessness of mankind's sin and our inadequacy before YHWH put on bloody display, in the most graphic and sobering symbolism. After centuries of these seemingly endless sacrifices, when the fullness of time in YHWH's redemptive plan had come, after the 69th shabuwa had run its course, the Son of God, Yeshua the Messiah, the Lamb of God, became the final sacrifice for mankind's sins.

Witnesses of the New Covenant

Today, you and I are blessed with the very words of YHWH, which testify to His love and desire to be reconciled with mankind, in what we call the Bible. These words were brought to us thanks to the Hebrew people who were chosen by YHWH to record His redemptive plan. The Old Testament is a record of this redemptive plan worked out through the descendants of Adam and Abraham and fulfilled in their seed, Yeshua.

The New Testament is the eyewitness record that tells of Yeshua's fulfillment of the Old Testament promises and prophecies that spoke of a coming Redeemer, that suffering servant who would pay the price for mankind's sins. But the New Testament goes further than that. It also tells us of a day after the full number of Gentiles have been added to the family of God when the Messiah will return, but this time as a conquering king to rule on the throne of David from Jerusalem.

For the purpose of understanding the final shabuwa, that 70th shabuwa of Daniel 9, it is the first-century Jewish eyewitnesses to Yeshua's death and resurrection who concern us now. If as we have suggested the "he" of Daniel 9:27 is in fact the Messiah Yeshua, then there is no reason to insert an undetermined gap in the prophecy of 70 shabuwa, as nearly all end-times scholars today do. Just as the 62 shabuwa directly followed the first 7 shabuwa, the most reasonable reading of the prophecy suggests that the final shabuwa begins where the 69th shabuwa ended: in the fall of 28 AD at the end of Yeshua's first year of ministry. We go back now to the fall of 28 AD and the end of the 69th shabuwa, just as Yeshua's first year of ministry is drawing to a close.

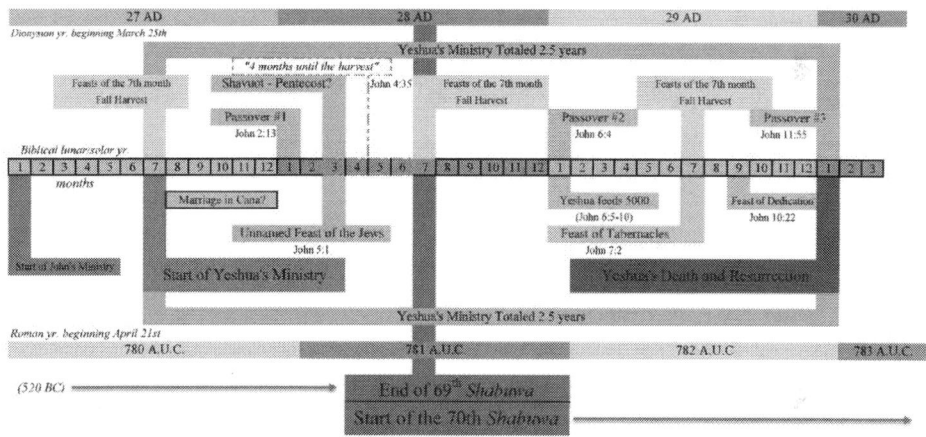

A Meeting of Seven

As the New Testament indicates, something remarkable took place at the start of the 70th shabuwa, a meeting that fundamentally altered the dynamics of Yeshua's ministry and marked the start of His strengthening of the covenant with the Jewish people, whom the text of Daniel 9:27 identifies as the "many." It was one of the most auspicious meetings recorded in the Bible, and appropriately, it was a meeting of seven individuals. In many ways it was a changing of the guard between the Old and New Covenants, and present at this meeting were representatives of both covenants. You and I know it as the transfiguration.

Representing the Old Testament Torah and Prophets were Moses and Elijah. Representing the New Testament were the apostles Peter, James, and John. YHWH, the living God of the Bible, officiated, and Yeshua was the man of honor.

It happened on an unnamed mountain sometime after the second Passover of Yeshua's ministry. The chronology of Matthew 16–17 and Mark 8–9 helps fix the transfiguration to a date after Yeshua fed the multitudes with the loaves and fish (see above chart). Sometime after this, Yeshua went to Bethsaida and healed the blind man, then traveled to Caesarea Philippi and began to teach His disciples that His ministry was to include His own suffering and death. From these events, the text tells us that six days later Jesus took Peter, James, and John (James's brother) up into an unnamed mountain and was transfigured before them. This event is related in both Matthew 17 and Mark 9. I've reproduced it below.

> And he said unto them, Verily I say unto you, That there be some of them that stand here, which shall not taste of death, till they have seen the kingdom of God come with power. And after six days Jesus taketh with him Peter, and James, and John, and leadeth them up into an high mountain apart by themselves: and he was transfigured before them.
>
> And his raiment became shining, exceeding white as snow; so as no fuller on earth can white them. And there appeared unto them Elias with Moses: and they were talking

with Jesus. And Peter answered and said to Jesus, Master, it is good for us to be here: and let us make three tabernacles; one for thee, and one for Moses, and one for Elias.

And there was a cloud that overshadowed them: and a voice came out of the cloud, saying, This is my beloved Son: hear him. (Mark 9:1–7)

Confirming the Covenant

In a setting reminiscent of the events at Mount Sinai in the days of Moses, Yeshua, Peter, James, and John meet with Elijah and Moses in the very shekinah presence of YHWH. Now, that must have been some meeting—but what was its purpose? I mean, we're talking here about a meeting with the living God of the Bible and six of its greatest heroes at a point in time which may very well have marked the first year of the 70th shabuwa. What was the purpose of this meeting, and what did it accomplish?

The answer that makes the most sense to me is that this meeting was YHWH's way of confirming to the apostles Peter, James, and John that indeed Yeshua was the Messiah promised in the Scriptures—that He was the Son of God who would fulfill the "covenant and mercy" promised to Abraham, that pivotal covenant which promised that in Abraham's seed all nations of the earth would be blessed.

In addition to confirming that Yeshua was His Son, YHWH also commanded Peter, James, and John, in the presence of Moses and Elijah, to listen to the words of Yeshua. In other words, the living God of the Bible personally told Peter, James, and John that Yeshua's words were equal to those of the Old Testament Torah and Prophets.

Think about Moses's and Elijah's presence at this meeting. These two witnesses represented the Torah (the Mosaic law) and the Prophets. The sacrificial law, as we have just learned in the previous chapters, was a definite picture of the Messiah's sacrifice on our behalf. Intertwined with the law were the prophets, who plainly spoke of the coming Messiah. These two men were witnesses to YHWH's testimony that Yeshua was the son of God, that promised Messiah. Less than a year later, just after His death and resurrection, Yeshua reminded the disciples that indeed the law and the prophets spoke of these events:

> And as they thus spake, Jesus himself stood in the midst of them, and saith unto them, Peace be unto you. But they were terrified and affrighted, and supposed that they had seen a spirit. And he said unto them, Why are ye troubled? and why do thoughts arise in your hearts?
>
> Behold my hands and my feet, that it is I myself: handle me, and see; for a spirit hath not flesh and bones, as ye see me have.
>
> And when he had thus spoken, he shewed them his hands and his feet. And while they yet believed not for joy, and wondered, he said unto them, Have ye here any meat? And they gave him a piece of a broiled fish, and of an honeycomb. And he took it, and did eat before them. And he said unto them, These are the words which I spake unto you, while I was yet

with you, *that all things must be fulfilled, which were written in the law of Moses, and in the prophets*, and in the psalms, concerning me. (Luke 24:36–44, emphasis mine)

The Living Witnesses

So let's take a step back for a moment. Daniel 9 and the 70 weeks countdown to the Messiah began with a divine "word" witnessed by the two Old Testament prophets Haggai and Zechariah. Now, 7 + 62 shabuwa later, we are at the start of the 70th shabuwa, that final epoch of Daniel 9, and once again the word of YHWH is given and witnessed by two Old Testament prophets. This time the word of YHWH was both a confirmation and a command given to three men who would form the nucleus of the New Covenant church. These men, Peter, James, and John, were the living witnesses, along with the other ten apostles Yeshua personally called, who for the next several decades would bear witness to the fact that indeed Yeshua (Jesus) was the Son of God, the very essence of the covenant and mercy promised to Abraham and mentioned in Daniel 9:4.

Take a moment to read the following passages, which speak not only of the evidence for the Messiah found in the law and the prophets, but also of those living eyewitnesses who saw this ancient covenant strengthened by the Messiah in a most wonderful way.

And he shall send Jesus Christ, which before was preached unto you: whom the heaven must receive until the times of restitution of all things, which God hath spoken by the mouth of all his holy prophets since the world began. (Acts 3:20–21)

He that despised Moses' law died without mercy under two or three witnesses: of how much sorer punishment, suppose ye, shall he be thought worthy, who hath trodden under foot the Son of God, and hath counted the blood of the covenant, wherewith he was sanctified, an unholy thing, and hath done despite unto the Spirit of grace? (Hebrews 10:28–29)

And, being assembled together with them, [Jesus] commanded them that they should not depart from Jerusalem, but wait for the promise of the Father, which, saith he, ye have heard of me . . . They asked of him, saying, Lord, wilt thou at this time restore again the kingdom to Israel? And he said unto them, It is not for you to know the times or the seasons, which the Father hath put in his own power. But ye shall receive power, after that the Holy Ghost is come upon you: *and ye shall be witnesses unto me both in Jerusalem, and in all Judaea, and in Samaria, and unto the uttermost part of the earth.* (Acts 1:4–8, emphasis mine)

Men and brethren, let me freely speak unto you of the patriarch David, that he is both dead and buried, and his sepulchre is with us unto this day. Therefore being a prophet, and knowing that God had sworn with an oath to him, that of the fruit of his loins, according to the flesh, he would raise up Christ to sit on his throne; he seeing this before spake of the resurrection of Christ, that his soul was not left in hell, neither his flesh did see corruption. This Jesus hath God raised up, *whereof we all are witnesses*. (Acts 2:29–32, emphasis mine)

And he commanded us to preach unto the people, and to testify that it is he which was ordained of God to be the Judge of quick and dead. To him give all the prophets witness, that through his name whosoever believeth in him shall receive remission of sins. (Acts 10:42–43)

Blessed be the Lord God of Israel; for he hath visited and redeemed his people, and hath raised up an horn of salvation for us in the house of his servant David; as he spake by the mouth of his holy prophets, which have been since the world began: that we should be saved from our enemies, and from the hand of all that hate us; *to perform the mercy promised to our fathers, and to remember his holy covenant* [beriyth]; *the oath which he sware* [*shaba*] *to our father Abraham*. (Luke 1:68–73, emphasis mine)

Renewing the Covenant

In summary, at the start of the 70th shabuwa of Daniel 9 comes a meeting of some of the Bible's greatest Old and New Testament heroes. This fantastic event, overshadowed by the very presence of YHWH, *confirmed* to all parties present that Yeshua was the Messiah, the Son of God promised in the law and prophets since the world began. For the next 70 years until the passing of the apostle John, we have a period of time when the early church was guided by men who had firsthand, eyewitness knowledge that Yeshua was the fulfillment of the covenant made by YHWH with the descendants of Adam, Noah, and Abraham. This strengthening of the covenant was the very basis for the New Testament church. In other words, as Daniel would say it, the Messiah strengthened the covenant with the many for one week.

This indeed is a fitting end to the greatest prophecy in the Bible! We are not left hanging at the death of the Messiah, but instead we are left with a record of a strengthened, prevailing covenant, recorded by living witnesses in the inspired book we know as the New Covenant.

"And as they did eat, Jesus took bread, and blessed, and brake it, and gave to them, and said, Take, eat: this is my body. And he took the cup, and when he had given thanks, he gave it to them: and they all drank of it. And he said unto them, This is my blood of the new testament [covenant]*, which is shed for many. Verily I say unto you, I will drink no more of the fruit of the vine, until that day that I drink it new in the kingdom of God."*
Mark 14:22–25

"And for this cause he is the mediator of the new testament [covenant]*, that by means of death, for the redemption of the transgressions that were under the first testament, they which are called might receive the promise of eternal inheritance."*
Hebrews 9:15

Chapter 12:

The 70ᵗʰ Shabuwa Fulfilled

"And now, brethren, I wot that through ignorance ye did it, as did also your rulers. But those things, which God before had shewed by the mouth of all his prophets, that Christ should suffer, he hath so fulfilled."
Acts 3:17–18

It is one thing to show that Yeshua strengthened or prevailed upon the covenant YHWH made with the Old Testament fathers, a strengthening which resulted in what we know as the New Testament covenant. Frankly, in my opinion, that is an indisputable fact. But admittedly, we have yet to prove how this satisfies all the events described in the 70ᵗʰ shabuwa—events which a majority of prophecy scholars believe will take place in the future. In order to do that, let's look once again at the text of Daniel 9:26–27 and our earlier list of people and events.

> And after threescore and two weeks shall Messiah be cut off, but not for himself:
>> *and the people of the prince that shall come shall destroy the city and the sanctuary; and the end thereof shall be with a flood, and unto the end of the war desolations are determined.*

And he shall confirm the covenant with many for one week: and in the midst of the week he shall cause the sacrifice and the oblation to cease, and for the overspreading of abominations he shall make it desolate, even until the consummation, and that determined shall be poured upon the desolate. (Daniel 9:26–27, 26b emphasized)

People Described:
- The Messiah
- The people who destroy the city
- The prince (of the people)
- He (the Messiah)

Events Described:
- After 62 shabuwa the Messiah is cut off.
- Jerusalem and the temple are destroyed (by the people of the prince).
- The Messiah confirms a covenant with the "many" for the 70th shabuwa.
- The Messiah causes the sacrifice and oblation to cease in the midst of the 70th shabuwa.
- On the "wings" of abomination, the Messiah makes it desolate until the consummation and those events which are to be poured upon the desolate/desolator.

The Numbers First

First, let's look at the final shabuwa from a chronological perspective so that we have a firm idea of its starting and ending points, and then we will explore the events that took place during those fateful years. Below is the chart from an earlier chapter that shows the end of the 69th shabuwa as it relates to Yeshua's ministry.

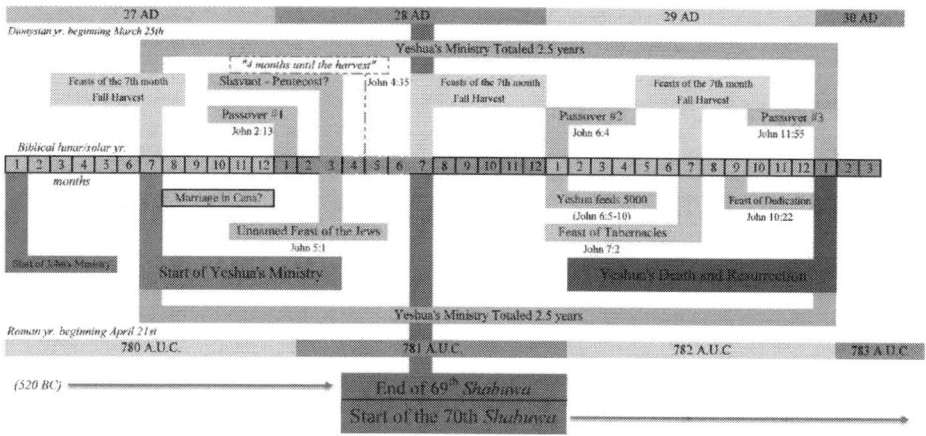

Here is the basic math of the final shabuwa. Using a 14-lunar-cycle period of time, the final (70th) shabuwa equals 7.92 solar years in length. (For those who would like to see the math reproduced in more detail, see the chart below.) According to our previous calculations, the 69th shabuwa ended in the fall of 28 AD at or near the end of Yeshua's first year of ministry. The first year of the 70th shabuwa, then, ran from the fall of 28 AD to the fall of 29 AD. This period of time marked the second year of Yeshua's ministry and likely included the transfiguration, when YHWH personally confirmed Yeshua's authority in the presence of Moses and Elijah (from the Old Testament) and Peter, James, and John (from the New Testament).

Biblical "time" & the Messiah Factors

Lunar month	29.53 days
Solar year	365.24 days

13 lunar cycle "year"	383.89 days	(13 x 29.53)
14 lunar cycle "year"	413.42 days	(14 x 29.53)

70 Sevens x 13 cycles	515.02 solar years	(490 x 13 x 29.53 / 365.24)
70 Sevens x 14 cycles	554.63 solar years	(490 x 14 x 29.53 / 365.24)

Starting in the fall of 28 AD, 7.92 solar years takes us to fall of 36 AD. The 70th shabuwa, then, is anchored by Yeshua's second year of ministry and the transfiguration on one end, but what about the other end? Is there any significance to the date 36 AD?

I believe there is. According to biblical scholars, the conversion of the apostle Paul took place sometime between the years 31–36 AD. The final shabuwa, then, is anchored on the other end by the conversion of Paul, who became Yeshua's primary apostle to the Gentiles. We will deal with the significance of this in the next chapter, but for now, we at least know the time frame encapsulated by the 70th shabuwa, a period that spans the years 28–36 AD. Let's now turn our attention to some of the events described in Daniel 9:26–27 to see how the final shabuwa played out.

The People of the Prince

We thoroughly dealt with the Messiah being "cut off," so now let's look at Daniel 9:26b and the events described there. First off, notice that the destruction of the city and sanctuary are not timed precisely. All we know is that sometime after the 69th shabuwa, the city and temple would be destroyed by "the people of the prince." Keep in mind, we have no compelling reason to consider Daniel 9:26b anything more than a brief change of focus to describe events that would befall Jerusalem before the main messianic theme of the prophecy is picked back up in verse 27. So this event does not have to fall before 36 AD in order for the prophecy to be fulfilled.

Historically, the destruction of the temple took place in 70 AD by the armies of the Roman general Titus. In fact, Josephus notes that Titus wanted to preserve the temple, but due to circumstances beyond his control, it was burned by his armies just as the Scripture predicted. Here is Josephus's description of the events:

> So Titus retired into the tower of Antonia, and resolved to storm the temple the next day, early in the morning, with his whole army, and to encamp around the holy house; but as for that house, God had, for certain long ago doomed it to the fire; and now that fatal day was come according to the revolution of ages; it was the tenth day of the month of Loos [Ab], (Niese: Aug. 29, Capellus: Aug. 10) upon which it was formerly burnt by the king of Babylon; although these flames took their rise from the Jews themselves, and were occasioned by them . . .

At which time one of the soldiers, without waiting for any orders, and without any concern or dread upon him at so great an undertaking, and being hurried on by a certain divine fury, snatched something out of the materials that were on fire, and being lifted up by another soldier, he set fire to a golden window, through which there was a passage to the rooms that were around the holy house, on the north side of it.

As the flames went upward, the Jews made a great clamour . . . And now a certain person came running to Titus, and told him of this fire, as he was resting himself in his tent after the last battle; whereupon he rose up in great haste, and, as he was, ran to the holy house, in order to have a stop put to the fire. (*The Jewish War* 6:249–254)

Causing the Sacrifice and Oblation to Cease

Daniel 9:27 tells us that "he"—whom we now know to be the Messiah—causes the sacrifice and oblation to cease in the midst of the final shabuwa. In the text of Daniel 9:27, the word "midst" comes from the Hebrew word *chetsiy,* and it means half or middle. In the Bible, *chetsiy* is used to denote exactly half, the middle, or some dividing part of the whole.

There are two ways to look at this. In the most literal sense, the actual sacrificial system and the priestly service did not end until the destruction of Jerusalem in 70 AD. That is just over forty years after the start of the final shabuwa. It's kind of hard to see that as being a literal fulfillment of the prophecy, isn't it? There may be a solution to this, but for the moment, let's move on and look at the end of the sacrificial system from YHWH's point of view rather than man's—that is, the end of the sacrificial system as seen from the spirit of the law.

The Bible is clear that Yeshua was the fulfillment of the sacrificial service. His death and resurrection forever ended the necessity for sacrifices to be offered in order for human beings to be considered right in the eyes of YHWH. Just a few examples are sufficient to make this point. Keep in mind here that this righteousness must be understood within the context of the sacrificial system and the temporary "rightness" which the blood of animals bestowed.

> Above when he said, Sacrifice and offering and burnt offerings and offering for sin thou wouldest not, neither hadst pleasure therein; which are offered by the law; Then said he, Lo, I come to do thy will, O God. He taketh away the first, that he may establish the second. By the which will we are sanctified through the offering of the body of Jesus Christ once for all. (Hebrews 10:8–10)

> For if, when we were enemies, we were reconciled to God by the death of his Son, much more, being reconciled, we shall be saved by his life. And not only so, but we also joy in God through our Lord Jesus Christ, by whom we have now received the atonement. (Romans 5:10–11)

> To wit, that God was in Christ, reconciling the world unto himself, not imputing their trespasses unto them; and hath

committed unto us the word of reconciliation. (2 Corinthians 5:19)

For verily he took not on him the nature of angels; but he took on him the seed of Abraham. Wherefore in all things it behoved him to be made like unto his brethren, that he might be a merciful and faithful high priest in things pertaining to God, to make reconciliation for the sins of the people. (Hebrews 2:16–17)

Although the majority of his own people did not realize it at the time, Yeshua's death and resurrection fulfilled the promise made to Abraham that in his seed all the nations of the world would be blessed. It was through the very framework of the sacrificial law that this promise was exemplified and brought to fruition. Although it took nearly forty years to become a physical reality for the Jewish people, the sacrificial system in the eyes of YHWH ended in 30 AD when Yeshua, the Lamb of God, took away the sins of the world.

Prophetic Milestone: The Desolations of Jerusalem

Daniel 9:27 goes on to tell us that "on the wings of abomination" there will be a period of desolation until "the consummation" and the events determined "shall be poured out upon the desolate." Before we look at the unusual phrase "wings of abomination," let's look first at the "he" who causes the desolation. I've read many different translations of this passage, but for the present let's look at the translation given by the KJV:

> And he shall confirm the covenant with many for one week: and in the midst of the week he shall cause the sacrifice and the oblation to cease, *and for the overspreading of abominations he shall make it desolate, even until the consummation*, and that determined shall be poured upon the desolate. (Daniel 9:27, emphasis mine)

The above translation seems to indicate that the "he" of verse 27 (the Messiah) has a part in the desolation of Jerusalem. It may come as a surprise to some, but Yeshua did indeed prophesy the desolation of Jerusalem and the judgment of His people. In Matthew 23, in a truly poignant and tragic condemnation of His own people, Yeshua laments the fact that His heart's desire was to gather the children of Israel together as a hen gathers her chicks, but they wanted none of it. He ends this passage by prophesying that their "house" would remain desolate until they say "Blessed is he that cometh in the name of the Lord."

> O Jerusalem, Jerusalem, thou that killest the prophets, and stonest them which are sent unto thee, how often would I have gathered thy children together, even as a hen gathereth her chickens under her wings, and ye would not! Behold, *your house is left unto you desolate.* For I say unto you, Ye shall not

see me henceforth, till ye shall say, Blessed is he that cometh in the name of the Lord. (Matthew 23:37–39, emphasis mine)

Few realize that not only did Yeshua predict the desolation of Jerusalem in this passage, but in Matthew 12, he also warned them of when it would take place. In a comparison most often associated with His death and resurrection, Yeshua gave the sign of Jonah as a warning to the scribes and Pharisees:

> Then certain of the scribes and of the Pharisees answered, saying, Master, we would see a sign from thee. But he answered and said unto them, An evil and adulterous generation seeketh after a sign; and there shall no sign be given to it, but the sign of the prophet Jonas:
> For as Jonas was three days and three nights in the whale's belly; so shall the Son of man be three days and three nights in the heart of the earth. The men of Nineveh shall rise in judgment with this generation, and shall condemn it: because they repented at the preaching of Jonas; and, behold, a greater than Jonas is here. (Matthew 12:38–41)

Yeshua's sign to the scribes and Pharisees was a comparison between himself and Jonah. Keep in mind that after spending three days and three nights in the belly of the fish, Jonah went to Nineveh and warned its inhabitants that they had forty days to repent or they would face judgment. That was Jonah's sign to the Ninevites.

Just as Jonah's resurrection from the whale's belly was the signal that gave his message the credibility of a man of God, so Yeshua's resurrection from the grave was the signal that warned His generation that judgment would also fall on them. Sadly, Yeshua also made it clear that the people of Nineveh would rise up in judgment of Yeshua's generation because the Ninevites repented at the preaching of Jonah, but those of Yeshua's generation would not repent even though someone far greater than Jonah had warned them—namely, the Son of God.

Sure enough, Yeshua's death and resurrection in 30 AD set in motion that fateful warning, and exactly forty years later Jerusalem was destroyed. Here too YHWH showed restraint by giving the people of Jerusalem not just forty days like the Ninevites were given: instead He increased their grace period by one magnitude larger, thus giving them forty years to repent. Tragically, they still did not realize their day of visitation. What is even more disconcerting is that they knew something bad was coming but were blinded to its true nature.

Forty Years of Signs

In one of the most unusual stories of the Second Temple era, the Jerusalem and Babylonian Talmuds record a series of signs that transpired between 30 AD and the destruction of Jerusalem in 70 AD. These signs were considered omens of impending disaster. It is fascinating to realize that these Talmudic records were written by Rabbinic sources which by most accounts were and in some cases still are hostile to early Christianity. In other words, they had no reason to provide evidence that might lend support to any early New Testament prophecies made by or about Yeshua. Still, it was during those forty years when Yeshua's "sign of Jonah" ran its course that they recorded several truly unsettling events that transpired in Jerusalem:

> Forty years before the destruction of the Temple, the western light (of the Lamp-stand, the Menorah) went out, the crimson thread remained crimson, and the lot for the LORD always came up in the left hand. They would close the gates of the temple by night and get up in the morning and find them wide open. *(The Yerushalmi.* 156–157)

> Our rabbis taught: During the last forty years before the destruction of the Temple the lot ("For the Lord") did not come up in the right hand; nor did the crimson-colored strap become white; nor did the western most light shine; and the doors of the Hekl (Temple) would open by themselves. (*Yoma* 39a)

> Said Rabban Yohanan Ben Zakkai to the Temple, "O Temple, why do you frighten us? we know that you will end up destroyed. For it has been said, Open your doors, O Lebanon, that the fire may devour your cedars." (*Sota* 6:3; quoting Zechariah 11:1)

In terms of the temple service and the sacrificial system, these signs had great significance in the eyes of the inhabitants of Jerusalem.
- The first omen or sign concerned the temple menorah (the lampstand), which was to be kept burning at all times. The

light in part represented the presence of God. After 30 AD, no matter the precautions taken, the light would go out every night.
- The second sign concerned the temple doors. Every night for forty years, the temple doors would open by themselves. As noted above, the rabbis considered this an omen of impending doom for the temple.
- The third sign concerned the scarlet thread or strip of cloth that had been stained with the blood of the goat sacrifice and then tied to the door of the temple on the Day of Atonement (Yom Kippur). Traditionally, it was believed that if the cloth turned white on this day, it meant their atonement sacrifice was accepted by God. From 30 AD until the destruction of Jerusalem in 70 AD, this red cloth never turned white.
- The fourth omen concerned the lot cast for the sacrificial goat and the scapegoat on the Day of Atonement. Each year on this day, lots were cast to determine which goat would be for "the LORD" and which goat would be the "Azazel" or scapegoat. The lot consisted of a white and a black stone. The priest would reach for a stone to make his determination. For two hundred years the results were random. But from 30 AD until the destruction in 70 AD, every year the black stone, the stone for the "Azazel" goat, was chosen. (The odds of that happening are 2 to the 40th power or just over one trillion to one. To look at it another way, if you placed one trillion dollar bills end to end, they would reach to our sun. Wow!)

Granted the above evidence is just circumstantial, but in conjunction with the biblical accounts and the testimony of Josephus, it demonstrates that 30–70 AD marked a very significant period in the history of the Second Temple.

The Great Escape

In the final years leading up to Jerusalem's destruction, those willing to heed Yeshua's warning of Jerusalem's impending demise were given an opportunity to escape. In Luke 21, Yeshua clarifies His earlier prophecy in Luke 13 concerning the desolation of Jerusalem:

> And when ye shall see Jerusalem compassed with armies, then know that the desolation thereof is nigh. Then let them which are in Judaea flee to the mountains; and let them which are in the midst of it depart out; and let not them that are in the countries enter thereinto. For these be the days of vengeance, that all things which are written may be fulfilled. But woe unto them that are with child, and to them that give suck, in those days! for there shall be great distress in the land, and wrath upon this people. And they shall fall by the edge of the sword, and shall be led away captive into all nations: and Jerusalem shall be trodden down of the Gentiles, until the times of the Gentiles be fulfilled. (Luke 21:20–24)

Over the years there has been much debate concerning the past or future fulfillment of Luke 21 and the similar passage in Matthew 24. Both chapters start out with warnings and admonitions to the apostles and new followers of Yeshua concerning the persecution that is coming to the early church. Then, as explained in Luke 21:20–24, the focus shifts to a brief description of what will befall Jerusalem and the Jewish people during what I will call "the desolation period."

For context's sake, keep in mind our earlier discussion of Luke 13 and Matthew 12, where Yeshua prophesied the desolation of Jerusalem, and how His sign of Jonah played into that prophecy. Now, in Luke 21, we find a further explanation of that prophesied desolation and the event that would tell them the time had come. That event, which He explicitly told His disciples to watch for, was Jerusalem surrounded by armies. He warned them to flee the city at that point and not return. Nearly forty years later, that is exactly what happened. In 66 AD the legate of Syria, Cestius Gallus, besieged Jerusalem in an attempt to put down the rebellion of the Jews in Judea, but unexpectedly he withdrew his army, thus giving those of the city an opportunity to heed Yeshua's warning and flee the city. But a few months later, in 67 AD, Vespasian and his son Titus returned with Roman armies to continue the siege. Those who did not take Yeshua's advice after Gallus's retreat lost their ability to do so. The following is Josephus's account of Cestius Gallus's unexpected withdrawal:

> Cestius . . . who, had he but continued the siege a little longer, would have certainly taken the city; but it was, I suppose, owing to the aversion God had already at the city and the sanctuary, that he was hindered from putting an end to the war that very day.

> It then happened that Cestius was not conscious either how the besieged despaired of success, nor how courageous the people were for him; and so he recalled his soldiers from the place, and, by despairing of any expectation of taking it, without having received any disgrace, he retired from the city, without any reason in the world. (*The Jewish War* 2:538–540)

Not many months later, anyone wanting to leave Jerusalem faced death from both sides in the conflict. The Jewish Zealots who controlled the city killed anyone trying to escape the terror inside, and the Romans who encircled the city would crucify anyone they caught who managed to elude the revolutionaries inside its walls.

The Wings of Desolation

This brings us back to the "wings of desolation." In a very unusual statement, Daniel 9:27 prophesies a specific event that would mark the start of Jerusalem's desolation. This trigger, if you will, is described as the "overspreading of abominations."

> *… and for the overspreading of abominations he shall make it desolate, even until the consummation*, and that determined shall be poured upon the desolate. (Daniel 9:27, emphasis mine)

All sorts of creative arguments have been made about the meaning of this unusual statement. The word "overspreading" comes from the Hebrew *kanaph,* and its primary meaning is simply "wing," as in the wing of a bird. Secondary meanings include "extremity," "edge," "winged," and "corner." The most natural reading of this passage would be "on the wings of abominations he shall make it desolate." We learned above that Yeshua prophesied the destruction of Jerusalem in 30 AD, and we know that YHWH used the armies of Titus, the "people of the prince," to accomplish this prophecy in 70 AD.

So what are the "wings of abomination"? Taken in its most natural context, there is only one event that fits this description perfectly—an event that every Jewish person still living in Jerusalem in 70 AD would have been able to witness. The Jewish historian Josephus gives a firsthand account of what happened. Please note the first passage is provided to clarify the context of the second. The quoted passages below are not taken from the same account.

> Then came the ensigns surrounding the eagle, which is at the head of every Roman legion, the king, and the strongest of all birds, which seems to them a signal of dominion, and an omen that they shall conquer all against whom they march; these sacred ensigns are followed by the trumpeters. (*The Jewish War* 3:123–124)

> And now the Romans, upon the flight of the seditious into the city, and upon the burning of the holy house itself, and of all the buildings around it, brought their ensigns to the temple and set them opposite its eastern gate; and there did they offer

> sacrifices to them, and there did they make Titus imperator, with the greatest acclamations of joy . . .
>
> So the Romans being now become masters of the walls, they both placed their ensigns upon the towers, and made joyful acclamations for the victory they had gained. (*The Jewish War* 6:316, 6:403)

In events reminiscent of Antiochus's abomination in the temple nearly two hundred years earlier, the armies of Titus planted their Roman eagle (which typically was surrounded by images of Caesar) on the temple mount and offered sacrifices to their gods. This infamous day marked the last time the Second Temple was seen by the Jewish people. From that point until today, nearly two thousand years have passed without a temple or sacrificial service in Jerusalem.

But Daniel 9:27 has more to say about this desolation. There is hope.

> . . . and in the midst of the week he shall cause the sacrifice and the oblation to cease, and for the overspreading [wings] of abominations he shall make it desolate, *even until the consummation, and that determined shall be poured upon the desolate.* (Daniel 9:27, emphasis mine)

Historicists who believe Daniel 9:27 has been fulfilled and the Jewish people have been replaced by the New Testament church often ignore the final part of Daniel 9:27. The text does not leave the destruction of Jerusalem open-ended. There is a limit to the desolations. In the KJV, the verse describes a period of time during which that "determined shall be poured upon the desolate." You see, while the primary focus of Daniel 9 is the covenant of the promised seed and mankind's reconciliation to YHWH, the covenant with Abraham also included an eternal promise to Abraham's descendants that they would inherit the land of Israel and would always be a special people in YHWH's eyes. After nearly two thousand years, it is both sobering and exciting to see the unfulfilled prophecies concerning the Jewish people and their inheritance in the land of Israel begin to be fulfilled once more.

> But this shall be the covenant that I will make with the house of Israel; After those days, saith YHWH, I will put my law in their inward parts, and write it in their hearts; and will be their God, and they shall be my people. And they shall teach no more every man his neighbour, and every man his brother, saying, Know YHWH: for they shall all know me, from the least of them unto the greatest of them, saith YHWH: for I will forgive their iniquity, and I will remember their sin no more. Thus saith YHWH, which giveth the sun for a light by day, and the ordinances of the moon and of the stars for a light by night, which divideth the sea when the waves thereof roar; YHWH of hosts is his name:
>
> If those ordinances depart from before me, saith YHWH, then the seed of Israel also shall cease from being a nation before me for ever. (Jeremiah 31:33–36)

It is tragically ironic that the very paradigm by which YHWH included the Gentiles into the family of God is used by some of those Gentiles who have most benefited from it to claim that YHWH's chosen people no longer have any role to play in His prophetic plan for mankind.

Yes, Daniel 9 was primarily fulfilled in the Messiah. But the desolation prophesied upon the children of Israel is limited to a specific period of time determined by YHWH. New Testament authors call this period of time, which has lasted over the last two thousand years, the "fullness of the Gentiles" or the "times of the Gentiles," and its official starting point is marked with the destruction of Jerusalem and the temple. As I will show you in the next chapter, the 70th shabuwa and the call of the apostle Paul was an important transitive period leading up to the desolations of Jerusalem. It was during this time that Gentiles in increasing numbers were added to the family of YHWH. Yet, during this period, YHWH never lost sight of His plan for His people Israel.

I think it only appropriate to end this chapter with the apostle Paul's thoughts on why YHWH has not cast away the children of Israel:

> I say then, Hath God cast away his people? God forbid. For I also am an Israelite, of the seed of Abraham, of the tribe of Benjamin. God hath not cast away his people which he foreknew . . . Even so then at this present time also there is a remnant according to the election of grace . . . I say then, Have they stumbled that they should fall? God forbid: but rather

through their fall salvation is come unto the Gentiles, for to provoke them to jealousy. Now if the fall of them be the riches of the world, and the diminishing of them the riches of the Gentiles; how much more their fulness? . . .

For I would not, brethren, that ye should be ignorant of this mystery, lest ye should be wise in your own conceits; that blindness in part is happened to Israel, until the fulness of the Gentiles be come in. And so all Israel shall be saved: as it is written, There shall come out of Sion the Deliverer, and shall turn away ungodliness from Jacob: For this is my covenant unto them, when I shall take away their sins. (Romans 11:1–27, excerpted for brevity's sake)

Chapter 13:

The 70ᵗʰ Shabuwa and the Times of the Gentiles

"And the Lord said unto him, Arise, and go into the street which is called Straight, and enquire in the house of Judas for one called Saul, of Tarsus . . . But the Lord said unto him, Go thy way: for he is a chosen vessel unto me, to bear my name before the Gentiles, and kings, and the children of Israel . . . Then was Saul certain days with the disciples which were at Damascus. And straightway he preached Christ in the synagogues, that he is the Son of God."
Acts 9:11–20

Sometime between the years 31–36 AD, one of the foremost enemies of the early church personally encountered Yeshua. Saul's conversion on the road to Damascus made him the last recorded apostle personally called by Yeshua, and it was a defining moment for YHWH's plan to reconcile all mankind through the Messiah.

For those who appreciate a little additional symbolism, this event marked the apostle Paul as the 13ᵗʰ apostle personally called by Yeshua—linking him to the Messiah factors and Daniel 9 in an even more personal way. Before Yeshua's death and resurrection there were only the 12, making a total of 13 with Yeshua; after the resurrection, Yeshua personally called Paul, who became the 13ᵗʰ—making Yeshua the 14ᵗʰ. It was Paul who explained in Ephesians 2:13–14 that Yeshua broke down the middle wall of partition that had prevented the Gentiles from approaching the presence of YHWH. That famous obstacle, as we learned in Book I, was accessed by 14 steps and guarded by 13 gates, an obstacle that promised death to all Gentiles who attempted to approach the presence of YHWH. This wall was "broken down" by Yeshua, the 13th and 14th generation of Matthew 1. Here, in the underlying dynamics of Paul's apostolic calling, we once again find the Messiah factors of 13 and 14 and YHWH's plan of reconciliation for all mankind, both Jews and Gentiles.

> But now in Christ Jesus ye who sometimes were far off are made nigh by the blood of Christ. For he is our peace, who hath made both one [Jews and Gentiles], and hath broken down the middle wall of partition between us. (Ephesians 2:13–14)

Paul's inclusion as an eyewitness with personal, firsthand knowledge of Yeshua's death and resurrection should not be ignored in the context of Daniel 9. Notice that in Acts 9:11–20 above, it is stated that Paul preached that Yeshua was the "Son of God." In other words, after his personal encounter on the road to Damascus, Paul realized that indeed Yeshua was the Messiah promised in the Scriptures, and it was He who had come in fulfillment of the Old Testament prophecies. This, as we have already seen, is a consistent theme of Paul's later epistles. For a moment, let's journey back in time to the second year of Yeshua's ministry in 28–29 AD. This year marked the start of the 70th shabuwa, and we saw that it was highlighted by the transfiguration, when YHWH confirmed with Moses, Elijah, Peter, James, and John that Yeshua was indeed "the Son of God."

Fascinating, isn't it, that in this final shabuwa—in which Daniel 9:27 describes the Messiah as confirming a covenant with the many—we find YHWH's covenant confirmed at the start with Peter, James, and John at the transfiguration and at the end with Paul on the road to Damascus? Those 13 men personally called by Yeshua are the foundation upon which you and I today rely for our understanding of how Yeshua fulfilled the covenants and promises made with the fathers "since the world began." Indeed, it was during this final epoch of the 70 sevens that Yeshua confirmed, strengthened, and yes, even prevailed upon the covenant of the promised seed. This covenant, exemplified and then executed through the framework of the sacrificial system, showed a fallen creation the true nature of YHWH's love and our desperate need for that love.

> And there came a voice out of the cloud, saying, This is my beloved Son: hear him. (Luke 9:35)

> And he was seen many days of them which came up with him from Galilee to Jerusalem, who are his witnesses unto the people. And we declare unto you glad tidings, *How that the promise which was made unto the fathers, God hath fulfilled the same unto us their children, in that he hath raised up Jesus again*; as it is also written in the second psalm, Thou art my Son, this day have I begotten thee. (Acts 13:31–33)

During the early years of the church, the gospel message was shared primarily with the Jewish people and those Gentiles living among them. Toward the end of the 70th shabuwa, with Paul's conversion and commission to take the gospel message to the Gentiles, Gentiles were added to the faith in increasing numbers. Remember, Daniel 9:4 began with a prayer to YHWH to remember His "covenant and mercy" promised to the fathers. That covenant and mercy we traced to the covenant YHWH swore (*shaba*) with Abraham that in his seed all nations of the earth would be blessed. Here, in the 70th shabuwa, that ancient promise went into full effect.

Through the intervening years between the 70th shabuwa and the destruction of Jerusalem, the early church, made up of Jewish and an increasing number of Gentile believers, thrived under incredibly difficult conditions. Then, with the destruction of Jerusalem and the end of the temple service in 70 AD, the biblical period described as "the times of the Gentiles" came into full force. In fulfillment of Yeshua's words and the prophecy of Daniel 9:27, the time of desolation had come for Jerusalem. Over the coming years, Jerusalem was all but deserted, and the Jewish people were dispersed into the nations.

It must not be ignored, though, that the desolation of Jerusalem and the dispersion of the Jewish people was limited by Yeshua and the prophecy of 70 sevens. Daniel 9 makes it clear that this desolation would last only until that "determined" desolation period ended. Yeshua clarifies this period in Luke 21 by linking the period of desolation with the times of the Gentiles:

> . . . and Jerusalem shall be trodden down of the Gentiles, *until the times of the Gentiles be fulfilled.* (Luke 21:24b, emphasis mine)

After two thousand years, our generation has witnessed firsthand the beginning of the end of this period of the desolation of Jerusalem. For the first time in the millennia since Rome burned the city, the Jewish people control Jerusalem, and Jews from all over the world are returning to Israel in fulfillment of Old and New Testament prophecies. Clearly a transition is afoot. The times of the Gentiles are winding down, and YHWH's prophetic plan is once more focusing on the Jewish people and Jerusalem.

For those who might still doubt the relevance of the Jewish people and Jerusalem to YHWH's prophetic plan for mankind's redemption and restoration, in Book III of this series, *The Jubilee Code: Prophetic Milestones in the Bible,* I will provide reasonable chronological proof to confirm YHWH's guiding hand in history and demonstrate how it leads us to a startling understanding of today. You'll be thrilled to see that YHWH's covenantal promise has worked its way through the biblical ages in a discernable pattern and that the pivotal milestones in His grand redemptive plan have been marked out chronologically in a very special way. I think you will be astounded to learn that once again, the mysterious list of Yeshua's generations in Matthew 1 plays a central role in symbolically illustrating this redemptive plan as it relates to the Jewish people, the Gentile nations, and the chronology of the Bible.

As we finish up our look at the great prophecy of 70 sevens, keep in mind that Daniel 9 is but a messianic keystone that connects one biblical covenant age to another, and by so doing, once and for all proves that Yeshua is the Messiah promised in the Scriptures—and that for those looking for Him, He most definitely is coming again.

The Desolation of Jerusalem and the 70th Shabuwa

In the previous pages, we have explored an interpretation of Daniel 9 that sees the goal of "making sacrifice and oblation to cease" fulfilled symbolically during the 70th shabuwa, according to the spirit of the law, with Yeshua's death and resurrection as the event that marked the end of the sacrificial system in the eyes of YHWH. I realize that for some, a more "letter of the law" fulfillment is needed to satisfy the requirements of the prophecy. If that is you, let me offer you another way of looking at the 70th shabuwa. Please understand that I offer this merely as a possibility which may need further revision.

When we looked at Yeshua's "sign of Jonah" and its relationship to the destruction of Jerusalem, I noted that Yeshua's prophecy took the original sign of Jonah and increased it by one magnitude. In reality, the inhabitants of Jerusalem were given not just forty days but forty years to repent.

In like manner, when we looked at Daniel 9:25 and the prediction that the Messiah would come after one shabuwa, we saw there too that the text indicated, in a most clever way, a one-magnitude-larger fulfillment. Is it possible that here in Daniel 9:27 we have a similar fulfillment of the prophecy? I'll let you decide. Here is a chart with the math.

Biblical "time" & the Messiah Factors

Lunar month	29.53 days
Solar year	365.24 days

13 lunar cycle "year"	383.89 days	(13 x 29.53)
14 lunar cycle "year"	413.42 days	(14 x 29.53)

1 Seven x 13 cycles	7.35 solar years	(7 x 13 x 29.53 / 365.24)
1 Seven x 14 cycles	7.92 solar years	(7 x 14 x 29.53 / 365.24)
1 Seven x 15 cycles	8.49 solar years	(7 x 15 x 29.53 / 365.24)

1 Magnitude Larger Fulfillment (x 10)

1 Seven x 13 cycles	73.57 solar years	(70 x 13 x 29.53 / 365.24)
1 Seven x 14 cycles	79.23 solar years	(70 x 14 x 29.53 / 365.24)
1 Seven x 15 cycles	84.89 solar years	(70 x 15 x 29.53 / 365.24)

In the chart above, I've given examples for a 13-, 14-, and 15-lunar-cycle "year" using a one-magnitude-larger fulfillment of the final 7 sevens of Daniel 9. For our present purposes I'll use a 14-cycle year. Using the chart above, a final 7 shabuwa increased by one magnitude goes from 7.9 years to 79.23 years in length. This period then spans the time from the end of the 69th shabuwa in the fall of 28 AD until approximately the winter of 107 AD. The "midst" of this week would be 39.61 years and span the period from the fall of 28 AD until the spring of 67 AD, about the time Rome's armies returned to continue the siege of Jerusalem. A little over three years later the temple was burned and the sacrificial service ended. If there is any merit to this way of looking at the final shabuwa, this would fulfill the physical reality of Daniel 9:27 with the end of the sacrifice and oblation in the "midst" of the 70th shabuwa.

The Final Eyewitness

If the final shabuwa should be stretched to the year 107 AD, you might be wondering what that does to the rest of the prophecy. How does it work with the view that Yeshua strengthened the covenant with the many during the final shabuwa? As I demonstrated in chapter 11, a shorter version of the 70th shabuwa began in the year YHWH confirmed with Moses, Elijah, Peter, James, and John that Yeshua was the Messiah, the Son of God. That shorter shabuwa ended with Paul's conversion. Paul was the last apostle personally called by Yeshua and the one apostle specifically charged with taking the gospel message to the Gentiles.

Personally, I think it awesome to consider the implications if the final shabuwa was *also* meant to be seen in a one-magnitude-larger fulfillment, because this takes us to the start of the second century—the time that traditionally marks the death of the apostle John, the last living eyewitness personally called by Yeshua. This was the very same John who was there at the start of the final shabuwa and the apostle who gave us the final words of Yeshua concerning the consummation of this age and the second coming in the book of Revelation. Thus, Yeshua's strengthening of the covenant with the many ends with the death of John, the last living eyewitness personally called by Yeshua, and in a sense with the end of the New Testament writings. Some of the key events are outlined in the chart below.

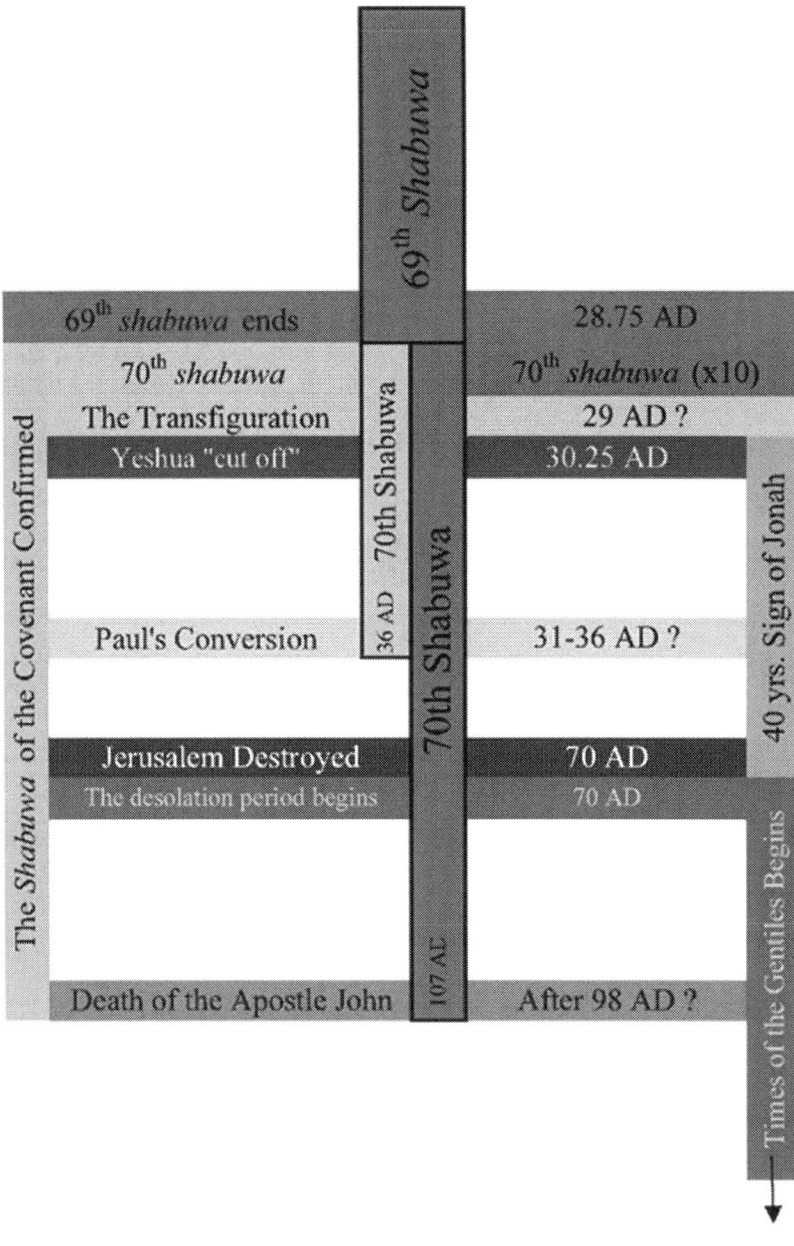

With the conversion of the apostle Paul and the death of John, we can see that the 70th shabuwa marked two pivotal events in YHWH's plan to reconcile all mankind to himself. From that final shabuwa until today, Paul's epistles and John's Revelation are the biblical writings that have most defined for us the nearly two thousand intervening years since the Messiah's first coming. That's the power of the 70th shabuwa!

Chapter 14:

Daniel 9 and the Messiah's Purpose

"Seventy weeks are determined upon thy people and upon thy holy city, to finish the transgression, and to make an end of sins, and to make reconciliation for iniquity, and to bring in everlasting righteousness, and to seal up the vision and prophecy, and to anoint the most Holy."

Daniel 9:24

For those who have made it this far, I have a question. After all the verses, charts, and explanations found in this book, what do *you* believe the prophecy of 70 shabuwa is really all about? Is Daniel 9 a prophecy about the death of the Messiah and the coming of the Anti-Messiah? Or is it a prophecy about the death of the Messiah and Israel's national restoration and redemption? After everything we've learned together, does either of those options completely satisfy the true spirit and depth of the prophecy of 70 shabuwa?

Lost in the Details

When exploring a subject as rich and complex as Daniel 9, it is really easy to lose our focus and get lost in the details. Both of the above options have one major failing: *both options take the focus off the Messiah and put it on someone else.* Daniel 9:24, at the very beginning of the prophecy, sets out six goals that only the Messiah could have accomplished. But those six goals must be understood within the larger context of Daniel's plea for YHWH to remember His "covenant and mercy" promised to Abraham and his seed. Too often the real beauty and purpose of the 70 sevens are lost when we narrow our focus without this context in mind.

> And I prayed unto YHWH my God, and made my confession, and said, O Lord, the great and dreadful God, keeping the *covenant and mercy* to them that love him, and to them that keep his commandments; we have sinned, and have committed iniquity, and have done wickedly, and have rebelled, even by departing from thy precepts and from thy judgments . . .
>
> And whiles I was speaking, and praying, and confessing my sin and the sin of my people Israel, and presenting my supplication before YHWH my God for the holy mountain of my God . . . (Daniel 9:4–5, 20)

You see, Israel was the people and Jerusalem the place whereby YHWH chose to demonstrate His incredible love for mankind. Because of Abraham's faith, YHWH chose the seed of Abraham to bring forth the Messiah. Daniel 9 is nothing more and nothing less than YHWH's ancient promise at work through the agency of the Jewish people.

Please don't jump to conclusions here. I am not saying or implying that the Jewish people were just a useful tool whom YHWH used to bring forth the Messiah and then discarded to make room for the New Testament church. Nothing could be further from the truth.

As I've said before, YHWH keeps His promises. To believe anything less undermines the very foundation of our faith. So while I believe that Jews and Gentiles become one spiritual family in the Messiah, I also believe the Bible is clear that the Jewish people, as the physical descendants of Abraham, have a distinctive and important role to play in YHWH's eternal plan for mankind, one that continues even to our own day.

But let's turn back to Daniel 9. This prophecy is not about Israel's national restoration, though it hints at it. It is about Israel's and mankind's reconciliation to God through the promised seed by which all nations of the earth were to be blessed.

> Christ hath redeemed us from the curse of the law, being made a curse for us: for it is written, Cursed is every one that hangeth on a tree: that the blessing of Abraham might come on the Gentiles through Jesus Christ; that we might receive the promise of the Spirit through faith. Brethren, I speak after the manner of men; though it be but a man's covenant, yet if it be confirmed, no man disannulleth, or addeth thereto.
>
> *Now to Abraham and his seed were the promises made. He saith not, And to seeds, as of many; but as of one, And to thy seed, which is Christ.*
>
> And this I say, that the covenant, that was confirmed before of God in Christ, the law, which was four hundred and thirty years after, cannot disannul, that it should make the promise of none effect. (Galatians 3:13–17, emphasis mine)

> Wherefore remember, that ye being in time past Gentiles in the flesh . . . that at that time ye were without Christ, being aliens from the commonwealth of Israel, and strangers from the *covenants of promise,* having no hope, and without God in the world:
>
> [13] *But now in Christ Jesus ye who sometimes were far off are made nigh by the blood of Christ.* [14] *For he is our peace, who hath made both one, and hath broken down the middle wall of partition between us;*
>
> Having abolished in his flesh the enmity, even the law of commandments contained in ordinances; for to make in himself of twain one new man, so making peace; and that he might reconcile both unto God in one body by the cross, having slain the enmity thereby: and came and preached peace to you which were afar off, and to them that were nigh. *For through him we both have access by one Spirit unto the Father.* (Ephesians 2:11–18, emphasis mine)

The testimony of both the Old and the New Testaments shows that the essence of Daniel 9 was YHWH's plan to reconcile all mankind through the promised seed. That covenantal promise was worked out through the ages and brought to fulfillment through the framework of the sacrificial law given to Israel by YHWH. In its initial form, the sacrificial service showed that animal sacrifices brought only temporary righteousness in the eyes of YHWH. It was through the promised seed of Abraham that Daniel's people brought forth the Messiah, whose sacrifice of Himself brought the eternal righteousness all men have desperately needed since the fall in Eden. This we must never forget.

Many people question how the six goals of Daniel 9:24 could have been fulfilled in relation to the Jewish people and Jerusalem at the death and resurrection of Yeshua in 30 AD. My question is, how could we have narrowed our focus so much that we cannot understand how those six goals of Daniel 9:24 were fulfilled in the Messiah?

By taking the six goals of Daniel 9:24 out of their messianic, sacrificial, redemptive context, we have unhinged them from their purpose and emptied them of their power. I find it disconcerting that many of my own futurist brethren believe that the events written about in the final shabuwa, that 70th week of Daniel 9, relate specifically to the Jewish people left behind during the Great Tribulation—yet that very premise leaves the Jewish people, in regards to Daniel 9, with a dead Messiah and a living Antichrist. Think about the implications. By removing the six goals of the 70 shabuwa from their sacrificial context in the Messiah's death and resurrection, we have cut out the very heart of the prophecy's redemptive message.

A Poor Trade-Off

What we've really done as futurists is taken the single most important biblical prophetic proof text for the Messiah's identity and redemptive purpose and weakened it so that we might use it to buttress a biblical truth about the Jewish people's restoration—a truth which already stands secure in its own right. In so doing, we've weakened both arguments. Daniel 9 without the redemptive message of the cross simply testifies to the Messiah's death. The Jewish people's status at the end of this age, and indeed their very inheritance in the land of Israel, depends on their acceptance of the biblical truth that Yeshua finished the transgression, made an end of sins, made reconciliation, and brought in everlasting righteousness nearly two thousand years ago. As Paul explains below, there is no hope in the death of the Messiah. It is the resurrection of Yeshua that brought the end of sins and the hope of mankind's eternal redemption. Daniel 9 without the resurrection means the Jewish people and indeed all of mankind are without hope and still in their sins.

> And if Christ be not risen, then is our preaching vain, and your faith is also vain. Yea, and we are found false witnesses of God; because we have testified of God that he raised up Christ: whom he raised not up, if so be that the dead rise not. For if the dead rise not, then is not Christ raised:
>
> *And if Christ be not raised, your faith is vain; ye are yet in your sins. Then they also which are fallen asleep in Christ are perished. If in this life only we have hope in Christ, we are of all men most miserable.*
>
> But now is Christ risen from the dead, and become the firstfruits of them that slept. For since by man came death, by man came also the resurrection of the dead. For as in Adam all die, even so in Christ shall all be made alive. But every man in his own order: Christ the firstfruits; afterward they that are Christ's at his coming. (1 Corinthians 15:14–23, emphasis mine)

O Jerusalem, Jerusalem, thou that killest the prophets, and stonest them which are sent unto thee, how often would I have gathered thy children together, even as a hen gathereth her chickens under her wings, and ye would not! Behold, your house is left unto you desolate. For I say unto you, *Ye shall not see me henceforth, till ye shall say, Blessed is he that cometh in the name of the Lord.* (Matthew 23:37–39 emphasis mine)

A Risen Redeemer

Instead of looking at Daniel 9 with eyes that only see the Messiah's death in Daniel 9:26, let's look at Daniel 9 with the hope of a risen Redeemer. With these new eyes, let's look at the six goals of Daniel 9:24, but this time within the context of the sacrificial law that Daniel's people were required to follow and the sacrificial system that saw its fulfillment in the Messiah.

70 Sevens will...

- Finish the Transgression
- Make an End of Sins
- Make Reconciliation for Iniquity
- Bring in Everlasting Righteousness
- Seal up the Vision & Prophecy
- Anoint the Most Holy

490

1. Finish the Transgression

Transgressions and the necessity for their atonement must be seen within the context of the sacrificial law given to Israel. There are numerous passages in the Bible that illustrate this, and in a moment we will look at two: one from the Old Testament looking forward and one from the New Testament looking back. Both of these passages show that transgressions in the eyes of YHWH are covered once and for all by the blood of Yeshua. All transgressions, whether Jew or Gentile, were atoned for in 30 AD.

> But he was wounded for our transgressions, he was bruised for our iniquities: the chastisement of our peace was upon him; and with his stripes we are healed . . . for he was cut off out of the land of the living: for the transgression of my people was he stricken . . .
>
> Yet it pleased YHWH to bruise him; he hath put him to grief: when thou shalt make his soul an offering for sin, he shall see his seed, he shall prolong his days, and the pleasure of YHWH shall prosper in his hand. He shall see of the travail of his soul, and shall be satisfied: by his knowledge shall my righteous servant justify many; for he shall bear their iniquities.
>
> Therefore will I divide him a portion with the great, and he shall divide the spoil with the strong; because he hath poured out his soul unto death: and he was numbered with the transgressors; and he bare the sin of many, and made intercession for the transgressors. (Isaiah 53:5–12, emphasis mine)

> But Christ being come an high priest of good things to come, by a greater and more perfect tabernacle, not made with hands, that is to say, not of this building; neither by the blood of goats and calves, but by his own blood he entered in once into the holy place, *having obtained eternal redemption for us.*

> For if the blood of bulls and of goats, and the ashes of a heifer sprinkling the unclean, sanctifieth to the purifying of the flesh: How much more shall the blood of Christ, who through the eternal Spirit offered himself without spot to God, purge your conscience from dead works to serve the living God? And for this cause he is the mediator of the new testament [covenant], *that by means of death, for the redemption of the transgressions that were under the first testament* [covenant], they which are called might receive the promise of eternal inheritance. (Hebrews 9:11–15, emphasis mine)

In the passage above, you can see that the prophet Isaiah looked forward to the cross for Israel's messianic redemption and reconciliation. In Hebrews 9 above, the author looks back toward the cross for the same. Both show that eternal redemption for transgressions under the law was accomplished at the cross.

2. Make an End of Sins

Did Yeshua's death and resurrection "make an end of sins" for Daniel's people in the context of the law and the sacrificial system? If this goal was not accomplished at the Messiah's first coming, how will Yeshua's second coming better accomplish it? If making an end of sins only applies to Daniel's people in the end of time, as many futurists would have it, in what way does salvation differ for Daniel's people than for the rest of humanity living at the time of the second coming? Note especially Isaiah 44:21–22 below, where the Scripture testifies that Israel's sins and transgressions were blotted out *before* the people returned unto YHWH. The redemptive price has already been paid.

> And she shall bring forth a son, and thou shalt call his name JESUS: for he shall save his people from their sins. (Matthew 1:21)

> For then must he often have suffered since the foundation of the world: but now once in the end of the world hath he appeared to put away sin by the sacrifice of himself. (Hebrews 9:26)

> Remember these, O Jacob and Israel; for thou art my servant: I have formed thee; thou art my servant: O Israel, thou shalt not be forgotten of me. I have blotted out, as a thick cloud, thy transgressions, and, as a cloud, thy sins: return unto me; for I have redeemed thee. (Isaiah 44:21–22)

> And they shall teach no more every man his neighbour, and every man his brother, saying, Know YHWH: for they shall all know me, from the least of them unto the greatest of them, saith YHWH: for I will forgive their iniquity, and I will remember their sin no more. (Jeremiah 31:34)

> For this is the covenant that I will make with the house of Israel after those days, saith the Lord; I will put my laws into their mind, and write them in their hearts: and I will be to them a

God, and they shall be to me a people: and they shall not teach every man his neighbour, and every man his brother, saying, Know the Lord: for all shall know me, from the least to the greatest. For I will be merciful to their unrighteousness, and their sins and their iniquities will I remember no more. (Hebrews 8:10–12)

And for this cause he is the mediator of the new testament, that by means of death, for the redemption of the transgressions that were under the first testament, they which are called might receive the promise of eternal inheritance. (Hebrews 9:15)

Who is a God like unto thee, that pardoneth iniquity, and passeth by the transgression of the remnant of his heritage? he retaineth not his anger for ever, because he delighteth in mercy. He will turn again, he will have compassion upon us; he will subdue our iniquities; and thou wilt cast all their sins into the depths of the sea. Thou wilt perform the truth to Jacob, *and the mercy to Abraham, which thou hast sworn unto our fathers from the days of old.* (Micah 7:18–20, emphasis mine)

3. Make Reconciliation for Iniquity

In the context of the law and the sacrificial system under which the Jewish people were obligated, did Yeshua make "reconciliation for iniquity" in 30 AD at His first coming, or will Daniel's people of the past, present, and future have to wait until the second coming for this promise to take effect?

If, as many of my futurist brethren believe, this reconciliation for iniquity does not take full effect for the Jewish people until the second coming, this creates a problem when considering how this "reconciliation for iniquity" applies to the Gentiles. If the reconciliation is given to the "Jew first," then when does "reconciliation for iniquity" for the Gentiles take place?

> He shall see of the travail of his soul, and shall be satisfied: by his knowledge shall my righteous servant justify many; for he shall bear their iniquities. (Isaiah 53:11)

> Wherefore in all things it behoved him to be made like unto his brethren, that he might be a merciful and faithful high priest in things pertaining to God, to make reconciliation for the sins of the people. (Hebrews 2:17)

> For if, when we were enemies, we were reconciled to God by the death of his Son, much more, being reconciled, we shall be saved by his life. (Romans 5:10)

> And all things are of God, who hath reconciled us to himself by Jesus Christ, and hath given to us the ministry of reconciliation; to wit, that God was in Christ, reconciling the world unto himself, not imputing their trespasses unto them; and hath committed unto us the word of reconciliation. (2 Corinthians 5:18–19)

> Having abolished in his flesh the enmity, even the law of commandments contained in ordinances; for to make in himself of twain one new man, so making peace; and that he might reconcile both unto God in one body by the cross, having slain the enmity thereby. (Ephesians 2:15–16)

> And, having made peace through the blood of his cross, by him to reconcile all things unto himself; by him, I say, whether they be things in earth, or things in heaven. (Colossians 1:20)

4. Bring in Everlasting Righteousness

In the context of the law and the sacrificial system to which the Jewish people were obligated, "righteousness" before YHWH required endless sacrifices. In 30 AD Yeshua's death and resurrection brought in everlasting righteousness in YHWH's sight to all who believe. Given that this is already a reality, if everlasting righteousness was not accomplished by Yeshua at His first coming, how could it possibly be better accomplished at His second?

> Whom God hath set forth to be a propitiation through faith in his blood, to declare his righteousness for the remission of sins that are past, through the forbearance of God; to declare, I say, at this time his righteousness: that he might be just, and the justifier of him which believeth in Jesus. (Romans 3:25–26)

> For Christ is the *end of the law for righteousness* to every one that believeth. For Moses describeth the righteousness which is

of the law, That the man which doeth those things shall live by them. (Romans 10:4–5, emphasis mine)

I do not frustrate the grace of God: for if righteousness come by the law, then Christ is dead in vain. (Galatians 2:21)

Is the law then against the promises of God? God forbid: for if there had been a law given which could have given life, verily righteousness should have been by the law. But the scripture hath concluded all under sin, that the promise by faith of Jesus Christ might be given to them that believe. (Galatians 3:21–22)

That as sin hath reigned unto death, even so might grace reign through righteousness unto eternal life by Jesus Christ our Lord. (Romans 5:21)

5. Seal Up the Vision and Prophecy

The prophecy of 70 shabuwa is a testimony to the Messiah's fulfillment of the ancient covenant and mercy promised to the fathers. In each biblical age, that covenant has been confirmed or sealed in blood. YHWH in Eden sacrificed an animal to clothe Adam and Eve after their sin. Centuries later, YHWH confirmed His covenant with Abraham by providing "Himself" a sacrifice instead of requiring Abraham to sacrifice Isaac. Moses confirmed the covenant of YHWH with Israel by sealing that covenant with the blood of a sacrifice. Finally, Yeshua with His own blood sealed, strengthened, and brought to completion YHWH's covenant to reconcile all mankind through the promised seed.

It's also worth considering here that a final shabuwa of one-magnitude-larger fulfillment stretches all the way to the time of the apostle John's prophetic revelation given to him by Yeshua. This record, which we call the book of Revelation, is the last recorded prophecy in the New Testament covenant Scriptures, and this book seals up or completes YHWH's written revelation to mankind. The 70 shabuwa spans biblical history from the point when the Messiah became flesh until He gave His final prophetic revelation to the apostle John. Indeed, the 70 shabuwa do seal up the Bible's prophetic record!

> And for this cause he is the mediator of the new testament, that by means of death, for the redemption of the transgressions that were under the first testament, they which are called might receive the promise of eternal inheritance.
>
> For where a testament is, there must also of necessity be the death of the testator. For a testament is of force after men are dead: otherwise it is of no strength at all while the testator liveth. *Whereupon neither the first testament was dedicated without blood.*
>
> For when Moses had spoken every precept to all the people according to the law, he took the blood of calves and of goats, with water, and scarlet wool, and hyssop, and sprinkled both the book, and all the people, Saying, *This is the blood of the testament* [covenant] which God hath enjoined unto you. (Hebrews 9:15–20, emphasis mine)

And Moses took half of the blood, and put it in basons; and half of the blood he sprinkled on the altar. And he took the book of the covenant, and read in the audience of the people: and they said, All that YHWH hath said will we do, and be obedient. And Moses took the blood, and sprinkled it on the people, and said, Behold the blood of the covenant, which YHWH hath made with you concerning all these words. (Exodus 24:6–8)

And he said unto them, These are the words which I spake unto you, while I was yet with you, that all things must be fulfilled, which were written in the law of Moses, and in the prophets, and in the psalms, concerning me. Then opened he their understanding, that they might understand the scriptures. (Luke 24:44–45)

Jesus answered them and said, Verily, verily, I say unto you, Ye seek me, not because ye saw the miracles, but because ye did eat of the loaves, and were filled. Labour not for the meat which perisheth, but for that meat which endureth unto everlasting life, which the Son of man shall give unto you: for him hath God the Father sealed. (John 6:26–27)

For now thou numberest my steps: dost thou not watch over my sin? My transgression is *sealed up* in a bag, and thou sewest up mine iniquity. (Job 14:16–17, emphasis mine)

6. Anoint the Most Holy

There is only one thing "anoint the Most Holy" could mean if the text is taken in its most natural context: of the Messiah and reconciliation being made for Daniel's people. I must admit I struggle with the length to which my futurist brethren go to apply this to anything but what the Scripture records. For your own knowledge and understanding, please don't skip over the Scripture below. It is worth every second of your time to see how the New Testament explains Yeshua's anointing of the Most Holy.

> And not only so, but we also joy in God through our Lord Jesus Christ, by whom we have now received the atonement. (Romans 5:11)

> But Aaron and his sons offered upon the altar of the burnt offering, and on the altar of incense, and were appointed for all the work of the place most holy, and to make an atonement for Israel, according to all that Moses the servant of God had commanded. (1 Chronicles 6:49)

> For he testifieth, Thou art a priest for ever after the order of Melchisedec. For there is verily a disannulling of the commandment going before for the weakness and unprofitableness thereof. For the law made nothing perfect, but the bringing in of a better hope did; by the which we draw nigh unto God . . .

By so much was Jesus made a surety of a better testament [covenant] . . . But this man, because he continueth ever, hath an unchangeable priesthood. Wherefore he is able also to save them to the uttermost that come unto God by him, seeing he ever liveth to make intercession for them . . . who needeth not daily, as those high priests, to offer up sacrifice, first for his own sins, and then for the people's: *for this he did once, when he offered up himself* . . .

Now of the things which we have spoken this is the sum: *We have such an high priest, who is set on the right hand of the throne of the Majesty in the heavens; a minister of the sanctuary, and of the true tabernacle, which the Lord pitched, and not man* . . .

But now hath he obtained a more excellent ministry, by how much also he is the mediator of a better covenant, which was established upon better promises. For if that first covenant had been faultless, then should no place have been sought for the second. For finding fault with them, he saith, Behold, the days come, saith the Lord, when I will make a new covenant with the house of Israel and with the house of Judah . . .

For this is the covenant that I will make with the house of Israel after those days, saith the Lord; I will put my laws into their mind, and write them in their hearts: and I will be to them a God, and they shall be to me a people: and they shall not teach every man his neighbour, and every man his brother, saying, Know the Lord: for all shall know me, from the least to the greatest. For I will be merciful to their unrighteousness, and their sins and their iniquities will I remember no more. In that he saith, A new covenant, he hath made the first old. Now that which decayeth and waxeth old is ready to vanish away. (Hebrews 7:17–8:13, emphasis mine)

For when Moses had spoken every precept to all the people according to the law, he took the blood of calves and of goats, with water, and scarlet wool, and hyssop, and sprinkled both the book, and all the people, Saying, This is the blood of the testament [covenant] which God hath enjoined unto you. Moreover he sprinkled with blood both the tabernacle, and all the vessels of the ministry. And almost all things are by the law purged with blood; and without shedding of blood is no remission . . .

It was therefore necessary that the patterns of things in the heavens should be purified with these; but the heavenly things themselves with better sacrifices than these. For Christ is not entered into the holy places made with hands, which are the figures of the true; but into heaven itself, now to appear in the presence of God for us:

Nor yet that he should offer himself often, as the high priest entereth into the holy place every year with blood of others; for then must he often have suffered since the foundation of the world: but now once in the end of the world hath he appeared to put away sin by the sacrifice of himself.

And as it is appointed unto men once to die, but after this the judgment: so Christ was once offered to bear the sins of many; and unto them that look for him shall he appear the second time without sin unto salvation. (Hebrews 9:19–28, emphasis mine)

A Final Question

Are there scriptural grounds to consider any of the above six goals of Daniel 9:24 to be fulfilled in Yeshua's death and resurrection in 30 AD? If your answer is yes to any of the above or any *part* of the above, then by the constraints of Daniel 9:24 and 26, the fulfillment must have taken place during the 70th shabuwa. Daniel 9:24 limits the above six goals to the period of 70 shabuwa. Daniel 9:26 tells us that Yeshua the Messiah was "cut off" after the 69th shabuwa. This means that the 70th shabuwa is the only period of time left for those six goals to be accomplished.

Think about the implications: either those six goals were accomplished by Yeshua at His death and resurrection, or we are left with a prophecy that tells us only of His death, leaves us without any hope of His resurrection, and adding further confusion, demands we look away from the Messiah and to a future Antichrist as the fulfillment of the final shabuwa. Do you really think that is how YHWH intended the prophecy of 70 shabuwa to be remembered?

For those of you who hold that none of the above goals will be accomplished until the second coming, I remind you of the words of Yeshua to His own brethren, words which remind us that Jerusalem's desolation will not end until His people acknowledge the truth of Isaiah 53 and Hebrews 9—truth which requires them to acknowledge that Yeshua did indeed finish the transgression, make an end of sins, make reconciliation for iniquity, and bring in everlasting righteousness, just as the prophecy of Daniel 9 foretold.

> *"O Jerusalem, Jerusalem, thou that killest the prophets, and stonest them which are sent unto thee, how often would I have gathered thy children together, even as a hen gathereth her chickens under her wings, and ye would not! Behold, your house is left unto you desolate. For I say unto you, Ye shall not see me henceforth, till ye shall say, Blessed is he that cometh in the name of the Lord."*
> Matthew 23:37–39

> *"I will go and return to my place, till they acknowledge their offence, and seek my face: in their affliction they will seek me early. Come, and let us return unto YHWH: for he hath torn, and he will heal us; he hath smitten, and he will bind us up. After two days will he revive us: in the third day he will raise us up, and we shall live in his sight. Then shall we know, if we follow on to know YHWH: his going forth is prepared as the morning; and he shall come unto us as the rain, as the latter and former rain unto the earth."*
> Hosea 5:15–6:3

Chapter 15:

Daniel 9: Keystone of the Covenants

"Remember the former things of old: for I am God, and there is none else; I am God, and there is none like me, declaring the end from the beginning, and from ancient times the things that are not yet done, saying, My counsel shall stand, and I will do all my pleasure."
Isaiah 46:9–10

YHWH, the living God of the Bible, loves you. From the very beginning of time He has had a plan to redeem each of us through the promised Messiah Yeshua. Daniel 9 and the prophecy of 70 shabuwa is just one of many biblical proofs of that love—but it is one of the most unique. One way to look at the prophecy of 70 shabuwa is as the keystone that holds together a doorway to YHWH's love. Supporting one side of that doorway is the Old Testament Torah and Prophets, which tell us of YHWH's covenant to redeem mankind through a coming Messiah. Supporting the other side of the doorway is the New Testament, which bears record that Yeshua was that promised Messiah. At the very center of this doorway is the keystone of Daniel 9 connecting both sides.

The Promised Seed

We started this book by looking at the covenant of the promised seed, and we traced that covenant through Adam, Noah,

Abraham, Isaac, Jacob, and David, and finally to its fulfillment in Yeshua, the "Salvation of YHWH." We learned in subsequent chapters that this covenant of the seed was what Daniel 9:4 refers to when Daniel reminded YHWH of the "covenant and mercy" He had promised to the fathers. Further, it is this covenant that is the underlying contextual theme of the prophecy of 70 shabuwa, a theme which finds its fulfillment in the coming of the promised Redeemer.

Looking back over the Bible's messianic symbolism, we saw that the lineage of Yeshua as given in Matthew 1 was no mere happenstance but a purposeful arrangement meant to emphasize the symbolic relationship between the sacrificial system, a biblical reckoning of time, the Messiah Yeshua, and the Bible's covenantal theme. That amazing list also drew our attention to the start of Daniel's captivity and to the numbers 13, 14, and 70. In hindsight, we now know this was also done with intent, because those very numbers and that symbolism are the key to Daniel 9, which proves the identity of the promised Messiah.

Do you realize the implications of Yeshua's fulfillment of the 70 shabuwa? YHWH in His infinite wisdom designed the very order of the heavenly cycles so that they would one day provide specific evidence that Yeshua was mankind's promised Redeemer. When YHWH gave Moses His unusual instructions concerning the sacrifices to be offered during the yearly feast days, He did it so that one day, a special generation would see them within the context of Daniel 9, and they would confirm that Yeshua was the Messiah promised in the Scriptures.

In light of Daniel 9, take another look at the messianic symbolism of 13 and 14 in the scriptural record. Ask yourself if the following could be just coincidence—or if it points instead to intentional design.

- The visible cycles of the moon wax and wane for 13 or 14 days each lunar cycle.
- Each of the biblical holy days has 13 or 14 sacrifices associated with it in some way.
- The list of Matthew 1 arranges Yeshua's lineage to show that He is both the 13th and 14th generation.
- The list of Matthew 1 arranges Yeshua's lineage to draw our attention to a single missing name between the 13th and 14th generations in the second column—a name which appropriately means "YHWH raises up."
- That missing name also reminds us of the start of the 70 years of Babylonian captivity and a young man named Daniel.
- The list of Matthew 1 sets out the missing names in such a way as to remind us of a similar countdown of sacrifices in the Feast of Tabernacles from 13 to 7, a countdown designed to equal 70 sacrifices.
- The burnt offering sacrifices for the first day of the Feast of Tabernacles are 13, 2, and 14 for a total of 29. The Bible's religious calendar is based upon the lunar cycle of two 13- or 14-day cycles of waxing and waning light within a full cycle of 29.53 days.

- The total burnt offering sacrifices during the Feast of Tabernacles are 182 (13 x 14).
- The priestly courses as defined in the Bible show that if Yeshua was born during the Feast of Tabernacles, He would have been born during the 13th or 14th priestly course.
- The biblical lunar/solar calendar is reconciled by a 13th month.
- The first epoch of Daniel 9, using a 13-lunar-cycle year times 7 shabuwa (plural masculine), equals the very year of Yeshua's conception/birth.
- The second epoch of Daniel 9, using a 14-lunar-cycle year times 7 + 62 shabuwa, takes us to the first year of the Messiah's ministry—thus confirming the New Testament chronology concerning Yeshua.
- The final epoch of Daniel 9, using a 14-lunar-cycle year, begins the same year as the transfiguration and ends about the time of Paul's apostolic calling.
- The final epoch of Daniel 9, using a 14-lunar-cycle year increased by one magnitude, encapsulates a period of time which begins with the transfiguration and ends at or near the time traditionally associated with the death of John, the last living eyewitness apostle of Yeshua. This was the same apostle who wrote the last recorded words of Yeshua in the book we call Revelation, a book that seals up or completes the Bible's prophetic record. In the midst of this larger shabuwa, the temple was destroyed and the sacrifices ceased, a condition which has remained to this day.

The sum of the matter is that Daniel 9 is the keystone of the prophetic record which testifies to a coming Redeemer. If the above evidence is not sufficient to give you a glimpse of YHWH's love for mankind, then I have failed in my efforts for this book. YHWH loves each of us so much that He became human flesh in the Messiah Yeshua so that He might reconcile us to Himself. My dear readers, Yeshua stands on the other side of that prophetic doorway knocking, hoping you'll open the door and believe what the Bible has to say about His love for you. Will you take that first step between the covenants and under the keystone of Daniel 9?

> Lift up your heads, O ye gates; even lift them up, ye everlasting doors; and the King of glory shall come in. Who is this King of glory? YHWH of hosts, he is the King of glory. Selah. (Psalm 24:9–10)

> Behold, I stand at the door, and knock: if any man hear my voice, and open the door, I will come in to him, and will sup with him, and he with me. (Revelation 3:20)

> For God so loved the world, that he gave his only begotten Son, that whosoever believeth in him should not perish, but have everlasting life. (John 3:16)

> But those things, which God before had shewed by the mouth of all his prophets, that Christ should suffer, he hath so fulfilled. Repent ye therefore, and be converted, that your sins

> may be blotted out, when the times of refreshing shall come from the presence of the Lord;
>
> And he shall send Jesus Christ, which before was preached unto you: whom the heaven must receive until the times of restitution of all things, which God hath spoken by the mouth of all his holy prophets since the world began. (Acts 3:18–21)

No Private Interpretation

Shortly before his death, the apostle Peter reminded his Jewish brethren in 2 Peter that his testimony of Yeshua was not a matter of "cunningly devised fables," but rather that he had seen firsthand YHWH's glory and heard His voice testify that Yeshua was His beloved son. Peter is referring to the transfiguration, an event which we learned earlier took place in the first year of the final shabuwa. In this context, Peter went on to explain that Old Testament prophecy should never be of "private interpretation," because its ultimate source is YHWH, the living God of the Bible, speaking through His servants. The prophecy of the Bible then must be interpreted and understood within a biblical context and rooted in biblical fact.

> Knowing that shortly I must put off this my tabernacle, even as our Lord Jesus Christ hath shewed me . . . For we have not followed cunningly devised fables, when we made known unto you the power and coming of our Lord Jesus Christ, but were eyewitnesses of his majesty.

> For he received from God the Father honour and glory, when there came such a voice to him from the excellent glory, This is my beloved Son, in whom I am well pleased. And this voice which came from heaven we heard, when we were with him in the holy mount.
>
> We have also a more sure word of prophecy; whereunto ye do well that ye take heed, as unto a light that shineth in a dark place, until the day dawn, and the day star arise in your hearts: knowing this first, that no prophecy of the scripture is of any private interpretation. For the prophecy came not in old time by the will of man: but holy men of God spake as they were moved by the Holy Ghost. (2 Peter 1:14–21)

It's really about stewardship. As believers, we have a profoundly awesome responsibility to handle the words of the YHWH with respect, humility, and integrity. When interpreting the prophetic record of the Bible this is especially true, because at their very core, the prophecies of the Bible are a testimony of Yeshua, the salvation of YHWH.

A good example of the kind of stewardship we should show regarding the prophetic record is found in the Jews of Berea. There, Paul preached that Yeshua was the Messiah, but the Bereans tested Paul's words by searching the Scriptures daily to see if what Paul told them was true. Keep in mind that back then there was no New Testament. The Bereans used the Torah and Prophets to verify whether Paul's words concerning Yeshua were true.

> And the brethren immediately sent away Paul and Silas by night unto Berea: who coming thither went into the synagogue of the Jews. These were more noble than those in Thessalonica, in that they received the word with all readiness of mind, and searched the scriptures daily, whether those things were so. (Acts 17:10–11)

Will You Be a Berean?

As you consider the prophecy of Daniel 9 in the coming days, I plead with you to search the Scriptures to see if these things be so. My hope is that you will use the biblical evidence I've provided in this book as a starting point, not an ending point. I encourage you to be a faithful steward of YHWH's words and make the effort to establish your understanding of Daniel 9 upon a solid biblical foundation. Don't take my word for it! Instead, search to see what the Bible says.

Here are a few questions that may help guide your own search:

1. Who gave the "word" to return and build Jerusalem of Daniel 9:25?
2. Are there any additional witnesses to this word?
3. What is the specific date of the word?
4. What does the Bible say about Ezra and Nehemiah's place in Second Temple chronology?
5. Who does the Bible define as the "Artaxerxes" of Ezra and Nehemiah?
6. What is a biblical definition of time?
7. Who is the Messiah of Daniel 9:25?

8. Who is the "he" of Daniel 9:26?
9. Is there reasonable biblical context for ending the messianic theme of Daniel 9 with the death of the Messiah and then turning the focus to the Anti-Messiah?
10. Is there reasonable biblical cause to ignore the messianic context of the "covenant" in Daniel 9:4 when interpreting the "covenant" of Daniel 9:27?

If we want to take the prophecy of 70 shabuwa out of the category of private interpretation, then it must be based upon real biblical evidence, not well-meaning traditions. My hope is that you will take this challenge to heart.

To the Historicists

To my historicist brethren, I admit that you were right, in part. Yes, Daniel 9 taken in its most natural and contextual sense shows that Yeshua fulfilled the six goals of Daniel 9:24 in the events surrounding His first coming. That being said, I see no justification to hold the Bible's unfulfilled prophecies concerning Yeshua's second coming and the Jewish people to a lesser biblical interpretational standard. By spiritualizing the remaining unfulfilled prophecies, your interpretation moves off solid contextual grounds into the realm of private interpretation. Sound biblical interpretive methods require a consistent standard. The prophecies of the Bible concerning Yeshua's first coming were fulfilled quite literally, and there is no sound biblical reason to believe that those which speak of His second coming should be interpreted any differently.

To the Futurists

To my futurist brethren, I say that in the few remaining years we have left before the Messiah Yeshua returns, we have a lot of serious work in front of us. Daniel 9, taken in its intended redemptive messianic context, was fulfilled in the death and resurrection of Yeshua. Our trading of the death and resurrection of the Messiah Yeshua for a yet-unfulfilled 70th week that centers around the Antichrist has influenced nearly every aspect of how we see the remaining unfulfilled prophecies of the Bible. As faithful stewards of the Word, we must now seriously consider an outline of end-time events that is independent of Daniel 9. I realize this will be challenging on many levels, but it must be done. The very credibility of futurist eschatology depends on it.

Prophetic Waypoints

Looking back over the prophetic record, it becomes obvious that YHWH loves mankind and has a plan to reconcile us to Himself. In this book we've looked at this plan in terms of His covenantal promise of the coming messianic seed. We've traced that covenant from Daniel 9:4 back to Moses, Abraham, and mankind's original sin in Eden. We've followed that covenant forward in Adam, Noah, Abraham, Isaac, Jacob, and David to its fulfillment in Yeshua, the "Salvation of YHWH," as is so beautifully described in Daniel 9 and the prophecy of 70 shabuwa.

But there is more. Daniel 9 has a specific place in an amazing master plan YHWH has for mankind. You see, YHWH is the author of order and purpose. It takes but a glance to see that truth reflected in every aspect of the created world around us. In the Bible, one of the most astounding ways that order and purpose is demonstrated is by looking at the Bible's internal chronology of events. Consider the words of Isaiah 46 below:

> Remember the former things of old: for I am God, and there is none else; I am God, and there is none like me, Declaring the end from the beginning, and from ancient times the things that are not yet done, saying, My counsel shall stand, and I will do all my pleasure. (Isaiah 46:9–10)

This passage makes it clear that YHWH has had a plan from the beginning, and parts of that plan are not yet done. As we have seen in this book, the overreaching theme of the Bible is YHWH's love for mankind and His desire to reconcile us to Himself. But here is what is fascinating to consider: YHWH's desire to reconcile mankind is based upon a plan He set in motion at creation when He ordered the cycles of the sun, earth, and moon. For thousands of years, these cycles and the Bible's prophetic calendar have proclaimed the coming of the Messiah. By its very nature, such a plan demonstrates order and purpose. By looking back over the major milestones in this redemptive plan, we should then be able to see that order and purpose reflected.

Prophetic Milestone

Throughout this book you've seen where I've highlighted several of the major prophetic milestones in YHWH's plan to redeem mankind. YHWH willing, in Book III, *The Jubilee Code: Prophetic Milestones in the Bible,* we will overlay these milestones on YHWH's redemptive plan and the Bible's own chronology. By showing these events relative to the Bible's overall chronological context, you will see the hand of YHWH at work in an amazing way. Let me give you just a glimpse.

41 Generations

By now you've probably realized the awesome prophetic implications of Yeshua's lineage in Matthew 1 as it relates to the Bible's messianic symbolism and the prophecy of Daniel 9. You'll be astounded to learn we have not yet plumbed the depths of this amazing list of names. Matthew 1, as written, gives us 41 names or generations between Abraham and Yeshua. Would it surprise you to learn that there are 41 Jubilee cycles between Abraham and Yeshua as well? What if I told you, using a straightforward contextual rendering of the Bible's chronological record, that there were also 41 Jubilee cycles between Adam and Abraham? I bet that got your attention!

Did you know that our generation, the generation that has seen the Jewish people return to the promised land after nearly two thousand years, is living in the 41st Jubilee cycle from Yeshua? Yes, you heard me correctly. Just as the lineage of Yeshua in Matthew 1 was separated into three chronological epochs, the Bible's own chronological record shows three chronological epochs when measured in Jubilee cycles.

Here are just a few of the many prophetic milestones we will place in the overall chronological context of the Bible in Book III, *The Jubilee Code: Prophetic Milestones in the Bible*. As you will see, each of these events shows evidence of YHWH's guiding hand in the history of mankind:

1. The creation of Adam
2. Enoch
3. The flood
4. The birth and call of Abraham
5. The birth of Isaac
6. The times of the Hebrew people relative to the times of the Gentiles
7. The 70 years captivity
8. Daniel 9 and the divine word to return and build
9. The death and resurrection of Yeshua
10. The destruction of Jerusalem and the temple
11. The 41st Jubilee cycle as it relates to our generation
12. The 123rd Jubilee cycle (3x41) as it relates to the millennium
13. The 144th Jubilee cycle as it relates to the New Jerusalem and the restitution of all things

I hope you'll join me on this next adventure as we once again dig into the treasures YHWH has hidden for us to find in His Word. Remember, those of you who subscribe to my blog will receive a free digital copy of my upcoming book *The Jubilee Code: Prophetic Milestones in the Bible* once it has been released. I look forward to continuing the adventure with you. You can subscribe here: http://www.the13thenumeration.com/Blog13/subscribe/

Maranatha!

Special Offer:

Do you want to learn more about the Bible's Jubilee Code? Subscribe to my blog, Where History and the Bible Meet and when it is released you'll receive a complimentary digital copy of Book III – <u>The Jubilee Code: Prophetic Milestones in the Bible</u> in your favorite digital media.

To learn more about the Bible's Jubilee Code visit my blog: http://www.the13thenumeration.com/Blog13/subscribe/

PROPHECIES & PATTERNS
BOOK III

THE JUBILEE CODE
PROPHETIC MILESTONES IN THE BIBLE

About the Author

William Struse is an author, blogger, and book reviewer with a love for Yeshua and his family. This book reflects his lifelong interest in Biblical history and Bible prophecy. William is the author of two books on Bible prophecy and three novels.

William resides in the desert of Southern Arizona with his love, Winnie, and their five children. You can connect with William on social media at:

His Blog: http://www.the13thenumeration.com/Blog13/
Twitter: @William_Struse
LinkedIn: William-Struse

Non-Fiction by William Struse (Prophecies & Patterns Series)
Book I - The 13th Enumeration: Key to the Bible's Messianic Symbolism
Book II - Daniel's Seventy Weeks: The Keystone of Bible Prophecy
Book III - The Jubilee Code: Prophetic Milestones in the Bible (to be released)

Christian Fiction by William Struse:
Book I - The 13th Enumeration
Book II - The 13th Prime: Deciphering the Jubilee Code
Book III - The 13th Symbol: Rise of the Enlightened One
Book IV - (to be released)

Made in the USA
Columbia, SC
25 September 2020